THE SECOND EPISTLE OF PAUL
TO THE
CORINTHIANS

AN INTRODUCTION AND COMMENTARY

by

COLIN G. KRUSE,
B.D., M.Phil., Ph.D.
New Testament Lecturer,
Ridley College, University of Melbourne

Inter-Varsity Press
Leicester, England

William B. Eerdmans Publishing Company
Grand Rapids, Michigan

The Tyndale New Testament Commentaries

General Editor:
THE REV. CANON LEON MORRIS, M.Sc., M.Th., Ph.D.

THE SECOND EPISTLE OF PAUL
TO THE CORINTHIANS

To my mother
DOROTHY ISOBEL KRUSE
and to the memory of my father
PETER WILLIAM KRUSE

Inter-Varsity Press
38 De Montfort Street, Leicester LE1 7GP, England

Wm. B. Eerdmans Publishing Company
255 Jefferson S.E., Grand Rapids, MI 49503

Published and sold only in the USA and Canada by Wm. B. Eerdmans Publishing Co.

Reprinted, April 1991

Unless otherwise stated, quotations from the Bible are taken from the Revised Standard Version, copyrighted 1946, 1952 © 1971, 1973 by the Division of Christian Education, National Council of the Churches of Christ in the USA, and used by permission.

British Library Cataloguing in Publication Data

Kruse, Colin G.
  The second epistle of Paul to the
  Corinthians: an introduction and
  commentary.—(The Tyndale New Testament
  commentaries).
  1. Bible. N.T. Corinthians, 2nd—
  Commentaries
I. Title   II. Bible. N.T. *Corinthians, 2nd*
  English   III. Series
  227′.307   BS2675.3

ISBN 0-85111-877-1

Library of Congress Cataloging-in-Publication Data

Kruse, Colin G.
  The Second Epistle of Paul to the Corinthians.

  (Tyndale New Testament commentaries)
  1. Bible.   N.T. Corinthians, 2nd — Commentaries.
I. Title.   II. Series.
BS2675.3.K78   1987   227′.307   87-17256

ISBN 0-8028-0318-0 (W. B. Eerdmans)

Set in Palatino
Typeset in Great Britain by Parker Typesetting Service, Leicester
Printed in USA by Eerdmans Printing Company, Grand Rapids, Michigan

*Inter-Varsity Press is the publishing division of the Universities and Colleges Christian
Fellowship (formerly the Inter-Varsity Fellowship), a student movement linking Christian
Unions in universities and colleges throughout the United Kingdom and the Republic of Ireland,
and a member movement of the International Fellowship of Evangelical Students. For information
about local and national activities write to UCCF, 38 De Montfort Street, Leicester LE1 7GP.*

GENERAL PREFACE

The original *Tyndale Commentaries* aimed at providing help for the general reader of the Bible. They concentrated on the meaning of the text without going into scholarly technicalities. They sought to avoid 'the extremes of being unduly technical or unhelpfully brief'. Most who have used the books agree that there has been a fair measure of success in reaching that aim.

Times, however, change. A series that has served so well for so long is perhaps not quite as relevant as when it was first launched. New knowledge has come to light. The discussion of critical questions has moved on. Bible-reading habits have changed. When the original series was commenced it could be presumed that most readers used the Authorized Version and comments were made accordingly, but this situation no longer obtains.

The decision to revise and up-date the whole series was not reached lightly, but in the end it was thought that this is what is required in the present situation. There are new needs, and they will be better served by new books or by a thorough up-dating of the old books. The aims of the original series remain. The new commentaries are neither minuscule nor unduly long. They are exegetical rather than homiletic. They do not discuss all the critical questions, but none is written without an awareness of the problems that engage the attention of New Testament scholars. Where it is felt that formal consideration should be given to such questions, they are discussed in the Introduction and sometimes in Additional Notes.

But the main thrust of these commentaries is not critical. These books are written to help the non-technical reader understand his Bible better. They do not presume a knowledge of Greek, and all Greek words discussed are transliterated; but the authors have the Greek text before them and their comments are made on the basis of the originals. The authors are free to choose their own modern translation, but are asked to bear in mind the variety of translations in current use.

The new series of *Tyndale Commentaries* goes forth, as the former series did, in the hope that God will graciously use these books to help the general reader to understand as fully and clearly as possible the meaning of the New Testament.

LEON MORRIS

CONTENTS

AUTHOR'S PREFACE

I want to express my thanks to the Inter-Varsity Press and the General Editor of the Tyndale New Testament Commentaries for their invitation to contribute this book to the revised series. I hope it will prove to be a worthy successor to the commentary of the late Professor R. V. G. Tasker which it replaces.

The major part of the work on this book was carried out during my sabbatical leave in 1985. I wish to record my thanks to the Council of Ridley College for leave granted to carry through this project, and also to the St Augustine's Foundation, Canterbury, for financial assistance to help cover the extra costs of living and studying abroad. I am grateful to Dr Murray Harris, the Warden of Tyndale House, Cambridge, and to other researchers who were working there during the latter part of 1985, for their friendship and encouragement. Also I want to thank my three sons who carried on alone at home while their father, mother and sister were in Canterbury, and especially I want to thank my wife for taking on the full responsibility for our family during the two months I spent in Cambridge.

This book is dedicated to my mother and to the memory of my father, in recognition of all that I owe them both.

It is my hope and prayer that this modest work will assist Christian people to better understand Paul's Second Epistle to the Corinthians and, in so doing, help them to appreciate more the incredible grace of the God whom he served.

COLIN G. KRUSE

9

CHIEF ABBREVIATIONS

Standard abbreviations, including those for journal titles, follow the scheme set out in the *New Bible Dictionary* (²1982), pp. x–xiii.

Allo	E. B. Allo, *Saint Paul: seconde épître aux Corinthiens*, Etudes bibliques (Gabalda, ²1956).
Alford	H. Alford, *The Greek New Testament*, 2 (Longmans, Green and Co., ⁷1895).
AV	Authorized (King James') Version, 1611.
BAGD	W. Bauer, *A Greek-English Lexicon of the New Testament and Other Early Christian Literature,* translated and adapted by W. F. Arndt and F. W. Gingrich; second edition revised and augmented by F. W. Gingrich and F. W. Danker (University of Chicago Press, 1979).
Barrett	C. K. Barrett, *The Second Epistle to the Corinthians* (A. and C. Black, 1968 and 1973).
Bornkamm	G. Bornkamm, 'The History of the Origin of the So-called Second Letter to the Corinthians', *NTS* 8 (1961–1962), pp. 258–264.
Bruce	F. F. Bruce, *1 and 2 Corinthians*, New Century Bible (MMS, 1971).
Bultmann	R. Bultmann, *The Second Letter to the Corinthians,* ET by R. A. Harrisville (Augsburg, 1985).
Calvin	John Calvin, *The Second Epistle of Paul the Apostle to the Corinthians and the Epistles to Timothy, Titus and Philemon,* ET by T. A. Smail (St Andrew Press, 1964).
Chrysostom	John Chrysostom, *Homilies on the Epistles of Paul to*

	the Corinthians, Nicene and Post-Nicene Fathers of the Christian Church 12 (Eerdmans, 1969).
Denney	J. Denney, *The Second Epistle to the Corinthians*, The Expositor's Bible (Hodder & Stoughton, 1894).
ET	English translation.
Furnish	V. P. Furnish, *II Corinthians*, Anchor Bible 32a (Doubleday, 1984).
GNB	Good News Bible (Today's English Version): Old Testament, 1976; New Testament, ⁴1976.
Harris	M. J. Harris, '2 Corinthians', *The Expositor's Bible Commentary* 10, ed. F. E. Gaebelein (Zondervan, 1976), pp. 299–406.
Héring	J. Héring, *The Second Epistle of St Paul to the Corinthians*, ET by A. W. Heathcote and P. J. Allcock (Epworth, 1967).
Hughes	P. E. Hughes *Paul's Second Epistle to the Corinthians*, New London Commentary (MMS, 1962).
JB	The Jerusalem Bible, 1966.
Kümmel	W. G. Kümmel, *Introduction to the New Testament*, ET by H. C. Kee (SCM, 1975).
Lietzmann	H. Lietzmann *An die Korinther I/II*, Handbuch zum Neuen Testament 9, augmented by W. G. Kümmel (J. C. Mohr, 1969).
LSJ	*A Greek-English Lexicon*, compiled by H. G. Liddell and R. Scott, new edition revised by H. S. Jones and R. Mackenzie (Oxford, ⁹1940).
Martin	R. P. Martin, *2 Corinthians*, Word Biblical Commentary 40 (Word Books, 1986).
MM	J. H. Moulton and G. Milligan, *The Vocabulary of the Greek Testament Illustrated from the Papyri and Other Non-Literary Sources* (Hodder & Stoughton, 1914–1929).
Murphy-O'Connor	J. Murphy-O'Connor, *St. Paul's Corinth: Text and Archaeology* (Michael Glazier, 1983).
NEB	The New English Bible: Old Testament, 1970; New Testament, ²1970.
NIV	The New International Version: Old Testament, 1978; New Testament, ²1978.

Plummer   A. Plummer, *A Critical and Exegetical Commentary on the Second Epistle of St Paul to the Corinthians*, International Critical Commentary 47 (T. & T. Clark, 1915).

RSV   Revised Standard Version: Old Testament, 1952; New Testament, ²1971.

RV   The Revised Version, 1884.

Schmithals   W. Schmithals, *Gnosticism in Corinth: An Investigation of the Letters to the Corinthians*, ET by J. E. Steely (Abingdon, 1971).

Strachan   R. H. Strachan, *The Second Epistle of Paul to the Corinthians*, Moffatt New Testament Commentary (Hodder & Stoughton, 1935).

Str-B   [H. L. Strack and] P. Billerbeck, *Kommentar zum Neuen Testament aus Talmud und Midrasch*, 6 vols. (Beck, 1922–1956).

Tasker   R. V. G. Tasker, *The Second Epistle of Paul to the Corinthians*, Tyndale New Testament Commentaries 8 (Tyndale, 1958).

TDNT   G. Kittel and G. Friedrich, eds., *Theological Dictionary of the New Testament*, ET by G. W. Bromiley, 10 vols. (Eerdmans, 1964–1976).

Wendland   H. D. Wendland, *Die Briefe an die Korinther*, Das Neue Testament Deutsch 7 (Vandenhoeck & Ruprecht, 1965).

Weiss   J. Weiss, *Earliest Christianity: A History of the Period AD 30–150*, 2 vols. (Harper & Row, 1959).

INTRODUCTION

I. THE CITY OF CORINTH

The ancient city of Corinth lay upon the narrow isthmus con-
necting the Peloponnesus with the Greek mainland. Situated
about three and a half miles south-west of present-day Corinth,
the ancient city was built on a trapezium-shaped terrace at the
foot of a large rocky hill known as Acrocorinth. This hill rises to
a height of 1,886 feet above sea-level and dominates the sur-
rounding landscape.

The isthmus upon which Corinth was built separates the
waters of the Gulf of Corinth in the north-west from those of the
Saronic Gulf in the south-east. On the north-western side of the
isthmus, bordering the Gulf of Corinth, was the port-city of
Lechaeum, and on the south-eastern side, bordering the Saronic
Gulf, lay the port of Cenchreae (the port used by Paul when
travelling to or from Corinth by ship, cf. Acts 18:18). The overland journey between the two ports was approximately ten
miles, while the journey by sea around the southern tip of the
Peloponnesus (Cape Maleae) was about two hundred miles. The
Cape Maleae region was notorious for its violent storms and
treacherous currents, so that ancient mariners used to quote the
proverb, recorded for us by Strabo: 'But when you double Maleae, forget your home.' Instead of undertaking the dangerous
journey around Cape Maleae, ancient sea captains would
unload their cargo on one side of the isthmus and have it
transported overland to the other. If the ship was not too large it
could then be strapped on to a wheeled vehicle and hauled
across the narrowest part of the isthmus on a stone-paved road

known as the Diolkos (from the verb *dielko*, 'to haul across'). The captain would then reload the cargo and continue on his journey.

Because of the danger of the voyage around Cape Maleae, and because of the expense of off-loading and reloading cargo and hauling ships across, plans were made from as early as the time of Periander (d. *c.*586 BC) to cut a channel through the isthmus. A serious attempt to do this was begun by the emperor Nero in AD 67 but was discontinued when he died. Work on the canal was only resumed in 1887 and completed in 1893.

Ancient Corinth, then, lay at the crossroads of two important trade routes. The first was the route via the isthmus between Attica and the Peloponnesus; the second was the route across the isthmus between Lechaeum and Cenchreae. Ships from the western end of the Mediterranean filled the harbour in Lechaeum, while those from Asia and the eastern end of the Mediterranean streamed into the port of Cenchreae. Corinth, being so strategically located, grew wealthy on the taxes levied on the movement of goods which it supervised and controlled.

However, ancient Corinth was renowned not only for its commercial importance, but also because it was responsible for the organization of the biennial Isthmian Games which attracted many visitors to the area. In addition to this, Corinth had gained a certain notoriety because of its worship of Aphrodite. A temple for Aphrodite stood on the highest point of Acrocorinth, the hill at whose foot the city was located. Strabo tells us that so wealthy was the cult of Aphrodite that it boasted a thousand courtesans dedicated to the goddess. Many sea captains, he says, squandered their money paying for the services of these cult prostitutes, so that the proverb, 'Not for every man is the voyage to Corinth', was in use among them.[1]

In 146 BC the city was overrun by the Romans under the leadership of Leucius Mummius. He had the city razed to the ground. Many of its treasures were carried away to Rome or

---

[1]Strabo (*c.* 63 BC – *c.* AD 22) completed his *Geography c.* 7 BC and included in this work a description of early Corinth as it was before its destruction in 146 BC. Recently some questions have been raised concerning the accuracy of his statements about cult-prostitution, *cf.* H. Conzelmann, *1 Corinthians* (Fortress, 1975), p. 12; Murphy-O'Connor, pp. 55–56.

destroyed. The inhabitants, the old Corinthians, were either killed or sold into slavery. The city lay in ruins and was uninhabited for more than a hundred years until 44 BC, when Julius Caesar ordered that it be rebuilt and freedmen were sent to occupy it.

Pausanias, writing about AD 174, said that 'Corinth is no longer inhabited by any of the old Corinthians, but by colonists sent out by the Romans.' The Corinth of Paul's day should not be envisaged as a Greek city, rather as a Roman colony, probably quite cosmopolitan in character. Even if the original freedmen sent in by Rome were Italians, we must allow that, by Paul's time, the location of Corinth and the opportunities to prosper as a result of the control of the trade routes would have attracted many others of different nationalities to the new city. We know that among these was a community of Jews. Their existence in Corinth, attested by Philo (*Embassy to Gaius,* 281), is confirmed by the discovery of a stone bearing the clear remains of an inscription, '[syn]agogue of Hebr[ews]'. This is usually dated from the period of the later occupation (between 100 BC and AD 200)[1] and may have served as the lintel over the entrance to the Jewish synagogue in Corinth where, according to Acts 18:4, Paul preached on first arriving in Corinth.

From Pausanias' description it is clear that the new Corinth became a centre for the worship of many of the old Graeco-Roman gods. He refers to temples or altars dedicated to Poseidon, Palaemon, Aphrodite, Artemis, Dionysus, Helius, Hermes, Apollo, Zeus, Isis, Eros and others. Strabo records that in his time there was a small temple to Aphrodite on the summit of Acrocorinth, while by the time Pausanias wrote the ascent to Acrocorinth was punctuated by places of worship dedicated to various deities including Isis, Helius, Demeter and Pelagian. On the summit there was still found the temple of Aphrodite with images of Helius, Eros and Aphrodite herself.

Clearly, then, the new Corinth of Paul's day was still a centre for the worship of Aphrodite, as the old city had been prior to its destruction in 146 BC. But it is a mistake to apply to it Strabo's

---

[1]It is impossible to ascribe an exact date to the inscription, but it does confirm that fairly early on the Jewish community had a meeting-place in Corinth. *Cf.* Murphy-O'Connor, pp. 78–79; Barrett, p. 2.

description of the worship of Aphrodite with its thousand cult-prostitutes which relates to the Corinth of the earlier period. We should think of Corinth in Paul's day as similar to any other cosmopolitan Roman trade centre, no worse and no better.

There is no doubt that Corinth was regaining its wealth and prestige in Paul's time. It was the capital of the Roman province of Achaia. Responsibility for the organization of the Isthmian Games (which had been assumed by the city of Sicyon when Corinth was destroyed in 146 BC) was restored to Corinth when the city was rebuilt in 44 BC by Julius Caesar. By the second century AD Corinth was probably the leading city in Greece.

Another matter of interest related to Paul's contacts with Corinth is the discovery during excavations of the remains of a large speaker's platform or rostrum. This is believed to be the tribunal (*bēma*) at which Paul was arraigned before Gallio (Acts 18:12–17). It was built around AD 44 from blue and white marble and consisted of a high, broad rectangular platform, originally carrying a superstructure and provided with benches at the back and along the two sides. However, in more recent times the identification of this structure with the tribunal at which Paul was arraigned before Gallio has been questioned. It is argued that the *bēma* was reserved for major official occasions, and that minor matters, such as the Jewish complaints against Paul, were more likely to have been heard in one of the basilicas which were used for administrative purposes. No matter at which exact spot Paul was arraigned, the whole episode seems to have provided him with the imagery for his statement in 2 Corinthians 5:10 that 'we must all appear before the judgment seat (*tou bēmatos*) of Christ'.

About five hundred yards north of the centre of ancient Corinth the remains of a shrine of Asklepios have been excavated. Asklepios, according to Greek mythology, was the son of the god Apollo and a human mother. He became a renowned healer. Shrines to this divine healer were to be found in many places, including Rome, Pergamum, Cyrene, Athens and Corinth. Cures were effected when, after bathing in the sea, the patients underwent token ablutions at the shrine, and then made offerings of honey cakes at the altar. Further ablutions followed before the patients entered the main hall of the shrine, where they were urged to sleep. While they slept the god would appear to them in a dream and practise his medical art upon them. When they woke worshippers found themselves cured. Votive thank offerings in the form of life-size terracotta models of the patients' affected parts where then presented to the god at the shrine. Many such terracotta models have been found at the Asklepieion in Corinth (*e.g.* hands, feet, legs, arms, eyes, ears, breasts, genitals), and are on display in a special room at the museum at ancient Corinth.[1]

If such cures were being claimed in the shrine of Asklepios in ancient Corinth, we can appreciate the Corinthians' tendency to be greatly impressed by anyone who came to them claiming to be able to perform cures. Paul's opponents in Corinth claimed such powers and implied that Paul was lacking in this area. In response the apostle had to remind his readers that 'The signs of a true apostle were performed among you in all patience, with signs and wonders and mighty works' (2 Cor. 12:12).

In 1858 the city of Corinth was destroyed by a major earthquake; as a result, the site at the foot of Acrocorinth was abandoned and the modern city built about three and a half miles to the north-east.

II. PAUL AND THE CORINTHIANS

Paul's relationship with the Corinthian Christians, which stretched over a period of several years (*c.* AD 50–57), was a very complex affair. The apostle made three visits to Corinth. Emissaries of Paul made visits to Corinth, and members of the Corinthian congregation visited Paul when he was ministering in Ephesus. In addition, Paul sent several letters to the Corinthians during this period, and received at least one from them.

Due to the fragmentary nature of the information available to us, it is very difficult to reconstruct the details of the historical relationship between Paul and the Corinthians with any degree

---

[1]M. Lang, *Cure and Cult in Ancient Corinth: A Guide to the Asklepieion* (American School of Classical Studies at Athens, 1977).

of certainty. Both our primary sources (extant letters of Paul) and the major secondary document (the Acts of the Apostles) provide only partial information. To add to the difficulty, our main primary sources (1 and 2 Corinthians) present us with some puzzling literary problems which need to be resolved before a compelling historical reconstruction can be made, but the literary problems themselves can be resolved properly only by recourse to an adequate historical reconstruction.

In order to provide a framework for understanding 2 Corinthians, a suggested reconstruction of the sequence of events in Paul's relationship with the Corinthian church is provided below. This reconstruction assumes certain decisions regarding the literary and historical problems involved. However, in the interests of a clear statement of the suggested sequence of events, the discussion of these critical issues is omitted from the reconstruction, and taken up later (see pp. 25–53), where reasons for the decisions taken are provided.

A. PAUL'S FIRST CONTACT WITH CORINTH

According to the Acts of the Apostles, Paul's first visit to Corinth was made in the last phase of his second missionary journey. After leaving Athens he came to Corinth, where he met up with a Jewish couple, Aquila and Priscilla, recently arrived in the city after being evicted from Rome. They, along with all other Jews, had been commanded to leave the imperial city under an edict of Claudius (generally believed to have been promulgated in AD 49). Paul plied the same trade of tentmaking (or leatherworking) as this couple, so he worked with them during the week, and every sabbath argued and persuaded Jews and Greeks in the synagogue (Acts 18:1–4).

After some time the Jews in Corinth rejected Paul's message, opposed and reviled him. Paul thereupon turned his full attention to the Gentiles of the city, many of whom believed and were baptized. The apostle apparently felt vulnerable and afraid, for we are told, 'The Lord said to Paul one night in a vision, "Do not be afraid, but speak and do not be silent; for I am with you, and no man shall attack you to harm you; for I have many people in this city." ' Following this he stayed eighteen months longer, teaching in Corinth (Acts 18:9–11).

Eventually the Jews did mount an attack against Paul and brought him before the tribunal (*bēma*), to Gallio the proconsul of Achaia, accusing him of teaching people to worship God in ways contrary to the law. But Gallio drove the Jews from his tribunal, refusing to judge in matters related to Jewish law. Paul continued to minister in Corinth for 'many days longer', then set sail for Syria, thus concluding his first visit to Corinth. He called in at Ephesus on the way and spoke in the synagogue there, but declined a request to stay longer, promising to return if God willed (Acts 18:19–21). When he arrived back in Syria his second missionary journey had been completed.

B. CONTACTS WITH CORINTH DURING THE EPHESIAN MINISTRY

After spending some time in (Syrian) Antioch, Paul began his third missionary journey, travelling 'from place to place through the region of Galatia and Phrygia, strengthening all the disciples' (Acts 18:23). Paul then made his way across to Ephesus, arriving just after Apollos, an outstanding Alexandrian Jew, had crossed from there to Corinth (Acts 18:24 – 19:1).

When Paul arrived in Ephesus he entered the synagogue and 'spoke boldly, arguing and pleading about the kingdom of God' (Acts 19:8). Once again he was opposed by Jews and so withdrew from them, taking the disciples with him. Then for two years he argued daily in the hall of Tyrannus and 'all the residents of Asia heard the word of the Lord, both Jews and Greeks' (Acts 19:10). During this time extraordinary miracles were wrought through Paul (healings and exorcisms), leading to many conversions and a mass burning of magical books. These conversions disturbed the guild of silversmiths in Ephesus who earned their living making shrines of Artemis, the god of the Ephesians; and led by one Demetrius they precipitated a great riot (Acts 19:8–41). Paul's ministry in Ephesus, then, was marked by great success and much opposition. It was during this tumultuous period that many of Paul's contacts with the Corinthian church which form the historical background to 2

Corinthians took place. The various contacts during this period are listed below.

(i) Paul's 'previous' letter

We learn of a letter sent by Paul to the Corinthians in which he urged them 'not to associate with immoral men'. What Paul wrote in this letter was misunderstood by the Corinthians to mean that they should cut themselves off from social contact with the non-Christian world (1 Cor. 5:9).

(ii) Visitors from Corinth

While at Ephesus, Paul was visited by Stephanus, Fortunatus and Achaicus (1 Cor. 16:15–18), and also by those referred to as 'Chloe's people', who reported to Paul the quarrelling and division which had occurred in the Corinthian church (1 Cor. 1:11–12).

(iii) The Corinthians' letter to Paul

Also during his Ephesian ministry, Paul received a letter, sent by the Corinthians themselves, which raised a number of issues about which they sought advice (marriage, 1 Cor. 7:1, 25; food offered to idols, 1 Cor. 8:1; spiritual gifts, 1 Cor. 12:1; the collection, 1 Cor. 16:1, 12).

(iv) Tension between Paul and the Corinthians

A close reading of 1 Corinthians reveals that the acute tension in the relationship between Paul and the Corinthians which is reflected in 2 Corinthians 10 – 13 was already beginning to mount during the early stages of Paul's Ephesian ministry. Hints of this are found throughout 1 Corinthians. Three statements will serve as examples: 'Some are arrogant, as though I were not coming to you. But I will come to you soon, if the Lord wills, and I will find out not the talk of these arrogant people but their power' (1 Cor. 4:18–19); 'This is my defence to those who would examine me. Do we not have the right to our food and drink?' (1 Cor. 9:3–4); 'If any one thinks that he is a prophet, or spiritual, he should acknowledge that what I am writing to you is a command of the Lord. If any one does not recognise this, he is not recognised' (1 Cor. 14:37–38).

(v) The writing of 1 Corinthians

It was, then, to clarify the intention of his 'previous' letter, to respond to news brought by (Stephanus and) Chloe's people, to answer the enquiries made in the Corinthians' letter, and to head-off some emerging criticisms of his own person and ministry that Paul wrote 1 Corinthians during his time in Ephesus. He took the opportunity also to give instructions about the 'contribution for the saints' (a collection that was being taken up among the Gentile congregations to assist poor Christians in Jerusalem), and to advise the Corinthians of his intended visit. Paul planned to travel via Macedonia to Corinth, and after spending some considerable time there, to journey on to Jerusalem, accompanying the bearers of the collection, if that seemed desirable (1 Cor. 16:1–9; *cf.* Acts 19:21–22).

(vi) Timothy's visit to Corinth

Paul sent Timothy to Corinth (1 Cor. 4:17; 16:10–11), though we have no explicit information concerning what transpired when he was there. However, it is clear that Paul eagerly awaited his return (1 Cor. 16:11). By the time Paul began writing 2 Corinthians, Timothy had already returned (2 Cor. 1:1) and the relationship between Paul and the Corinthians had passed through a very difficult period.

(vii) Paul's 'painful' visit

Apparently when Timothy arrived back in Ephesus he brought disturbing news of the state of affairs in Corinth. This made Paul change the plans for travel he had outlined in 1 Corinthians 16:5–9. Instead of journeying through Macedonia to Corinth and then on to Jerusalem, he sailed directly across to Corinth. It was now his intention, after visiting the church there, to journey north into Macedonia and then return again to Corinth on his way to Jerusalem. By so doing he hoped to give the Corinthians 'a double pleasure' (2 Cor. 1:15–16). However, when Paul arrived in Corinth from Ephesus he found himself the object of a hurtful attack (2 Cor. 2:5; 7:12) made by an individual, while no attempt was made by the congregation as a whole to support Paul (2 Cor. 2:3). It proved to be a very painful visit, and one which the apostle did not wish to repeat. Once again he changed his travel plans; instead of returning to Corinth after the projected journey into Macedonia, he made his way straight back to Ephesus (2 Cor. 1:23; 2:1).

(viii) Paul's 'severe' letter

Once back in Ephesus, Paul wrote his so-called 'severe' letter to the Corinthians. This letter is probably no longer extant, though some have suggested that it is preserved in whole or in part in 2 Corinthians 10 – 13 (see pp. 27–29). It called upon the Corinthian church to take action against the one who had caused Paul such hurt, and so to demonstrate their innocence in the matter and their affection for Paul (2 Cor. 2:3–4; 7:8, 12). It is not clear who carried the 'severe' letter to Corinth. It may have been Titus. In any case it was from Titus, returning from a visit to Corinth, that Paul expected news of the Corinthians' response to this letter. Paul was apparently fairly confident of a positive response. He expressed his confidence in them to Titus before the latter left for Corinth (2 Cor. 7:14–16), and may have even asked Titus to take up with the Corinthians the matter of the collection (2 Cor. 8:6). Plans had been made for the two to meet in Troas. So Paul left Ephesus and made his way to Troas. He found there a wide-open door for evangelism, but because Titus had not yet come, and because he was so anxious to meet him, he left Troas and crossed over into Macedonia hoping to intercept him on his way through that province to Troas (2 Cor. 2:12–13).

C. CONTACTS WITH CORINTH WHILE IN MACEDONIA

When Paul reached Macedonia he found himself embroiled in

the bitter persecution which the churches of Macedonia themselves were experiencing (2 Cor. 7:5; 8:1–2) and this only com-
pounded his anxiety.

(i) Titus' arrival in Macedonia and Paul's letter of relief

When Titus finally arrived, Paul found great consolation (2 Cor.
7:6–7), the more so when he heard from him of the Corinthians'
zeal to demonstrate their affection and loyalty to their apostle by
punishing the one who had caused him such hurt. Paul responded to this good news by writing another letter, 2 Corinthians 1
– 9 (see pp. 29–33). He said how glad he was that their response
to the 'severe' letter and Titus' visit had justified his pride in
them, especially seeing that he had boasted about them to Titus
before sending him to Corinth (7:4, 14, 16). He also went to great
lengths to explain the changes to his travel plans (1:15 – 2:1) and
why, and in what frame of mind, he had written them previously such a 'severe' letter (2:3–4; 7:8–12). Although Paul was
overjoyed because the Corinthians had acted so vigorously to
clear themselves, nevertheless he urged them now to forgive
and restore the one who had caused the pain, 'to keep Satan
from gaining the advantage' (2:5–11).

This letter of relief deals with two other subjects at some
length. First, there is a long explanation of the way in which
Paul's apostolic ministry was upheld and empowered in the
midst of the many afflictions and anxieties which he experienced both in Asia (Ephesus) and in Macedonia (1:3–11; 2:12 –
7:4). Second, we find detailed instructions and exhortations
about the contribution for the saints (2 Cor. 8 – 9). The Corinthians had made a beginning 'a year ago' (8:10) when they wrote
to Paul, and he had replied giving basic directions about this
matter (1 Cor. 16:1–4). In fact Paul had actually boasted to the
Macedonians about the Corinthians' readiness to contribute to
the collection, and was now becoming anxious lest they fail to
vindicate his boasting (9:1–4).

(ii) Titus returns to Corinth

Paul wanted to ensure that neither he nor the Corinthians

would be embarrassed because of their unreadiness in the matter of the collection. So he sent Titus and two others to Corinth to make sure certain matters were finalized before Paul himself arrived, possibly accompanied by some of the very Macedonians to whom he had boasted of the Corinthians' readiness (8:16 – 9:5).

However, when Titus and the others arrived in Corinth they found a situation which had seriously deteriorated. Men whom Paul called 'false apostles' were levelling all sorts of accusations against Paul and his emissaries. Apparently the Corinthian church had been deeply influenced by these men, had accepted their 'gospel' (11:1–4) and submitted to their overbearing demands (11:16–20). Titus brought back news of the terrible situation in Corinth to Paul, who was still in Macedonia.

(iii) Paul's final letter to Corinth

In response to this major crisis situation, Paul wrote his most severe and apparently final letter to the Corinthians, our 2 Corinthians 10 – 13 (see pp. 34–35). It was written to answer the accusations of the 'false apostles' and to dispel the suspicions they had raised in the minds of the Corinthians. It reads like a last desperate attempt to bring the church to its senses, to secure again their pure devotion to Christ and to revive once more their loyalty to their spiritual father. In it Paul warns them of his planned third visit when he would demonstrate his authority, if need be, though clearly he hoped the Corinthians' response to this final letter would make that unnecessary (12:14; 13:1–4, 10).

D. PAUL'S THIRD VISIT TO CORINTH

According to Acts 20:2–3, Paul did travel to Greece after the time in Macedonia, and spent three months there. We may assume that at this time he made his promised third visit to Corinth. Apparently, either as a result of his letter or because of his own coming to Corinth for the third time, the problems in the Corinthian church were settled for the time being. This can be inferred from Paul's letter to the Romans, which was written from Corinth during these three months. In that letter he wrote: 'At present, however, I am going to Jerusalem with aid for the saints. For Macedonia and Achaia have been pleased to make some contribution for the poor among the saints at Jerusalem' (Rom. 15:25–26). If the Achaians (who must for the most part have consisted of the Corinthians) had now contributed to the collection, obviously their misgivings reflected in 2 Corinthians 11:7–11 and 12:13–18 had been overcome. And if Paul spent three months in Greece, in a frame of mind which allowed him to write Romans, then the situation in Corinth must have improved markedly.

It would be gratifying to be able to say that after all these things the Corinthian church went from strength to strength. Unfortunately this was not the case. Evidence from the First Epistle of Clement (written *c*. AD 95) indicates that disharmony had become a problem once more.

III. LITERARY PROBLEMS

At the beginning of the preceding section, in which an attempt was made to reconstruct the course of Paul's relationship with the Corinthians, it was noted that such an enterprise can be carried out only when certain decisions about literary problems have been taken. Clearly, then, the reconstruction offered above rests on certain assumptions concerning the literary make-up of 1 and 2 Corinthians. It is now time to state those assumptions and give reasons why they have been made, for they not only underline the historical reconstruction of events suggested above, but also influence the commentary provided below.

A. PAUL'S CORINTHIAN CORRESPONDENCE: HOW MANY LETTERS?

One of the most perplexing problems related to Paul's relationship with the Corinthians concerns the number of letters he wrote and whether or not all those letters have been preserved (in whole or in part). Views vary widely. The viewpoint underlying the reconstruction of events adopted in this commentary is that Paul wrote five letters to the church in Corinth. The first was the 'previous' letter (now lost) mentioned in 1 Corinthians 5:9, then followed our 1 Corinthians. The third was the 'severe' letter spoken of in 2 Corinthians 2:3–4; 7:8, 12, while the fourth letter was our 2 Corinthians 1 – 9. The fifth and final letter is that preserved substantially in 2 Corinthians 10 – 13.[1]

However, there are a number of other views. Some argue that there were only three letters: the 'previous' letter (now lost), then 1 Corinthians (which is to be identified as the 'severe' letter of 2 Cor. 2:3–4; 7:8, 12) and finally 2 Corinthians.[2] Others assume four letters were written: the 'previous' letter (2 Cor. 6:14 – 7:1 sometimes being seen as a fragment of this), 1 Corinthians, the 'severe' letter (largely preserved in 2 Cor. 10 – 13) and 2 Corinthians 1 – 9.[3] In addition to these major and more or less 'straightforward' viewpoints, there are suggestions that fragments of at least four (or as many as six) letters, including the 'previous' and 'severe' letters, can be found scattered throughout our 1 and 2 Corinthians. Such views are based upon the recognition of apparent points of discontinuity in 1 and 2 Corinthians.[4] As mentioned above, the viewpoint adopted in this commentary is that Paul wrote five letters to Corinth. In what follows, each of these letters is discussed in turn and reasons given for the stance adopted.

(i) The 'previous' letter

The fact that Paul wrote a letter prior to the writing of 1 Corinthians is uncontested. Such a 'previous' letter is implied by 1 Corinthians 5:9. The letter dealt, at least in part, with the matter

[1]There appears to be an emerging consensus of opinion in support of this view among more recent commentators. Cf., e.g., Bruce, pp. 23–25; 164–170; Barrett, pp. 3–11; Furnish, pp. 26–46; Martin, p. xl.

[2]Cf. Allo, pp. lii–liii; Lietzmann, pp. 139–140; Tasker, pp. 30–35; Hughes, pp. xxiii–xxxv; Kümmel, pp. 287–293; W. H. Bates, 'The Integrity of II Corinthians', NTS 12 (1965–66), pp. 56–59; A. M. G. Stephenson, 'A Defence of the Integrity of 2 Corinthians', The Authorship and Integrity of the New Testament (SPCK, 1965), pp. 82–97.

[3]So, e.g., Plummer, pp. xvii–xix; Strachan, pp. xxxix–xl.

[4]So, e.g., Bultmann, pp. 16–18; Schmithals, pp. 87–110. The latter detects the remains of six letters: (A) 2 Cor. 6:14 – 7:1; 1 Cor. 6:12–20; 9:24 – 10:22; 11:2–34; 15; 16:13–24, (B) 1 Cor. 1:1 – 6:11; 7:1 – 9:23; 10:23 – 11:1; 12:1 – 14:40; 16:1–12, (C) 2:14 – 6:13; 7:2–4, (D) 10:1 – 13:13, (E) 9:1–15, (F) 1:1 – 2:13; 7:5–16; 8:1–24.

of association with Christians who behaved immorally. Many commentators believe that this letter has been lost; however, some argue that part of it is preserved in 2 Corinthians 6:14 – 7:1.[1] This passage does appear to interrupt the flow of thought in its present context, and for that reason it has been regarded by some as an interpolation and identified as a fragment of Paul's 'previous' letter (see pp. 37–40). However, there is a major difficulty involved with this suggestion. While it is true that Paul's 'previous' letter had been misunderstood by the Corinthians to mean that they should have no contact with anyone who was immoral, Paul responds in 1 Corinthians 5:9–13 by saying that his remarks had applied only to 'any one who bears the name of brother if he is guilty of immorality'. He did not intend them to apply to unbelievers. Yet the passage in 2 Corinthians 6:14 – 7:1, which some claim to be a fragment of the 'previous' letter, clearly refers to contact with *unbelievers*: 'Do not be mismated with unbelievers.' If this were a fragment of the 'previous' letter, Paul would be guilty of a blatant contradiction.

(ii) 1 Corinthians

The great majority of scholars accept the unity of 1 Corinthians, and agree that it is the second of the letters sent by Paul to Corinth. A small number do question its unity and suggest that several sections belonged originally to the 'previous' letter.[2] However, their arguments have not been found convincing, and as the whole matter does not impinge directly upon the exegesis of 2 Corinthians it may be left aside.

(iii) The 'severe' letter

That Paul wrote a 'severe' letter is clearly implied by 2 Corinthians 2:3–4; 7:8, 12. The view adopted in this commentary is that this letter is no longer extant. The older traditional view, still supported by some scholars, is that the 'severe' letter to which Paul refers is in fact 1 Corinthians.[3] The writing of that letter, it

---

[1] *E.g.* Strachan, p. xv; Schmithals, p. 95.   [2] *E.g.* Schmithals, pp. 95–96.
[3] So, *e.g.*, Hughes, pp. xxviii–xxx.

is argued, both caused Paul many tears and produced grief in the recipients. Paul had to reprimand his converts for a number of reasons, but especially because of their lax attitude towards immoral practices indulged in by certain members of the congregation. One factor supporting the traditional view is that 1 Corinthians does contain a demand for disciplinary action against an offender (1 Cor. 5:3–5, 7, 13), and the one thing we know about the contents of the 'severe' letter is that it contained such a demand, to which the apostle expected his readers to be obedient (2 Cor. 2:5–11). However, the majority of commentators today reject the view that 1 Corinthians is to be identified as Paul's 'severe' letter. The reason is that, despite the demand for disciplinary action against the incestuous person, and some strong words about party-spirit, libertarianism and disorder in public worship, 1 Corinthians just does not read like a letter written 'out of much affliction and anguish of heart and with many tears' (2 Cor. 2:4). It does not seem to be a letter which Paul would have regretted writing and that would have caused such grief to its recipients (2 Cor. 7:8–9).

The dominant view for many years was that the 'severe' letter has survived, in part at least, and is preserved in 2 Corinthians 10 – 13.[1] In support of this it is argued first that it would have been psychologically impossible for Paul to have written 2 Corinthians 1 – 9 and 10 – 13 at the same time to the same people. The change in tone from warm encouragement to his readers to complete what they had begun in the matter of the collection found in chs. 8–9, to the strident rebukes and impassioned personal defence in chapters 10 – 13, is just too great. Second, it is asserted that a number of passages in chs. 1 – 9 refer to statements made *previously* in chs. 10 – 13 (*cf.*, *e.g.* 1:23/13:2; 2:3/13:10; 2:9/10:6; 4:2/12:16; 7:2/12:17), and that this shows that chs. 1 – 9 were written after chs. 10 – 13. Third, in 10:16 Paul says he is looking forward to preaching the gospel 'in lands beyond you'. This, it is argued, could not have been written from Macedonia to Corinth (as would have to be the case if 2 Corinthians were a unity), but could have been written quite

[1]So, *e.g.*, Plummer, pp. xxvii–xxxvi; Strachan, p. xix; Bultmann, p. 18; Wendland, p. 8; Schmithals, p. 96.

appropriately from Ephesus (the probable place of writing of the 'severe' letter). Fourth, it is argued that if 2 Corinthians were a unity Paul would be guilty of making contradictory statements within the one letter (cf. 1:24/13:5; 7:16/12:20–21).

The positive aspects of the view that chs. 10 – 13 constitute the greater part of Paul's 'severe' letter are that it offers an explanation for the dramatic change in tone which occurs at 10:1, that the content of these chapters is such that they could have been written 'out of much affliction and anguish of heart', and that it would no doubt have caused much pain to the readers. However, this view does have a number of weaknesses. First, chs. 10 – 13 do not contain the one thing which we know was found in Paul's 'severe' letter, the demand to discipline the offender. Second, in 12:17–18 Paul asks, 'Did I take advantage of you through any of those whom I sent to you? I urged Titus to go, and sent the brother with him. Did Titus take advantage of you?' This seems to refer *back* to arrangements mentioned in 8:6, 16–24 and 9:3–5. If we accept that chs. 8 – 9 belonged originally with chs. 1 – 7 (as do most, but not all, proponents of the view that chs. 10 – 13 constitute Paul's 'severe' letter), then it seems that chs. 10 – 13 were written *after* chs. 1 – 9. Third, Paul wrote his 'severe' letter instead of making the return visit to Corinth which he had promised earlier, and so as not to cause his readers pain (1:23 – 2:4), whereas chs. 10 – 13 were written when the apostle was ready to make a visit (12:14) and threatening strong disciplinary action (13:1–4).

The view adopted in this commentary, then, is that the 'severe' letter is to be found neither in 1 Corinthians nor 2 Corinthians 10 – 13, but that it is no longer extant.

(iv) 2 Corinthians 1 – 9

There appears to be an emerging consensus in more recent works on 2 Corinthians that chs. 1 – 9 constitute Paul's fourth letter to the church in Corinth.[1] Such a consensus rests upon the acceptance of two propositions: first, that chs. 8–9 belong together with chs. 1 – 7, and second that chs. 1 – 9 and 10 – 13

---

[1] Bruce, p. 169; Barrett, p. 9; Furnish, pp. 30–41; Martin, p. xl.

could not have been written at the same time to the same people.

The first proposition has been questioned by a number of scholars. It has been variously suggested that either ch. 8 was originally a separate letter, and that it was ch. 9 that followed ch. 7, or that ch. 9 was originally a separate letter and only subsequently added in after ch. 8.[1]

There are three main arguments supporting this line of questioning. First, the wording of 9:1, with its introductory formula, *peri men gar* ('now it is') and full description of the subject-matter, 'the offering for the saints', reveals that Paul is taking up a new subject, rather than continuing one already broached in ch. 8. While it is true that Paul uses similar (but not identical) formulae elsewhere when taking up new subjects (*e.g.* 1 Cor. 7:1; 8:1; 12:1; 16:1), this does not mean that wherever such formulae are found we must assume the introduction of a new subject. Also the use of the full description, 'the offering for the saints', where we might expect something briefer if ch. 9 continues the treatment begun in ch. 8, does not compel us to regard ch. 9 as a letter originally separate from ch. 8. The use of a full description in 9:1 is understandable following the large amount of material set down after the first mention of the collection in 8:4.

Second, Paul's appeal to the example of the Macedonians to stir up the Corinthians in 8:1–5 and his reference to the example of the Corinthians which he used to stir up the Macedonians in 9:1–2 are seen to be in contradiction if chs. 8 and 9 belong together. However, such a contradiction is more apparent than real. In ch. 8 Paul tells of a completed action by the Macedonians to stimulate the Corinthians to complete what they had only begun. In ch. 9 Paul tells how earlier on he had used the readiness of the Corinthians to be involved in providing relief to stir the Macedonians to the action they had now taken. There is no inherent contradiction here.

Third, chs. 8 and 9 present different purposes for sending the 'brethren' on ahead to Corinth. In ch. 8 Paul says he is sending

---

[1]*Cf., e.g.*, Weiss, 2, p. 353, who regards ch. 8 as the later addition, and Bornkamm, p. 260; Schmithals, pp. 97–98; Bultmann, p. 18, who regard ch. 9 as having been added subsequently.

highly accredited envoys so as to avoid accusations of impropriety as far as the collection is concerned. In ch. 9 the purpose of their being sent is to ensure everything is ready when Paul himself arrives. In response it can be said that these two purposes are complementary and do not demand a separation of chs. 8 and 9.

In favour of the unity of chs. 8 and 9, it can be shown that there is a discernible progression in the argument begun in one chapter and carried through the other. In ch. 8 Paul begins to stimulate the Corinthians to action by citing the example of the Macedonians (vv. 1–7) and the example of Christ's self-giving (vv. 8–12), while assuring them that he was not seeking to burden them so that others might be eased (vv. 13–15). He then describes the arrangements that have been made for receiving and transporting the collection, so that the whole project will be seen clearly to have been carried out in an exemplary fashion (vv. 16–24). In ch. 9 the apostle continues to stir the Corinthians to action by stressing how embarrassed they would feel if, after all, they proved unprepared when some of the Macedonians arrived, for Paul had earlier boasted to them about the Corinthians' readiness (vv. 1–5). He strengthens his appeal for action by emphasizing that God loves the cheerful giver and that 'he who sows bountifully will also reap bountifully' (vv. 6–7). Finally Paul reminds his readers that God is able to provide them with every blessing that they may abound in their generosity, and that by responding positively they will demonstrate their obedience to the gospel (vv. 8–15).

It can be further argued in favour of chs. 8 and 9 belonging together that Paul's reference to 'sending the brethren' in 9:3 presupposes some knowledge of who they are such as is provided in 8:16–24. In addition, 9:3–5 implies that the Corinthians understood the obligation resting upon them to contribute to the collection, an obligation Paul had stressed to them in 8:6–15.

All in all, there seem to be insufficient reasons to overthrow the conclusion that chs. 8 and 9 belong together in their present position, and this is supported by the fact that there is no known manuscript in which these chapters are found anywhere but in their traditional location.

The second proposition rests upon the belief that the change in tone which occurs at 10:1 is so great that it is psychologically improbable that chs. 1 – 9 and 10 – 13 were written at the same time to the same people. In the earlier chapters, especially chs. 7 – 9, the apostle expressed his joy and relief upon hearing how the Corinthians had shown their loyalty to him by disciplining the offender (7:6–11), affirmed his confidence in the Corinthians (7:14–16), and felt free to raise once more the matter of the collection with his hearers (chs. 8 – 9). At 10:1 the tone of the letter changes dramatically. Paul proceeds to warn of disciplinary action he may have to take (10:2, 5–6; 13:2–4, 10), to counter accusations made against him and entertained by his readers (10:9–11; 11:7–11; 12:16–18), to express his dismay at the Corinthians' readiness to accept another gospel (11:3–4), and to attack vigorously the integrity of those who are seeking to turn his converts against him (11:12–15). What we see then in chs. 1 – 9 is basically Paul's response to a crisis resolved (a crisis which was precipitated by the action of one individual), whereas in chs. 10 – 13 we find the apostle's reaction to a fresh crisis, one which was far from resolution at the time of writing (and which was brought on by a group of intruders whom the apostle calls 'false apostles'). These facts, it may be argued, are best accounted for by regarding chs. 1 – 9 as Paul's response to the good news which Titus brought of the Corinthians' reaction to the 'severe' letter, and by seeing in chs. 10 – 13 a subsequent letter written by the apostle when news reached him of a far more serious crisis precipitated by the activities of the 'false apostles' in Corinth.

There are, however, scholars who reject this view and argue for the unity of the Epistle.[1] They too recognize the change of tone at 10:1 but suggest that this can be understood without postulating two letters. Some suggest that while the apostle was in process of writing his letter of relief and joy he received further news from Corinth saying that a fresh crisis had been precipitated, and so he responded by adding chs. 10 – 13 to what he had already written. Others argue that the change in tone at 10:1 is not as great as has been suggested. They point to a

[1]So, e.g., Allo, pp. lii–liii; Lietzmann, pp. 139–140; Tasker, pp. 30–35; Hughes, pp. xxiii–xxxv; Kümmel, pp. 287–293; Bates, op. cit., pp. 56–59; Stephenson, op. cit., pp. 82–97.

common theme of strength through weakness running through both parts of the letter. They point out also that the apostle indulges in personal defence in both parts of the letter. Finally they note that there are no existing manuscripts which reproduce 2 Corinthians in any other form than that in which we know it today.

These are important considerations and need to be taken seriously. In response it must be said first, that it is possible the change in tone which occurs at 10:1 is to be accounted for by the apostle receiving fresh disconcerting news from Corinth while in process of writing his letter of relief. However, if this were the case, we would expect Paul to have written something to the effect that while he had just been commending them for their loyalty, in the light of the latest news he was forced now to rebuke them for their disloyalty to him and his gospel.

Second, it is true that the theme of strength through weakness is present in both chs. 1 – 9 and chs. 10 – 13, and that there is personal defence in both as well. But the intensity of the defence in the latter is far greater than in the former, and the reason for the incorporation of the theme of strength through weakness in chs. 1 – 9 is different from the reason for its incorportion in chs. 10 – 13. In the former he included it to show how, despite all his apostolic privations and difficulties, the power of God is still at work through his ministry. In the latter he includes it as part of his deliberate inversion of his opponents' criteria for evaluating apostleship.

Third, it is true that there are no extant manuscripts supporting the division of the letter as suggested, but this can be accounted for if we envisage two originally separate letters being copied on to one scroll very early in the history of the transmission of the text.

If we accept these two propositions (that chs. 8 and 9 belong together and with chs. 1 – 7, and that chs. 10 – 13 represent a letter written some time after chs. 1 – 9 were sent to Corinth), then there is no reason why chs. 1 – 9 should not be regarded as Paul's fourth letter to Corinth.

(v) 2 Corinthians 10 – 13

The arguments against the view that chs. 10 – 13 belonged originally with chs. 1 – 9 have been set out above (pp.29–33), as also have the arguments against seeing in chs. 10 – 13 Paul's 'severe' letter (pp. 28–29). The view adopted by the majority of more recent interpreters is that chs. 10 – 13 constitute the major part of a fifth letter which Paul wrote to Corinth after the writing of chs. 1 – 9,[1] and this is the approach adopted in this commentary.

One advantage of this view is, as we have seen, that it accounts better for the marked change in tone that takes place at 10:1. A second advantage is that it takes better account of the fact that in chs. 10 – 13 Paul is preparing the way for his imminent third visit. Thus in 12:19 – 13:10 he shows that the purpose of all he has said was for the Corinthians' upbuilding in the hope that when he makes his third visit he would not have to be severe in the use of his authority. Such a declared purpose fits in well with the content of chs. 10 – 13 so long as they are not regarded as belonging with chs. 1 – 9, for the latter bear no hint of a threat of imminent disciplinary action. Further, this declared purpose is also understood better when chs. 10 – 13 are not identified with Paul's 'severe' letter. Paul wrote the 'severe' letter *instead of* making another visit, not to prepare the way for one.

A third advantage of this view is that it makes better sense of Paul's references to Titus' behaviour in 12:17–18. There Paul asks whether Titus and the others whom he sent to Corinth on the business of the collection had been instrumental in Paul's taking advantage of the Corinthians. This question implies that chs. 10 – 13 were written *after* chs. 1 – 9, in which Paul tells his readers he is about to send these men to them (8:6, 16–24; 9:3–5).

Finally this view recognizes the difference in the nature of the opposition to Paul which is reflected in chs. 1 – 9 and chs. 10 – 13 respectively. In the former the opposition was from an individual (the offender of 2:5; 7:12) and it had been dealt with already by the Corinthians. In the latter the opposition came from a number of intruders whom Paul called 'false apostles',

[1]Bruce, pp. 166–172; Barrett, pp. 9–10,21; Furnish, pp. 30–41; Martin, p. xl.

and this opposition was at its height when these chapters were written. Furthermore, the outcome of the crisis precipitated by this opposition was by no means clear.

B. INTERPOLATIONS IN 2 CORINTHIANS?

There are two passages in 2 Corinthians which on first reading appear to interrupt the flow of Paul's presentation. Because of this a number of scholars have suggested that the passages concerned did not originally occupy their present position within the letter. The whole problem is related to the wider question of the number of letters Paul wrote to Corinth and what traces of these remain embedded in our 1 and 2 Corinthians. The passages which concern us here are 2:14 – 7:4 and 6:14 – 7:1.

(i) 2:14 – 7:4

Paul brings the first part of the letter (1:1 – 2:13) to a close by telling how his anxiety while awaiting Titus' arrival had prevented him from taking full advantage of the door that was opened for him to preach the gospel in Troas; indeed, he had left that work and crossed over to Macedonia (2:12–13). At this point there is an abrupt change in the letter. What follows, 2:14 – 7:4, is basically an extended description of the way God had enabled him to carry on an effective ministry despite many difficulties and criticisms. It is only at 7:5 that Paul returns once again to the matter of the meeting with Titus. In fact, if the whole of 2:14 – 7:4 is omitted and in reading the letter we jump from 2:13 directly to 7:5 it still makes good sense. Various explanations have been offered for this phenomenon.

First, there are those who argue that 2:14 – 7:4 is definitely an interpolation, being either the whole of or a portion of a separate letter written by Paul and included here by an editor of his letters. Accordingly some suggest that 2:14 – 7:4 along with chs. 10 – 13 constitute the 'severe' letter mentioned in 2:3–4,[1] while

___
[1]Weiss, p. 349; Bultmann, p. 18.

others say it is an interim letter, penned earlier than the 'severe' letter, at a time before the Corinthians had fallen prey to Paul's opponents.[1] There are serious problems with these views. The view which connects 2:14 – 7:4 with chs. 10 – 13 fails to take sufficient note of the very different attitude adopted by Paul in the two blocks of material. In 2:14 – 7:4 he expresses great confidence in the Corinthians' loyalty (7:14, 16) whereas in chs. 10 – 13 he is convinced that they had capitulated to his opponents (11:2–4, 19–20). And both views fail to explain adequately the close connection between 7:4 and 7:5ff. In the latter the idea of affliction is taken up again and related to 7:2–4 by the use of the word 'for' (*gar*). Also, both views take insufficient account of the repetition in 7:5ff. of ideas found in what precedes it (*e.g.* 7:4: 'I have great confidence in you'; 7:14, 16: 'I have expressed to him some pride in you . . . our boasting before Titus has proved true'; 'I have perfect confidence in you').

Second, and in contrast, there are those who regard 2:14 – 7:4 as an integral part of 2 Corinthians. To maintain this position they have to account for the rough transition from 2:13 to 2:14ff. Numerous explanations have been made:

(a) In 2:14 – 7:4 Paul makes a conscious digression to express his gratitude to God for the relief from anxiety experienced when he finally met with Titus, a digression evoked by the mention of his name in 2:13.[2]

(b) In 2:14ff. Paul refers all his journeyings to God, to counterbalance his earlier acknowledgments (1:8–11; 1:23 – 2:1; 2:12–13) that the 'compulsion of affairs' had frustrated his desire either to journey or to tarry.[3]

(c) The contrast of human weakness and the power of God found in 1:8–11 is repeated when, following the admission of his weakness in 2:12–13, Paul strikes the note of triumph again in 2:14ff.[4]

---

[1]Bornkamm, pp. 259–260; Wendland, p. 9; Schmithals, pp. 98–100.

[2]Plummer, p. 67; Tasker, pp. 56–57; Kümmel, p. 291; Harris, pp. 303,331. Allo, p. 45, broadens the base of thanksgiving to include not only relief of anxiety when Titus arrived but also the reminder of the universal triumph of the gospel evoked by the mention of Macedonia in 2:13 and thereby of the faithful Christians in that part of the world.

[3]Chrysostom, p. 301.

[4]P. Bachmann, *Der zweite Brief des Paulus an die Korinther* (Erlangen, ⁴1922), pp. 126–127, cited by M. Thrall, 'A Second Thanksgiving Period in II Corinthians', *JSNT* 16 (1982), p. 105.

(d) Paul was eager to prevent misunderstanding following his acknowledgment of acute anxiety while in Troas (2:13), so he either stresses there was no spiritual defeat involved for him personally[1] or claims that his preaching had proved successful everywhere (including Troas),[2] as God always led him in triumph.

(e) The mention of Titus in 2:13 prompted Paul to leap forward, overlooking for the present the intermediate stages which are disclosed in 7:5ff., and to burst forth with a theological expression of the basis upon which his restored relationship with the Corinthians now rested.[3]

(f) A more recent suggestion is that, while a break between 2:13 and 2:14 is acknowledged, this is not evidence for an interpolation, but rather is occasioned by Paul's introduction of a second traditional thanksgiving period (2:14–16). This thanksgiving period foreshadows, as most of Paul's thanksgivings do, what is to be argued in detail in what follows.[4]

The major argument in favour of the view that 2:14 – 7:4 is an integral part of 2 Corinthians is the presence of the idea of comfort in affliction which is found in both 1:1 – 2:13; 7:5–16 and 2:14 – 7:4 (cp. 1:3–11; 7:5–7, 12–13 with 4:7 – 5:8; 6:1–10; 7:4). This idea runs as a thread throughout the first seven chapters. In addition, this view takes proper notice of the logical connection between 7:4 and 7:5. In both these matters, then, the view that 2:14 – 7:4 is not an interpolation is to be preferred so long as some adequate explanation for the abrupt transition from 2:13 to 2:14 can be found. Suggestions, as we have seen, are not lacking, and so long as we can see possible ways of negotiating the transition we ought not to accept too easily the idea that 2:14 – 7:4 is an interpolation.

(ii) 6:14 – 7:1

It is quite easy to see why these six verses have been regarded by many as an interpolation (within the larger interpolation 2:14

[1]Hughes, pp. 76–77.

[2]T. Zahn, *Introduction to the New Testament* (T. & T. Clark, [3]1909), p. 343, n. 1, cited by Thrall, *op. cit.*, p. 106.

[3]Barrett, p. 97.   [4]Thrall, *op. cit.*, pp. 111–119.

– 7:4). In 2:14 – 6:13 Paul stresses the nature and conduct of his apostolic ministry, apparently defending himself against the accusations that had been voiced by the offender and entertained by the congregation. He follows this defence with a heartfelt plea: 'Our mouth is open to you, Corinthians; our heart is wide . . . In return – I speak as to children – widen your hearts also' (6:11–13). This plea is then abruptly broken off and an exhortation to have no contact with pagans follows (6:14 – 7:1). At 7:2 the plea to the Corinthians to open their hearts to Paul is taken up once more.

All modern commentators recognize the abrupt changes in subject-matter at 6:14 and 7:2. Several different explanations for these have been made. Some suggest that 6:14 – 7:1 is a non-Pauline interpolation.[1] The apocalyptic dualism (righteousness/iniquity; light/darkness; Christ/Belial) reminiscent of the Qumran Scrolls, the use of *hapax legomena* (words found only here in Paul's writings), the incompatibility of Paul's exclusivism here with his more liberal approach in 1 Corinthians 5:9–10, and the unusual conjunction of 'body' (*sarx*, lit. 'flesh') and 'spirit' (*pneuma*) (which are usually contrasted by Paul) are all cited as evidence that this passage is not of Paul's composition. Such arguments have not proved compelling for most scholars. The unusual apocalyptic vocabulary could be accounted for by the nature of the exhortation, as could the use of *hapax legomena*. The so-called exclusiveness of 6:14 – 7:1 is not necessarily in conflict with the so-called liberalism of 1 Corinthians. Even in that letter Paul is quite adamant about the need to avoid compromise with idolatrous worship (1 Cor. 10:14–22). He distinguishes between social contact with pagans and involvement in pagan worship. Finally, it is true that Paul does, in theological argument, place 'flesh' and 'spirit' over against one another where 'spirit' refers to the Holy Spirit (*cf.* Gal. 5:16–25), but in the present passage the expression 'body (lit. flesh) and spirit' stands as a designation for the whole person .

Most modern scholars, then, accept 6:14 – 7:1 as Pauline. However, many still regard it as an interpolation into the text of 2 Corinthians made by a later redactor. Most of those who do so

---

[1] *Cf.*, *e.g.*, Bultmann, p. 180, and n. 202.

identify it as a fragment of the lost 'previous' letter mentioned in 1 Corinthians 5:9.[1] One problem with this view is that 6:14 – 7:1 calls for a separation of believers from *unbelievers* in the matter of idolatrous worship, whereas Paul's words in 1 Corinthians 5:9–13 indicate that in the 'previous' letter his concern had been that the Corinthians should avoid contact with *believers* who were behaving immorally. Another problem is the very difficulty of explaining *why* any later redactor would deliberately interpolate such a passage into this context (accidental insertion is ruled out when it is recalled that first-century copies of Paul's letters were written on papyrus scrolls, not on leaves of a codex which could have been accidentally displaced).[2]

In the light of all this, there are many scholars who, while recognizing the rough transitions (6:13 to 6:14 and 7:1 to 7:2) still argue that 6:14 – 7:1 has always been an integral part of 2 Corinthians and has always been located in its present position.[3] They, of course, have to explain why there are such abrupt changes in subject-matter at both 6:14 and 7:2. A number of suggestions have been made:

(a) There was a pause in dictation of the letter at 6:13.[4]

(b) Having established his spiritual authority in preceding chapters, Paul boldly warns against the ever-present threat of paganism, but not in a spirit of censoriousness, as 6:11–13 (which precedes) and 7:2–4 (which follows) indicate.[5]

(c) Paul, knowing that the Corinthians were having dealings with other apostles who proclaimed a different gospel, opens his heart to reveal his longing for a restored relationship with his converts, and urges them to reciprocate. However, he reminds them: 'If you turn to God and to me his messenger, it means a break with the world.'[6]

(d) Paul's main concern is for a restored relationship, as is evidenced by the thrust of 6:11–13 which is resumed again in 7:2–4. However, he realized that the main hindrance to the relationship was the Corinthians' unwillingness to renounce all

---

[1]Wendland, p. 212; Weiss, p. 356; Strachan, pp. xv,3–4; Schmithals, pp. 94–95.
[2]*Cf.* Allo, pp. 189–193.
[3]Plummer, pp xxiii–xxvi; Lietzmann, p. 129; Allo, pp. liii,193–194; Tasker, pp. 29–30; Hughes, pp. 241–244; Barrett, pp. 23–25; Harris, p. 303.
[4]Lietzmann, p. 129.   [5]Hughes, p. 244.   [6]Barrett, p. 194.

compromise with paganism, and this fact accounts for the inclusion of 6:14 – 7:1 between 6:13 and 7:2.[1]

An interesting suggestion has been made by N. A. Dahl. He argues that 6:14 – 7:1, with its marked parallels with certain features of the Qumran Scrolls, was originally a non-Pauline composition but was included by Paul (or less probably by some later redactor) in its present context as part of the apostle's warning to the Corinthians not to side with the false apostles. To join them 'in their opposition to Paul would mean to side with Satan/Belial in his opposition to Christ'.[2] While Dahl's view of the original composition of 6:14 – 7:1 is problematical, the explanation he gives concerning the interrelation of the passage and its present context is attractive. It has the advantage of relating the passage to the undercurrent of opposition to Paul reflected in chs. 1 – 7 and which had become quite overt by the time Paul wrote chs. 10 – 13.

IV. OPPOSITION TO PAUL IN CORINTH

In our reconstruction of the events involved in Paul's relationship with the church in Corinth (pp. 17–25) it was suggested that the opposition to Paul had two phases. In the first phase the opposition emanated primarily from one individual. It was news that the church had taken disciplinary action against the offending individual that produced in Paul the relief and joy which are expressed in chs. 1 – 7. While the opposition in this first phase was concentrated in one individual, there are hints in chs. 1 – 7 of an undercurrent of opposition in the background.

The second phase of the opposition is reflected in chs. 10 – 13. Here Paul responds vigorously to the attacks of those whom he calls 'false apostles'. According to our suggested reconstruction of events this phase of the opposition only became overt after Paul had succeeded in having disciplinary action taken against the individual offender mentioned above. The 'false apostles' may have been in Corinth during the first phase of opposition,

---

[1]Plummer, p. xxv; Harris, p. 303.

[2]N. A. Dahl, 'A Fragment and Its Context: 2 Cor. 6:14 – 7:1', *Studies in Paul: Theology for the Early Christian Mission* (Augsburg, 1977), p. 69.

and an undercurrent of criticism emanating from them may have strengthened the attacks of the offending individual. However, it was only after disciplinary action had been taken against this offender, and after Paul had urged members of the church to reinstate this person in their affection, that the opposition of the 'false apostles' moved from the background into the foreground.

The purpose of this section of the Introduction is to discuss the identity of the opposition to Paul in Corinth, and this can be done conveniently under two main headings.

A. THE OPPOSITION REFLECTED IN CHAPTERS 1 – 7

As described above (pp. 21–22), Paul, when he made his second visit to Corinth, became the object of a bitter personal attack mounted by some particular individual (the one who caused pain, 2:5; the one who did wrong, 7:12). The church as a whole did not provide the defence for its apostle one might have expected (2:3) and Paul felt forced to withdraw, but not before uttering dire warnings of disciplinary action (*cf.* 13:2).

Traditionally the offending individual has been identified as the incestuous person referred to in 1 Corinthians 5,[1] and then accordingly Paul's second visit to Corinth was believed to have taken place *before* the writing of 1 Corinthians, which then came to be regarded as the 'severe' letter.[2] However, this view has been abandoned by most twentieth-century commentators on two major counts: (a) Paul, having in 1 Corinthians 5 called so strongly for the excommunication of the incestuous person, could hardly then turn around and plead for his reinstatement in 2 Corinthians 2. This is not a very compelling objection, because it underestimates the effects of the gospel of forgiveness in the apostle's own life. (b) The offence Paul alludes to in 2 Corinthians 2 is not immoral behaviour, rather a personal attack upon himself and his apostolic authority. This is a far more weighty objection

[1] *Cf.*, *e.g.*, Chrysostom, pp. 296, 351–352; Alford, p. 637; Denney, pp. 1–6; Hughes, pp. 59–65.
[2] Alford, p. 53; Denney, pp. 3–5; Hughes, pp. 50–51.

Other scholars have identified the individual who mounted this attack against Paul as one of the 'false apostles' whom Paul castigates in 11:12–15,[1] but this identification is also problematical. It would seem unreasonable for Paul to expect the church to exercise discipline against one who was not only not one of its members, but one whom the church had accepted as an apostle of Christ on the strength of letters of recommendation (from Jerusalem). Others have been content to leave aside the question of the offender's actual identity, simply regarding him as an unknown person who, for some unknown reason, mounted a personal attack against Paul.[2] However, it is possible at least to suggest a more positive identification: that the offending individual was none other than the incestuous person against whom Paul previously demanded disciplinary action, and that this person was now guilty of an additional offence. In support of this view the following sequence of events is suggested.

In the libertarian atmosphere which pertained in Corinth (1 Cor. 5 – 6), one of the church members had committed incest with his stepmother (1 Cor. 5:1). Hearing of this, Paul was scandalized and demanded that disciplinary action be taken by the church against the offender, that they 'deliver this man to Satan for the destruction of the flesh, that his spirit may be saved in the day of the Lord Jesus' (1 Cor. 5:1–5). This demand was heard by the church when 1 Corinthians was received and read. Some time afterwards, Timothy, sent by Paul (1 Cor. 4:17 mg.; 16:10–11), arrived in Corinth. Apparently he discovered that all was not well in the church. Paul's demand for disciplinary action had not been complied with, and the incestuous person himself was resisting the apostle's authority. Timothy returned to Ephesus, where he informed Paul of this state of affairs. The apostle then made his second and 'painful' visit to Corinth (2 Cor. 2:1), during which he expected to resolve the problem with the support of the church. However, what in fact happened was that the incestuous man, far from being brought to repentance or intimidated, mounted a personal attack against

---

[1] So, *e.g.*, Barrett, p. 7.
[2] This is the majority opinion today, supported, *e.g.*, by Plummer, pp. 54–55; Strachan, p. 70; Bruce, p. 185; Bultmann, pp. 47–48; Furnish, p. 168.

Paul and questioned his credentials and authority. The church members did not come to Paul's defence as he expected they would (2 Cor. 2:3).

This questioning of Paul's credentials and authority was not done in a vacuum. Even at the time of writing 1 Corinthians, Paul was aware that his apostolate was under critical review in Corinth (1 Cor. 4:3–5), and that questions were being asked by some who felt a certain antipathy towards him (1 Cor. 4:18–21). It is possible that Peter may have visited Corinth, and that afterwards there emerged a Cephas party (1 Cor. 1:12). While it is unlikely that Peter himself would have raised questions about Paul's credentials, the Cephas party which claimed him as their patron may have done so. However, there seem to have been others lurking in the background as well, those to whom Paul referred later as 'peddlers of God's word' (2 Cor. 2:17), whose 'disgraceful, underhanded ways' the apostle refused to imitate (2 Cor. 4:1–2), but who seem to have come to Corinth armed with letters of recommendation and criticized Paul's lack of the same (2 Cor. 3:1–3). While these people would hardly support the incestuous man in his sin, their own muffled criticisms of Paul could have been used by the offender as extra ammunition when he mounted his attack against him. If this was the case, we have one clue as to the reason the Corinthian church as a whole did not spring to Paul's defence. Though they may have agreed with Paul that the offender ought to be disciplined, they were at the same time entertaining questions about his authority, questions raised by others but taken up and used against Paul by the offender. While the members of the church were considering such questions about Paul they would feel pulled in two directions, and so were rendered powerless in the situation with the result that they did not support Paul as he expected they would have done (2 Cor. 2:3).

Paul thus found himself without support in Corinth, and was forced to withdraw without resolving the problem, but not before uttering dire warnings of the action he intended to take subsequently (2 Cor. 13:2). He returned to Ephesus where he wrote the 'severe' letter 'out of much affliction and anguish of heart and with many tears' (2 Cor. 2:4). It was a letter Paul regretted writing, and which caused much grief to the Corinthian believers. In it he apparently rebuked them sternly for their failure to act against the offender and support their apostle (2 Cor. 2:1–4; 7:8). However, the letter had the desired effect. The Corinthians were stung into action. They took vigorous disciplinary action against the offender. He was excommunicated from the church, delivered to Satan, as Paul had demanded (1 Cor. 5:3–5, 13; *cf.* 2 Cor. 7:6–13). When Paul heard from Titus that the offender had been severely disciplined by the Corinthians he was relieved and overjoyed because his confidence in them had been vindicated at last (2 Cor. 7:6–16). At the same time he became concerned for the well-being of the one who had been disciplined, fearing that he might be overwhelmed by excessive sorrow, and for the church, fearing it may be disadvantaged by Satan through it all. He therefore urged members of the church to reaffirm their love for the offender and comfort him (2 Cor. 2:6–11).

In support of the suggested identification of the offender as the incestuous person of 1 Corinthians 5:1 several points can be made. First, it is clear that the general problem of immorality persisted throughout the period of Paul's written communications with Corinth. The 'previous' letter contained an exhortation to avoid contact with immoral men, by which Paul meant 'any one who bears the name of brother if he is guilty of immorality' (1 Cor. 5:9–11). When the apostle wrote 1 Corinthians the problem of immorality was manifesting itself in both the behaviour of the incestuous man (1 Cor. 5:1–2) and the use of prostitutes by others (1 Cor. 6:15–20). When Paul wrote his final letter to Corinth he was still concerned about the problem of immorality in the church (2 Cor. 12:21). The persistence of the general problem of immorality in the church before and after the mention of the sin of incest shows that the atmosphere was present in which the incestuous person could have opposed, rather than have submitted immediately to, the discipline Paul demanded.

Second, it needs to be realized that there are *no* indications that 1 Corinthians, which contained the demand for disciplinary action against the offender, actually induced the church to carry through that action. Third, it is possible, therefore, that when Timothy arrived in Corinth he faced an unrepentant offender and a church still hesitating to carry through the action Paul had demanded.

Fourth, 2 Corinthians 2:5 describes the offender as the one who has caused pain 'to you all'. In 1 Corinthians 5:6–8, where Paul speaks about the effect of the incestuous man's sin, he reminds his readers that 'a little leaven leavens the whole lump'. It was impossible for the church to allow the continued presence of the incestuous person in its midst without all its members being harmed to a certain extent as well. There is, then, this possible link between the leavening of the whole lump which Paul warned of in 1 Corinthians 5:6–8 and the harm done to all by the offender spoken of in 2 Corinthians 2:5.

Fifth, once Paul knew the church had taken severe disciplinary action against the offender, he began to be concerned that the individual involved might be overcome with excessive sorrow. Therefore he urged the Corinthians to reaffirm their love for the offender, forgiving and comforting him, so that Satan might not gain the advantage in the situation (2 Cor. 2:6–11). It will be remembered that in Paul's original demand for disciplinary action he called upon the church to 'deliver this man to Satan'. There is here another possible link, suggesting that the offender of 2 Corinthians 2:5; 7:12 is to be identified with the incestuous man of 1 Corinthians 5:1. Paul, who had demanded that the man be delivered to Satan in the first place, now, presumably seeing that he has been brought to repentance, wants him forgiven and restored so that it is not Satan who at the end of the day gains the advantage (by depriving the church of one of its members indefinitely).

B. THE OPPOSITION MET IN CHAPTERS 10 – 13

The second phase of the opposition involved a bitter personal attack upon Paul by those whom he called 'false apostles', and this is the opposition which Paul confronts in chs. 10 – 13. As noted above, the influence of these men may have already been felt at the time Paul wrote 1 Corinthians, and their muffled criticisms may have provided some of the ammunition used against Paul by the incestuous offender during the apostle's 'painful' visit to Corinth. In that case we could understand why, in responding to the challenges of this man, Paul had to defend the fact that he carried no letters of recommendation as others did (2 Cor. 3:1–3). Also, knowing that the 'false apostles' laid great store by their Jewish connections (2 Cor. 11:22), we can understand the significance of Paul's comparison and contrast between the glory of ministry under the new covenant and that under the Mosaic covenant (2 Cor. 3:4–18).

(i) The 'false apostles' and their attack against Paul

The nature of the attack made by the 'false apostles' upon Paul is reflected in his spirited response to it in chs. 10 – 13. They accused him of practising boldness while absent and at a safe distance, but of being only humble and meek when present (10:1). He acted in a 'worldly fashion' (10:2). He used to frighten people with stern letters from afar, but lacked a commanding presence and impressive speech when present among them (10:9–10). They criticized Paul's apostolate, saying it was inferior to their own, both because he was unskilled in speaking (11:5–6) and because, they implied, his ministry lacked apostolic signs (12:11–12). And, perhaps most cruelly, they attacked Paul's personal integrity in financial matters. They insinuated that his refusal to accept financial support from the Corinthians (as they themselves obviously did) was both evidence that Paul did not really love them (11:7–11) and a smokescreen behind which he intended to extract an even greater amount for himself through the collection ploy (12:14–18).

What have just been listed are criticisms levelled against Paul by the 'false apostles'. However, it is important that we also try to understand what these people stood for positively, so that we can fill in as far as possible the background to what the apostle says in chs. 10 – 13. Once again we are dependent upon hints available in Paul's response to them which is found in chs. 10 – 13. But from this we can deduce the following. They were proud to belong to Christ (10:7). They preached a gospel different from the one Paul preached (11:4) and prided themselves on their speaking ability (11:6). They presented themselves in Corinth (perhaps only initially) as those who carried out their mission on the same basis as Paul had done (11:12). They adopted an authoritarian stance in Corinth and succeeded in imposing their authority upon the church (11:19–21). They were proud of their Jewish ancestry and that they were servants of Christ (11:21–23). They stressed the importance of having enjoyed visionary experiences and revelations from God (12:1), as well as the performance of signs and wonders, which they regarded as the signs of a true apostle (12:11–13). They also emphasized the need for evidence that Christ spoke through anyone who claimed to be his emissary, evidence which consisted of some display of power (13:3).

From the various hints provided in chs. 10 – 13 it emerges that Paul's opponents were Jewish Christians[1] who were proud both of their Jewish credentials and that they were servants of Christ. If, as suggested above (p. 43), the demand for letters of recommendation to which Paul responded in 3:1–3 emanated originally from these men, it seems reasonable to conclude that they themselves bore such commendatory letters, most likely from Jerusalem. In that case they would have had a natural affinity with the Cephas party, which had already formed in Corinth and which would have favoured the Jewish form of Christianity associated with Peter.

As far as Paul was concerned, these men were not true apostles of Christ at all. In fact he accused them of preaching another Jesus and a different gospel (11:4), and this reminds us of the letter to the Galatians in which Paul attacks others who proclaim another gospel (Gal. 1:6–9). In that case the opponents of Paul were Judaizers, a name coined to describe Christian Jews who sought to impose upon Gentile converts the obligation of the law and to make them submit to circumcision. However, there are no indications in 2 Corinthians that Paul's opponents in Corinth were trying to impose these things.

There are, in addition to the matters of the law and circumcision, other significant differences between the Judaizers of the Galatian letter and the opponents Paul confronts in chs. 10 – 13. Paul's Corinthian opponents laid great stress upon oratorical

---

[1]Most scholars would go at least this far in the identification of Paul's opponents. However, Schmithals, pp. 293–295, concludes that they were Jewish Gnostics.

skills (11:5–6), not something which was predicated of the Jerusalem hierachy (Acts 4:13), nor presumably of the Judaizers who
represented them. In addition the 'false apostles' at Corinth
stressed the importance of visionary experiences and revelations
(12:1), displays of power to prove that Christ spoke through
them (13:3) and the so-called apostolic signs (12:11–13). These
things also, as far as we know, did not feature as part of the
Judaizers' approach. In the Hellenistic world there was stress
upon the importance of oratorical skill and a fascination with
wonder-workers who sought to demonstrate their validity by
appeals to visions and revelations (*cf.* Col. 2:18) and by the
performance of mighty works (*cf.* Acts 8:9–13). Perhaps the
Jewish Christian opposition to Paul in Corinth had borrowed
something from the Hellenistic world, or even accommodated
their approach to the Corinthian outlook. It is clear from 1
Corinthians that the believers in Corinth both prided themselves on such things and needed to be warned by Paul against
placing too much importance upon them (1 Cor. 1:5; 4:8–10;
13:1–2).

It would seem then that Paul's opponents were either Jewish
Christians who had themselves been influenced by exposure to
the Hellenistic world and incorporated into their own understanding of apostleship certain Hellenistic ideas, or that they
were Jewish Christians from the mother church in Jerusalem
who had accommodated themselves to ideas prevalent among
the Corinthians so as to more easily influence the latter against
Paul.[1]

(ii) 'False apostles' and 'superlative apostles'

Up until this point in the discussion we have assumed that Paul
has only one group in mind throughout chs. 10 – 13, where he
attacks his opponents and compares himself with others. Thus it
has been assumed that those whom Paul calls 'false apostles'
(11:12–15) and those whom he refers to as 'superlative apostles'
(11:5; 12:11) are one and the same. However, not all com-

[1]Barrett, pp. 29–30, argues that Paul's opponents were 'Jews of Palestinian origin, who
exercised a Judaizing influence', who for strategic reasons when in Corinth adopted certain
Hellenistic characteristics.

mentators agree with the assumption involved here. Barrett, for example, argues that while the expression 'false apostles' refers to Paul's opponents active in the church at Corinth, the expression 'superlative apostles' does not. The latter denotes rather the leadership of the Jerusalem church, the Jerusalem apostles including Peter. Even though Paul admits no inferiority *vis-à-vis* these 'superlative apostles', he will not criticize or attack them as he does the 'false apostles'.[1]

One of the positive features of this view is that it makes it possible for us to see parallels between the problems Paul was confronting in Corinth and those he faced in Galatia. Paul's converts in Galatia were troubled by Judaizers who demanded that Gentile converts take upon themselves the yoke of the law and submit to circumcision. At the time this issue was being debated in the early church, things were made more difficult by Peter's ambivalence in Antioch (Gal. 2:11–21). If Paul's opponents in Corinth were appealing to the example and teaching of the 'superlative apostles' including Peter, then Paul would have been caught on the horns of a dilemma. On the one hand he needed to attack the views advocated by his opponents, but on the other hand he would be reticent to criticize either Peter or the other 'superlative apostles', for they were the 'pillars' of the Jerusalem church who had recognized the validity of his mission and gospel, and given to him the right hand of fellowship (Gal. 2:1–10). Thus Paul, though forced to claim that he was in no way inferior to the 'superlative apostles', so that he could strengthen his position against those who were appealing to them against him, refused to criticize or attack them as he did the 'false apostles'.

While this viewpoint which distinguishes between 'false apostles' and 'superlative apostles' in chs. 10 – 13 is quite attractive, there are a couple of factors which militate against it. First, in 11:1–6, where Paul first uses the term 'superlative apostles', he does so in the context of reproaching the Corinthians for receiving a different Jesus, a different spirit and a different gospel. It is unlikely that Paul would so describe the content of

<hr />

[1] C. K. Barrett, 'Paul's Opponents in 2 Corinthians', *Essays on Paul* (SPCK, 1982), pp. 60–86.

the preaching of the 'pillars' of the Jerusalem church, for he and they had reached an accord and made mutual recognition of the gospels they preached as well as the mission areas for which they were responsible (Gal. 2:6–9). Second, in the same context (11:1–6) Paul concedes that he may be less skilled in speaking than the superlative apostles, but claims he is in no way deficient in knowledge. It seems highly unlikely that Paul would need to concede any inferiority in speaking ability when comparing himself with the 'superlative apostles' if the latter are to be identified with the Jerusalem apostles. None of them had had the advantage of a formal education as far as we know (cf. Acts 4:13), whereas Paul, though possibly unskilled in the rhetoric of the Hellenistic world, had had the great advantage of training under a famous Jewish rabbi (Acts 22:3). It seems, therefore, that when Paul concedes inferiority to the 'superlative apostles' in speaking ability, he cannot be doing so to the Jerusalem apostles. It is more likely that he concedes such inferiority to his opponents in Corinth, men who had gained some skill in the rhetorical arts as taught in the Hellenistic world.

Seeing, therefore, that Paul both connects the 'superlative apostles' with a different gospel, a different Jesus and a different spirit, and concedes a certain inferiority to them in speaking ability, the identification of the 'superlative apostles' with the Jerusalem 'pillars' is unlikely. It is better to regard 'superlative apostles' and 'false apostles' as two designations for the one group, those whom Paul opposed in Corinth and whom he accused of leading his converts astray from their pure devotion to Christ (11:2–6), and this is the view adopted by most modern commentators.

(iii) Theological differences between Paul and the 'false apostles'

If we bring together the scraps of information which Paul provides about the teaching of his opponents, two major areas of theological disagreement between these men and the apostle Paul may be discerned. The first relates to the gospel itself, and we have seen that Paul regards theirs as a different gospel in which a different Jesus is preached and by which a different spirit is received (see Introduction, pp. 46–47, and Commentary, pp. 184–185).

The second area of disagreement relates to the whole matter of apostleship and the criteria for evaluating claims people make to be apostles of Christ. Such criteria were necessary, for the title 'apostle' was claimed by individuals other than the Twelve in the early church, and Christians needed to be able to evaluate their claims. Paul's opponents, at least as far as Paul lets us see them through his letter, embraced what may be called a triumphalist viewpoint. They expected an apostle to be personally impressive, have a commanding presence and good speaking ability (10:10). He will be authoritative in his dealings with those under him (11:20–21). His claim to be an apostle will rest upon visions and revelations of God experienced by him (12:1), and will be supported by the performance of apostolic signs (12:11–13). He will act as a spokesman of Christ and be known as such because of the manifestations of power in his ministry (13:2–4). And on the more formal side, the apostle of Christ will have proper Jewish connections (11:21–22) and bear letters of recommendation (3:1), most likely from the Jewish leadership of the mother church in Jerusalem.

For the sake of the Corinthian church, Paul felt obliged to answer his opponents according to their folly. So he points out that his own ministry does not lack commendation (3:2–3), knowledge (11:6) or authority (11:20–21; 13:10). He points out also that he has experienced visions and revelations of God (12:1–5), that he does perform the signs of an apostle (12:11–13) and that he can show evidence that Christ speaks through him (13:3–4). However, it is patently clear that Paul rejects this whole approach to evaluating claims to apostleship, and the triumphalist criteria involved. For Paul the marks of true apostolic ministry are its fruit (3:2–3), the character in which it is carried out (*i.e.* in accordance with the meekness and gentleness of Christ) (10:1–2), and the sharing of Christ's sufferings (4:8–12; 11:23–28). He who preaches the gospel of Christ crucified as Lord will exemplify in his ministry both the weakness in which Christ was crucified and the power exercised by Christ as the risen Lord (4:7–12; 12:9–10; 13:3–4).

We have here, then, two quite different ways of evaluating authentic ministry. The one is triumphalist and stresses only the manifestations of power and authority, without any place for weakness and suffering. The other, while also affirming the importance of power and authority, insists that these do not inhere in the apostle, but depend wholly upon the activity of God, who chooses to let that power rest upon his servants in their weakness and to manifest his power through the folly of gospel preaching (12:9–10; 1 Cor. 1:17 – 2:5).

V. DATE

The historical circumstances in which 2 Corinthians (both chs. 1 – 9 and 10 – 13) was written have been discussed at length above (pp. 17–35). It now only remains to try to give actual dates to the writing of these chapters.

Assigning dates to the various points in Paul's career and to the time of writing of his letters is fraught with difficulties. In the case of his relationship with the Corinthians, we do have a couple of possible reference points which may help us. First, Acts 18:2 tells us that when Paul arrived in Corinth on his first visit 'he found a Jew named Aquila, a native of Pontus, lately come from Italy with his wife Priscilla, because Claudius had commanded all the Jews to leave Rome'. This edict of Claudius is generally held to have been promulgated in AD 49.[1] Second, in Acts 18:12–17 we read that during Paul's first visit to Corinth he was brought before Gallio, the proconsul of Achaia. Fragments of an inscription found during excavations at Delphi contain a reproduction of a letter from the emperor Claudius. From the contents of this inscription it can be inferred that Gallio held office in Corinth from the spring of AD 51 to the spring of AD 52. However, a statement made by Seneca, the Stoic philosopher and brother of Gallio, informs us that Gallio did not complete his term of office, and it is therefore impossible to date Paul's encounter with him in the latter part of his term of office. It must have taken place then between July and October AD 51.[2]

Working from these reference points and taking note of the

---

[1]Murphy-O'Connor, pp. 130–140, raises some questions about this dating.
[2]*Ibid.*, pp. 146–150.

information provided about Paul's movements in the Acts of the Apostles (and assuming that this is essentially compatible with what may be inferred from Paul's letters), the following chronology for Paul's contacts with the Corinthians can be suggested. He arrived in Corinth for his first visit early in AD 50. After spending eighteen months there he was arraigned before Gallio (latter half of AD 51). He stayed on in Corinth 'many days longer' after the arraignment, then sailed for Antioch. After spending 'some time' there Paul travelled through Galatia to Ephesus, where he spent two years and three months (AD 52–55). After leaving Corinth, and quite possibly during his stay in Ephesus, the apostle wrote the 'previous' letter. Towards the end of his time in Ephesus (AD 55) he wrote 1 Corinthians, made the 'painful' visit, and wrote the 'severe' letter. Paul then left Ephesus, travelling via Troas to Macedonia, where he met Titus and from where he wrote 2 Corinthians 1 – 9, and shortly afterwards 2 Corinthians 10 – 13 (AD 56). He then made his third visit to Corinth and spent three months in Greece before setting out with the collection to Jerusalem, hoping to arrive there in time for Pentecost AD 57.

ANALYSIS

A. PAUL'S RESPONSE TO A CRISIS RESOLVED (1:1 – 9:15)

I. PREFACE (1:1–11)
   a. *Greeting* (1:1–2)
   b. *Thanksgiving* (1:3–11)

II. THE BODY OF THE RESPONSE (1:12 – 7:16)
   a. *Paul's change of plans* (1:12 – 2:4)
      1. *General defence of integrity* (1:12–14)
      2. *Defence of changed travel plans* (1:15 – 2:4)
   b. *Forgiveness for the offender* (2:5–11)
   c. *Waiting for Titus* (2:12–13)
   d. *Led in triumph* (2:14–17)
   e. *Letters of recommendation* (3:1–3)
   f. *Ministers of the new covenant* (3:4–6)
   g. *Two ministries compared and contrasted (3:7–18)*
      1. *Exposition of Exodus 34:29–32* (3:7–11)
      2. *Exposition of Exodus 34:33–35* (3:12–18)
   h. *The conduct of Paul's ministry* (4:1–6)
   i. *Treasure in earthen vessels* (4:7–12)
   j. *The spirit of faith* (4:13–15)
   k. *The object of faith* (4:16 – 5:10)
      1. *We do not lose heart* (4:16–18)
      2. *The heavenly dwelling* (5:1–10)
   l. *The ministry of reconciliation* (5:11 – 7:4)
      1. *Response to criticism* (5:11–15)
      2. *God's reconciling act in Christ* (5:16–21)
      3. *An appeal for reconciliation* (6:1–13)
      4. *A call for holy living (6:14 – 7:1)*

5. *A further appeal for reconciliation* (7:2–4)
m. *Paul's joy after a crisis resolved* (7:5–16)

III. THE MATTER OF THE COLLECTION (8:1 – 9:15)
  a. *The example of the Macedonians* (8:1–6)
  b. *Paul exhorts the Corinthians to excel* (8:7–15)
  c. *Commendation of those who will receive the collection* (8:16–24)
  d. *Be prepared and avoid humiliation* (9:1–5)
  e. *An exhortation to be generous* (9:6–15)

B. PAUL RESPONDS TO A NEW CRISIS (10:1 – 13:14)

  I. THE BODY OF THE RESPONSE (10:1 – 13:10)
  a. *An earnest entreaty* (10:1–6)
  b. *Paul responds to criticisms* (10:7–11)
  c. *Boasting within proper limits* (10:12–18)
  d. *The Corinthians' gullibility* (11:1–6)
  e. *The matter of financial remuneration* (11:7–15)
  f. *The fool's speech* (11:16 – 12:13)
    1. *Accept me as a fool* (11:16–21a)
    2. *Paul's Jewish ancestry and apostolic trials* (11:21b–33)
    3. *Visions and revelations* (12:1–10)
    4. *Signs of an apostle* (12:11–13)
  g. *paul refuses to burden the Corinthians* (12:14–18)
  h. *The real purpose of Paul's fool's speech* (12:19–21)
  i. *Paul threatens strong action on his third visit* (13:1–10)

II. CONCLUSION (13:11–14)
  a. *Final exhortations and greeting* (13:11–13)
  b. *The benediction* (13:14)

COMMENTARY

A. PAUL'S RESPONSE TO A CRISIS RESOLVED (1:1 – 9:15)

I. PREFACE (1:1–11)

A. Greeting (1:1–2)

Paul's opening words follow the formula found at the beginning of many ancient Greek letters: 'A to B, greeting.' But Paul has expanded the formula with words that emphasize his apostolic authority (which had been called into question at Corinth), and by the inclusion of specifically Christian sentiments.

1. Paul describes himself as *an apostle of Christ Jesus by the will of God*. For Paul, an apostle of Christ was one who had seen the risen Lord (1 Cor. 15:3–10; Gal. 1:15–16), been entrusted with the gospel by him (Gal. 1:11–12; 2:7), and in whose gospel ministry the grace of God was evident (Rom. 1:5; 15:17–19; Gal. 2:8–9). It was on the Damascus road that Jesus Christ apprehended Paul, entrusted him with the gospel, and commissioned him to 'bring about the obedience of faith for the sake of his name among all the nations' (Rom. 1:5). While Paul describes himself as *an apostle of Christ*, he insists that he was so *by the will of God*. There is a distinct parallel between the authority that Paul claimed and that exercised by the Twelve whom Jesus sent on the Galilean mission. To them Jesus said, 'He who receives you receives me, and he who receives me receives him who sent me' (Mt. 10:40). The commission to be Christ's emissary is backed by the will of God the Father. Paul needed to emphasize this authority at the beginning of his letter because it had been called in question at Corinth.

Included with Paul in the opening greeting is *Timothy our brother*. According to Acts 16:1–3, it was at Lystra, while on his second missionary journey, that Paul met Timothy. He was the son of a Jewish mother and a Greek father. Paul saw Timothy's potential and recruited him as a member of the small missionary band. During Paul's extended ministry in Ephesus on the third missionary journey he sent Timothy to Corinth (1 Cor. 4:17 mg.; 16:10), probably as the bearer of 1 Corinthians. If Timothy was the bearer of 1 Corinthians, then we may assume he did in fact reach Corinth, though there is no explicit evidence that he did so, or of what transpired there if he did. What we do know is that Titus subsequently replaced Timothy as Paul's emissary to that city. In any case, by the time Paul dictated the opening greeting of 2 Corinthians, Timothy had rejoined him and things had taken a turn for the worse in Corinth as far as Paul's relationship with the congregation there was concerned.

The letter is addressed *to the church of God which is at Corinth*. Paul frequently describes the churches as God's possession (*cf.*, *e.g.* 1 Cor. 1:2; 10:32; 11:16, 22; 15:9; 1 Thes. 2:14; 2 Thes. 1:4) and this reminds us that, properly understood, they are not just assemblies of like-minded individuals with a religious bent, but communities which belong to God and enjoy a special relationship with him. Because the church at Corinth was God's possession, any threat to its purity or its devotion to Christ was a matter of deep concern to the apostle (*cf.* 1 Cor. 3:16–17; 5:6–8; 2 Cor. 11:2).

Included with the Corinthian church in the address are *all the saints who are in the whole of Achaia*. The word *saints* here carries none of the twentieth-century ideas of canonization, rather its use reflects the fact that all believers are called of God to be his special possession. The Roman province of Achaia covered the southern half of present-day Greece, and included, as well as Corinth, the port-city of Cenchreae and Athens. However, what Paul means by the whole of Achaia may not be coextensive with this Roman province. In 1 Corinthians 16:15–18 he referred to the household of Stephanus (of Corinth) as the first converts in Achaia. We know Paul made converts in Athens (Acts 17:34) before coming to Corinth, so it would seem that the region he speaks of as Achaia here did not include Athens, and was therefore not coextensive with the Roman province so named.[1] We know there were believers in Cenchreae (Rom. 16:1), and these are probably to be seen as included among Paul's addressees here.

2. In ancient Greek letters the word *chairein* ('greeting') was used in the introductory formula, 'A to B, greeting.' In New Testament epistolary contexts *chairein* is found only in Acts 15:23; 23:26 and James 1:1. In Paul's letters *chairein* is replaced by the characteristically Christian word *charis* (*grace*), and in most cases this is expanded, as here, to read: *Grace to you and peace from God our Father and the Lord Jesus Christ.* The word *grace* in these contexts means God's care or help. Such grace was primarily shown in the sending of his Son into the world to effect salvation for mankind (*cf.* Rom. 5:8; 2 Cor. 8:9), but that having been done it is now shown by repeated gracious acts of love, help and provision (*cf.* Rom. 8:32).

Peace is a translation of the word *eirēnē*, which in classical Greek had a predominantly negative meaning (absence of hostility). But in the LXX *eirēnē* was used as an equivalent for the Hebrew word *shalôm*; a word which carried the positive notions of well-being, wholeness and prosperity enjoyed by those who were the recipients of God's grace (*cf., e.g.* Nu. 6:22–27). It was this positive idea that *eirēnē* bore for the New Testament writers and especially for Paul. The peace which Paul invoked for his readers was primarily that objective peace with God won through Christ's death (*cf.* Eph. 2:13–18), the realization of which produces in believers the subjective awareness of peace and well-being.

B. *Thanksgiving* (1:3–11)

Ancient Greek letters generally included, following the introductory greeting, a short expression of prayerful concern or thanksgiving for the recipients. Paul's letters usually include a

[1]But *cf.* Leon Morris, *The First Epistle of Paul to the Corinthians* (IVP/Eerdmans, ²1985) on 1 Cor. 16:15.

thanksgiving after the introductory greeting and 2 Corinthians is no exception. However, the thanksgiving in this letter is unusual in that it focuses not upon the grace of God evident in the lives of the readers, as is the case in most of Paul's other letters, but rather upon the comfort which he and his colleagues had experienced in the midst of great affliction. His readers come into view only in so far as Paul tells them that his afflictions are for their comfort and salvation, and that he hopes as they share his sufferings they will share in the comfort he has experienced as well. Despite the unusual nature of this thanksgiving section, it nevertheless performs the usual function of a thanksgiving in Paul's letters, *i.e.* to foreshadow some major theme which is taken up throughout the Epistle (4:7–18; 6:3–10; 7:4–7; 11:23 – 12:10; 13:3–4).

3. *Blessed be the God and Father of our Lord Jesus Christ.* Old Testament ascriptions of praise to God (*e.g.* Ex. 18:10; Ru. 4:14; 1 Ki. 1:48; Pss. 28.6; 41:13) as well as first-century Jewish liturgies (*e.g.* the eighteen benedictions of the synagogue service) often began with the words 'Blessed be God' which closely parallel the words that open Paul's thanksgiving here. However, by describing God as the *Father of our Lord Jesus Christ* Paul reveals the new Christian understanding of God. He is the one revealed in the Son whom he sent into the world (*cf.* Gal. 4:4).

When Paul describes God as *the Father of mercies* he is again drawing upon his Jewish literary heritage in which the mercies of God are frequently celebrated and invoked (*e.g.* Ne. 9:19; Ps. 51:1; Is. 63:7; Dn. 9:9; Wisdom of Solomon 9:1). However, Paul's appreciation of the mercies of God had been deepened by an understanding of God's saving action in Christ (Rom. 12:1 uses the expression 'the mercies of God' to denote the great saving acts of God in Christ as described in Rom. 1 – 11). It is noteworthy that the apostle uses both the noun, 'mercy', and the verb, 'to have mercy', more than any other writer in the New Testament, and this reflects how important the mercy of God was to him.

The . . . God of all comfort. With this added description of God, Paul introduces the main theme of the thanksgiving section and foreshadows much of what is to follow later in the Epistle. The word here translated *comfort* (*paraklēsis*) belongs to an important word group (which also includes *parakaleō* (to ask, to exhort or encourage, to comfort); *paraklētos* (advocate or comforter)). Significantly the use of *parakaleō* meaning 'to exhort', which was common in both the Greek and Hellenistic Jewish worlds, is almost completely absent from the LXX. On the other hand, the use of *parakaleō* meaning 'to comfort', which is rare in writings from the Greek and Hellenistic Jewish worlds, is common in the LXX. Outstanding examples of the use of this word in the LXX are found in Isaiah 40:1; 51:3; 61:2; 66:13, where the comforting spoken of is God's deliverance of his people.[1] The word *paraklēsis* is used by Luke in his Gospel when describing those who, like the aged Simeon, were 'looking for the consolation (*paraklēsin*) of Israel' (Lk. 2:25), and here too the comfort expected is the deliverance which God will provide (through the coming of the Messiah). For Paul, the messianic age had already begun, albeit while the old age was still running the last stages of its course, and it is the overlapping of the two ages which accounts for the surprising coincidence of affliction and comfort of which he speaks in the present passage. The final consolation of the children of God awaits the day of the revelation of Jesus Christ in glory. But because the messianic age has been inaugurated by Christ at his first coming, the believer experiences in the present time the comfort of God as a foretaste of that final consolation.

4. In this verse Paul moves from the general description of the 'God of all comfort', to speak of him as the one *who comforts us in all our affliction.* There are two things we need to know. What was the affliction, and what was the nature of the comfort? It is fairly easy to identify what Paul meant by *affliction.* In 2 Corinthians itself there are a number of references to the affliction Paul experienced (1:8–10; 4:7–12; 11:23–29). These included the physical hardships, dangers, persecutions and anxieties he experienced as he carried out his apostolic commission.

The answer to the second question is not so easily determined. On the one hand, it is true that sometimes the comfort which Paul received was deliverance *out of* his affliction. In vv. 8–11 he

[1] See O. Schmitz, G. Stahlin, '*Parakaleō, paraklēsis*', *TDNT* 5, pp. 773–799.

speaks of deliverance *from* deadly peril, and in 7:5ff., where Paul describes the events immediately preceding the writing of this letter, he speaks of the release *from* anxiety experienced when Titus rejoined him in Macedonia. It is clear that Paul was not exempt from persecution and affliction because he received comfort from God. The references to affliction in 2 Corinthians which were mentioned above are enough to show that. Nevertheless, it is obvious that up to the time of writing God had delivered Paul out of all his afflictions in the sense that none of them had proved fatal (vv. 8–11; *cf.* Acts 9:23–25; 14:19–20; 16:19–40).

On the other hand, it is equally true that Paul understood comfort in the sense of encouragement and strengthening grace *in* afflictions. This is evident when Paul, in this verse, explains to his readers one of the positive aspects of Christian suffering. It is allowed *so that we may be able to comfort those who are in any affliction, with the comfort with which we ourselves are comforted by God.* One human being cannot effect divine deliverance *from* affliction for another, but it is possible to share with another sufferer the encouragement received *in* the midst of one's own afflictions. The testimony of God's grace in one's life is a forceful reminder to others of God's ability and willingness to provide the grace and strength they need. It is this that Paul has in mind when he says to his readers in v. 6 that the comfort he received was 'for your comfort'. (For unambiguous references to Paul's being encouraged by God to stand firm in face of reviling, and his being assured that God's grace is sufficient to enable him to cope with weakness, suffering and persecution, see Acts 18:9–11 and 2 Cor. 12:8–10 respectively.)

5. In vv. 3–4 Paul blessed God for comfort in affliction, and here he goes on to explain that the honour of sharing in Christ's sufferings is always accompanied by the joy of sharing God's comfort. Because the old age still persists he and his co-workers *share abundantly in Christ's sufferings.*

The idea of sharing Christ's sufferings has been variously interpreted: (a) Paul experienced suffering in his apostolic work just as Christ did in his work as Messiah.[1] (b) The sufferings

---

[1] J. Denney, *The Death of Christ*, ed. R. V. G. Tasker (Tyndale, 1956), p. 82.

experienced by Christ are extended so as to reach and be shared by others (Barrett). (c) The expression 'sharing the sufferings of Christ' is an allusion to Christian baptism (Allo). (d) The sufferings of Christ are no special sufferings, but those experienced by mankind in general. But Christians experience and understand them in a new way (Bultmann). (e) Paul's Jewish contemporaries expected the messianic age to be preceded and ushered in by a period of tribulations. These were known as the messianic woes or the birthpangs of the Messiah/Christ (Goudge).[1] (f) Christ, who suffered personally on the cross, continues to suffer in his people while the old age lasts (*cf*. Acts 9:4–5; Bruce, Harris).

Evaluating the various suggestions, we can say Allo's view that 'the sufferings of Christ' is an allusion to Christian baptism has found few supporters. Bultmann's suggestion that it refers to mankind's experience in general lacks cogency in the light of the lists of affliction in 2 Corinthians, all of which are related to Paul's ministry as an apostle. On the other hand, some of the remaining suggestions could be combined. We could say that 'the sufferings of Christ' here means suffering endured on behalf of Christ and experienced as a part of what the Jews called the birthpangs of the Messiah, while at the same time seeing some closer identification between Christ and the Christian sufferer. We could, for instance, say that while Christians endure the messianic woes for the sake of Christ, he at the same time suffers in his people (*cf*. Acts 9:4–5), or that united with Christ, they too fulfil the role of the Suffering Servant, and share his afflictions.[2]

While Paul and his co-workers *share abundantly in Christ's sufferings* because the old age still persists, they *share abundantly in comfort too* because the new messianic age has already begun. As we have seen, this comfort can take the form of either deliverance *out of* affliction or encouragement *in* affliction which enables them to endure.

6. In v. 4 Paul indicated one positive outcome of the endurance of affliction: the ability to comfort others who are in affliction.

---

[1] So also E. Best, *One Body in Christ: A Study in the Relationship of the Church to Christ in the Epistles of the Apostle Paul* (SPCK, 1975), pp. 131–136.

[2] C. Kruse, *New Testament Foundations for Ministry* (MMS, 1983), pp. 111–114.

Here in v. 6 he mentions a second positive aspect: *If we are afflicted, it is for your comfort and salvation.* There is a benefit to be received by the Corinthians as a result of Paul's afflictions. Pious Jewish expectation of the messianic age could be expressed in terms of a time of comfort for God's people (Is. 40:1–11; 51:1–6; 61:1–4; Lk. 2:25; *cf.* Mt. 5:4; 2 Thes. 2:16–17). Paul, through his preaching ministry which was accompanied by many afflictions, made it possible for the Corinthians to share in this comfort. This comfort was understood to include both the first-fruits of salvation which are experienced in the present time, and final salvation at the last day. For this reason Paul could say his afflictions were for their comfort and salvation.

Not only Paul's affliction, but also the comfort he received in the midst of it, was for the benefit of others: *and if we are comforted, it is for your comfort.* What he stated in general terms in v. 4, he now applies specifically to the Corinthians. It is true to say (but of course it is not the whole truth) that Paul was comforted *for (hyper)* his readers' comfort, *i.e.* that he might comfort them with the comfort he himself had received from God. He goes on to explain that this comfort *you experience when you patiently endure the same sufferings that we suffer.* Two aspects of this statement call for comment.

First, we must admit that we can only guess what the Corinthians' actual sufferings might have been. It is unlikely that they were of the same nature as those experienced by Paul in the course of his apostolic mission. Allo may be right when he suggests that the afflictions the Corinthians experienced were the conflicts among families and relatives, the painful problems and the small everyday vexations which the practice of the gospel would give rise to on all sides in the midst of a town submerged in paganism and its licentiousness. If so, Paul is recognizing that in such afflictions the Corinthians may be said to be sharing the sufferings of Christ (*cf.* v. 5; Phil. 1:29–30).[1]

Second, the comfort which the Corinthians received was not only the encouragement of Paul's testimony, but, perhaps awakened to the possibility by Paul's testimony, that they them-

---

[1]*Cf.* R. C. Tannehill, *Dying and Rising with Christ: A Study in Pauline Theology* (Alfred Topelmann, 1967), pp. 90–98.

selves experienced similar encouragement and strengthening grace from God himself.

7. Despite all the tension in the relationship between Paul and his converts after the writings of 1 Corinthians (see Introduction, pp. 21–23), he concludes this thanksgiving section with the affirmation: *Our hope for you is unshaken.* Up until, and including, the time of writing chs. 1 – 9, Paul had not lost confidence in his readers (*cf.* 2:3; 7:4), and even when he wrote the 'severe' letter he was sure that they would respond positively. He had expressed to Titus his confidence that they would do so (7:12–16). Undergirding Paul's confident hope in the Corinthians was the knowledge that God himself encouraged and strengthened them, *for we know that as you share in our sufferings, you will also share in our comfort.* Literally translated the statement would read: 'knowing that as you are partakers of the sufferings, so also of the comfort'. Two matters call for comment.

First, Paul speaks of 'the' sufferings and 'the' comfort, not *our* sufferings and *our* comfort. This suggests that the meaning is not that the Corinthians share the sufferings of Paul and his colleagues (as the RSV translation suggests), but rather that all (Paul, his colleagues and the Corinthians) share 'the' sufferings, *i.e.* the sufferings of Christ (see commentary on v. 5).

Second, in the original the latter clause lacks a verb (see literal rendering provided above), and this has to be supplied in translation. The RSV, in supplying a verb, makes the text imply that the Corinthians' share in comfort will be experienced in the future (*you will also share in our comfort*). However, as the verb in the first clause is in the present tense (*you share*), it is better to supply a present tense verb in the second clause, as does the NIV ('so also you share in our comfort'). In fact to do so provides a translation of the clause which fits better with the context, where Paul says that his hope for his readers is unshaken because he knows that as they are sharing the sufferings, they are sharing the comfort also.

8. In the preceding verse Paul told his readers that as they share in the sufferings, they also share in the comfort. In this verse Paul, using the formula, *For we do not want you to be*

ignorant, brethren, moves from the general to the particular in order to illustrate from his own recent experience both the suffering and the comfort of which he has just spoken. The word *brethren* is used generically, of course, and denotes both male and female believers (so also in 8:1; 13:11).

The afflictions we experienced in Asia. This was still vividly fresh in Paul's memory. We lack sufficient information for a positive identification of what this Asian affliction was. A number of suggestions have been made (see Additional Note, pp. 68–69), of which Jewish opposition stirred up against the apostle in Ephesus seems to commend itself the most. In any case the affliction proved to be a devastating experience for Paul. He says *we were so utterly, unbearably crushed that we despaired of life itself.*

9. Adding a further explanation of the seriousness of the situation he faced, Paul says, *Why, we felt that we had received the sentence of death.* This statement (lit. 'indeed we ourselves have received the sentence of death in ourselves') is difficult to interpret. Two factors are determinative: the meaning of the Greek word (*apokrima*) translated *sentence*, and the significance of the words 'in ourselves' (*en heautois*). Paul's reference to having received the sentence 'in ourselves' suggests that a subjective experience was involved. It was not so much a verdict pronounced by some external authority, but rather a perception in the heart and mind of the apostle himself. It follows then that *apokrima* was probably not a sentence of death pronounced by some magistrate. It was more likely either the verdict passed by Paul's own mind perceiving the dire straits in which he found himself (so most commentators), or possibly the answer (*apokrima* can mean either 'answer' or 'verdict') given by God to the apostle's prayer about this situation.[1] In any case, he was in a hopeless situation, and humanly speaking there was no escape.

Paul says he experienced this verdict/answer of despair *to make us rely not on ourselves but on God who raises the dead.* Reliance upon God rather than upon one's own native ability is of fundamental importance in the Christian life, yet such an attitude

[1]C. J. Hemer, 'A Note on 2 Corinthians 1:9', *Tyn B* 23 (1972), pp. 103–107, argues that 'There is no ground in contemporary usage for seeing a judicial metaphor here,' rather *apokrima* is best understood as an answer given by God to a petition made by the apostle.

does not come naturally. Very often, as in the case of even the apostle Paul, the facing of impossible situations is necessary *to make us rely not on ourselves but on God*. Paul perceived that one of the divine purposes involved when Christians are plunged into afflictions is to teach dependence on God. For Paul the deadly peril he faced in Asia must have been most distressing. Not only was the prospect of death involved (v. 8, 'we despaired of life itself') but it appeared that his missionary career was to be cut short and urgent projects be left incomplete. The problems in Corinth had not been resolved, the collection for the saints at Jerusalem (*cf.* chs. 8 – 9) had not been completed, and Paul's own ambition to evangelize the western part of the empire would not reach fruition (*cf.* Rom. 15:22–29). These seemingly God-given tasks were to come to nothing. As Hughes observes, 'His feelings must have been not unlike those of Abraham when faced with the offering of Isaac . . . But he learnt also to have a faith similar to that of Abraham, who accounted "that God is able to raise up, even from the dead".' It was when Paul himself faced death that he learnt to rely upon God as the one who raises the dead. Paul already knew that God was the one who had raised Christ from the dead and who would raise up with Christ those who trusted in him (1 Cor. 15:20–23; 1 Thes. 4:13–18). However, he seems to have learnt something more personal through his experience in Asia, *i.e.* reliance upon God as the one who will raise him from his own personal death.

10. Paul testifies that God *delivered us from so deadly a peril, and he will deliver us*. If the deadly peril from which Paul was delivered was a concerted attack by the Jews in Ephesus (see Additional Note, pp. 68–69), then just possibly it was by the heroic intervention of Priscilla and Aquila that divine deliverance for Paul was effected. According to Acts 18:24 – 19: 1 this couple was resident in Ephesus just before Paul arrived there on his third missionary journey, and may well have continued to be so during the apostle's Ephesian ministry, though by the time Paul wrote Romans the couple had moved to Rome (Rom. 16:3). If they were in Ephesus during Paul's ministry there, and if our preferred identification of Paul's affliction in Asia is correct, then they would have been present when Paul faced his 'deadly peril' in Ephesus. In Romans also Paul says 'Greet Prisca and Aquila, my fellow workers in Christ Jesus, who risked their necks for my life' (Rom. 16:3–4). These words, written shortly after the writing of 2 Corinthians, could refer to the couple's part in Paul's deliverance, provided of course the rest of the reconstruction suggested above is correct.

Having experienced a divine deliverance in the immediate past, Paul was encouraged to believe that God would act on his behalf again: *on him we have set our hope that he will deliver us again.* Paul was ever conscious of the threats to his safety which emanated from his fellow countrymen (Rom. 15:30–31; 1 Thes. 2:14–16), and according to Acts there were to be yet further attempts made by the Jews to kill him (Acts 20:3; 21:10–14; 23:12–15). Nevertheless, Paul expresses here his confidence that God will deliver him again. Some have suggested that this future deliverance which Paul anticipated was not deliverance from temporal dangers, but rather the final great deliverance of the last day. However, this is unlikely – the solicitation of his readers' prayers in the next verse suggests that deliverance from perils in the present time is uppermost in Paul's mind here.

11. *You also must help us by prayer.* Paul was convinced of the efficacy of intercessory prayer and repeatedly solicited the prayers of his friends (*cf.* Rom. 15:30–32; Eph. 6:18–20). But characteristic of the apostle was his concern not only for personal deliverance to be granted *in answer to many prayers* but also that thanksgiving should be given to the One who grants deliverance. He urged them to help in prayer *so that many will give thanks on our behalf for the blessing granted us in answer to many prayers.* The expression *many prayers* in this verse is a translation of *pollōn prosōpōn* (lit. 'many faces'). This is probably a figurative use of *prosōpōn*, meaning simply 'persons' or 'people', and the text can accordingly be rendered: 'so many will give thanks on our behalf for the blessing granted us in answer to [the prayers of] many people'. In the present context of prayer, it is possible that *prosōpōn* was used to give the idea of people's faces upturned in prayer to God. Then the text could be rendered: 'so that thanksgiving be made through many people for the blessing granted to us because of many faces upturned in prayer'.

Additional Note: Paul's Affliction in Asia

Numerous attempts have been made to explain the nature of Paul's affliction in Asia. While none of these explanations can be regarded as conclusive, due to lack of sufficient concrete evidence, nevertheless some commend themselves more than others. Denney suggested that it was the imminent danger of drowning implied by 2 Corinthians 11:25, but this is unlikely, not being the sort of experience one would describe as occurring 'in Asia'. Another view adopted by several more recent commentators (*e.g.* Allo, Barrett, Harris) is that the affliction Paul suffered was a grave illness. In favour of this view is the fact that it makes good sense of the perfect tense in 'we felt that we had received (*eschēkamen*) the sentence of death' (v. 9). If Paul had been afflicted with a grave illness, then he might have felt as though 'he had received the sentence of death', and that it was only the life-giving power of God which could prevent that sentence from being carried out. However, the view is not without its problems. It entails a highly unusual (though not unique) use of the word translated 'affliction' (*thlipsis*), which is rarely used to describe illness. Also, if it is accepted that vv. 8–11 are illustrative of the general truth of sharing comfort while sharing Christ's affliction (vv. 5–7), it is unlikely that Paul's affliction 'in Asia' was a grave illness. Elsewhere when the apostle speaks of his afflictions in such terms they are best understood as persecutions and sufferings encountered in the course of his apostolic ministry (*cf.* Gal. 6:17; Col. 1:24).

Tertullian identified Paul's affliction in Asia with the fighting with 'beasts at Ephesus' spoken of by the apostle in 1 Corinthians 15:32[1] (so too Plummer). Against this it is objected that the way Paul speaks of his affliction in 2 Corinthians 1:8 suggests that this was the first time he had mentioned it to the Corinthians, and that it must therefore have occurred after the writing of 1 Corinthians. Another explanation that has been suggested is that it was during an Ephesian imprisonment that Paul had been exposed to 'so deadly a peril' (Furnish). Provided we accept the hypothetical Ephesian imprisonment this is an

---

[1]'On the Resurrection of the Flesh', *The Ante-Nicene Fathers* 3 (Eerdmans, 1973), p. 582.

attractive explanation, more especially if along with it we also accept an Ephesian provenance for Philippians, in which there are possible allusions to an imminent death anticipated by Paul (Phil. 1:20–23; 2:17–18).

Other commentators (*e.g.* Calvin, Lietzmann) identify the affliction in Asia with the tumult in Ephesus following the charges brought against Paul by the guild of silversmiths led by Demetrius, a tumult in which the Jewish opposition to Paul was also mobilized (*cf.* Acts 19:23–41). R. J. Yates draws particular attention to the possible leading role played by Alexander in stirring up the Jews (Acts 19:33), for one by the same name is mentioned again in 2 Timothy 4:14 as having done 'great harm' to Paul. Also, in the address to the Ephesian elders Paul refers to the 'trials which befell me through the plots of the Jews' (Acts 20:19). Further, according to Acts it was 'Jews from Asia' who stirred up the crowd in the temple at Jerusalem so that rough hands were laid upon Paul (Acts 21:27). (Had these Jews travelled from Asia to carry through in Jerusalem the persecution they had begun in Ephesus?)[1] Against this view it is urged that according to Acts 19 Paul does not appear to have been in such deadly peril or despair of his life as 2 Corinthians 1:8–11 implies. This is a weighty objection, but can be largely neutralized when it is recognized that the writing of Acts was possibly some thirty years removed from the events described in its nineteenth chapter, whereas when Paul wrote 2 Corinthians 1:8–11 these events were still very fresh in his memory.

It is the last of these suggestions that commends itself most to the present writer. However, as was mentioned at the beginning of this note, every explanation can only be something of a conjecture, because of the paucity of hard evidence available. While we cannot be certain about the nature of Paul's affliction, we may be sure about the lesson he wishes to draw from it: dependence upon the God who raises the dead.

---

[1] R. J. Yates, 'Paul's Affliction in Asia: 2 Corinthians 1:8', *EQ* 53 (1981), pp. 241–245. See also J. E. Wood, 'Death at Work in Paul', *EQ* 54 (1982), pp. 151–155.

II. THE BODY OF THE RESPONSE (1:12 – 7:16)

A. Paul's Change of Plans (1:12 – 2:4)

In this section Paul, aware that there have been certain criticisms of his character and actions, defends his integrity in general terms (1:12–14) and then in relation to his travel plans and the 'severe' letter (1:15 – 2:4).

1. General defence of integrity (1:12–14)

Paul concluded the previous section (1:3–11) with a request for prayer. It may be that the general defence of his integrity in 1:12–14 is intended as a justification of this request, but it is more likely that it looks forward and paves the way for the specific defence of his integrity in relation to his travel plans and the writing of the 'severe' letter in 1:15 – 2:4.

12. *For our boast is this, the testimony of our conscience.* Paul uses the concept of boasting more than any other New Testament writer. Essentially it means confidence, and in Paul's writings it is used both negatively and positively. Used negatively it refers to an unwarranted self-confidence based on one's own merits, but used positively it denotes a legitimate confidence based upon what God has done and enabled one to do (*cf.* Rom. 15:17–19).

The word *conscience* (*syneidēsis*) is found more often in the Pauline corpus than in the rest of the books of the New Testament put together. Unlike the Stoics, Paul did not regard conscience as the voice of God within, nor did he restrict its function to a person's past acts (usually the bad ones), as was the case in the secular Greek world of his day.[1] For Paul the conscience was a human faculty whereby a person either approves or disapproves his or her actions (whether already performed or only intended) and those of others.[2] The conscience is not to be equated with the voice of God or even the moral law, rather it is a human faculty which adjudicates upon

[1] *Cf.* J. N. Sevenster, *Paul and Seneca* (Brill, 1961), pp. 84–102; C. Maurer, '*Synoida/ syneidēsis*', *TDNT* 6, pp. 898–919.

[2] M. E. Thrall, 'The Pauline Use of *syneidēsis*', *NTS* 14 (1967–1968), pp. 118–125.

human action by the light of the highest standard a person perceives.

Seeing that all of human nature has been affected by sin, both a person's perception of the standard of action required and the function of the conscience itself (as a constituent part of human nature) are also affected by sin. For this reason conscience can never be accorded the position of ultimate judge of one's behaviour. It is possible that the conscience may excuse one for that which God will not excuse, and conversely it is equally possible that conscience may condemn a person for that which God allows. The final judgment therefore belongs only to God (*cf.* 1 Cor. 4:2–5). Nevertheless, to reject the voice of conscience is to court spiritual disaster (*cf.* 1 Tim. 1:19). We cannot reject the voice of conscience with impunity, but we can modify the highest standard to which it relates by gaining for ourselves a greater understanding of the truth.

In this verse Paul explains the ground of his boasting in the testimony of his conscience, a conscience which acknowledges *that we have behaved in the world, and still more toward you, with holiness*[1] *and godly sincerity, not by earthly wisdom but by the grace of God.* Paul behaves in this way *in the world, i.e.* wherever he carries out his mission, but he says *still more toward you.* He had spent eighteen months among the Corinthians on his first visit to their city, and during that time, and in his subsequent contacts with them, he had been especially careful to act in an exemplary way. We can only guess at the reason Paul was so careful in Corinth. Perhaps the Corinthians were more critical than most of the behaviour of itinerants (whose methods were not always exemplary) and Paul wanted it to be abundantly clear that as a messenger of the gospel he renounced all such doubtful methods.

The contrast between behaviour that is according to *holiness and godly sincerity* and *by the grace of God* on the one hand, and that according to *earthly wisdom* on the other, is one which surfaces frequently in Paul's Epistles. For instance, later in this

---

[1]Other ancient manuscripts read 'simplicity' (*haplotēti*) instead of 'holiness' (*hagiotēti*). The evidence is finely balanced and it is difficult to choose between the alternatives. However, the main thrust of Paul's assertion in v. 12 is clear enough, and unaltered by tne choice made between the two alternatives.

same letter Paul asserts: 'We are not, like so many, peddlers of God's word; but as men of sincerity, as commissioned by God, in the sight of God we speak in Christ' (2:17; *cf.* 4:2). *Earthly wisdom* is that which resorts to cunning (*cf.* 4:2) or cleverness with words (*cf.* 1 Cor. 2:1) to impress the hearer. A ministry *by the grace of God* is one which relies upon, and sees, the power of God at work in it (*cf.* Rom. 15:17–19; 1 Cor 2:2–5; 2 Cor. 12:11–12). If God by his grace chooses to manifest his power, then the ministry will be effective; if not, then Paul will not seek to produce results by underhand means.

13a. Paul continues his general defence saying: *For we write you nothing but what you can read and understand.* The apostle apparently perceived that he had been criticized in Corinth by some who questioned the straightforward character of his letters. Later on (according to the reconstruction of events adopted in this commentary, see Introduction, pp. 23–24) Paul had to answer other criticisms concerning an alleged discrepancy between his attitude to the Corinthians when present and that reflected in his letters written to them while absent (*cf.* 10:10–11). But in the present context Paul seems to be responding to an insinuation that he wrote one thing but intended another. This he firmly denies.

13b–14. Here Paul directs his readers' attention to *the day of the Lord Jesus*, that day when every person's life and work will be subject to divine scrutiny. In that connection he says, *I hope you will understand fully, as you have understood in part, that you can be proud of us as we can be of you.* Paul speaks elsewhere of the pride and joy in his converts which he will have at the coming of the Lord (Phil. 4:1; 1 Thes. 2:19), but only here of the pride he expects his converts to feel in their apostle on that day. For his part, Paul will feel pride in his converts because they are the seal of his apostleship, the proof that he has successfully carried out his commission to bring about 'the obedience of faith for the sake of his name among all the nations' (Rom. 1:5). His converts should feel pride in their apostle as they realize fully in that day all they owe to him. All this helps us to make sense of Paul's hope, expressed in the present context, that the Corinthians will understand fully what heretofore they have only understood in part.

2. Defence of changed travel plans (1:15 – 2:4)

15–16. *Because I was sure of this.* Paul explains to his readers that it was with a sense of confidence in their pride in him and of his in them that he was desiring to come and visit them. In 1 Corinthians 16:5 he had promised to visit them *after* passing through Macedonia. But as he explains here, he made a change in those plans so as to visit them *before* going to Macedonia: *I wanted to come to you first, so that you might have a double pleasure.* The apostle explains in v. 16 how his change in plans was to have resulted in a *double pleasure* for the Corinthians: *I wanted to visit you on my way to Macedonia, and to come back to you from Macedonia and have you send me on my way to Judea.* By so doing he intended to make *two* visits instead of the one he had promised in 1 Corinthians 16:5–7.

The word *pleasure*[1] may simply denote the enjoyment the Corinthians were to have experienced when they saw their apostle again. However, because Paul no longer thought of his relationship with others in purely human terms (5:16), *i.e.* apart from the significance of Christ, it is more likely that the *pleasure* Paul had in mind should be understood in terms of the effects of his spiritual ministry among them (*cf.* Rom. 1:11–12).[2]

17. The confidence with which Paul spoke in v. 15 was to a certain extent misplaced, for criticism of him had been entertained among the Corinthians. It was criticism of his changed travel plans that forced him to ask: *Was I vacillating when I wanted to do this?* The form of the question in Greek indicates that a

[1] The word which the rsv renders *pleasure* is *charan* (lit. 'joy'). However, this is probably a scribal amendment of an original *charin* ('grace', 'kindness', 'favour'), which has slightly better support in the manuscripts and underlies the reading of the rsv margin.

[2] A different interpretation of *charin*, suggested by G. D. Fee ('*Charis* in II Corinthians 1:15: Apostolic Parousia and Paul–Corinth Chronology', *NTS* 24 (1978), pp. 533–538), is that it should be taken in an active sense. In this case the *double pleasure* the Corinthians were to experience was that they would have two opportunities to show 'kindness' to their apostle: when they helped him first on his way to Macedonia, and then on his journey to Judea. The weakness of this suggestion is that if the Corinthians had been encouraged to be critical of their apostle, an assertion that he intended to give them two opportunities to do him a favour would not be the best way to overcome their critical attitude.

negative answer was required. Paul in effect says: 'You do not think I was changing my plans in an off-hand manner, do you?' The next question relates to Paul's personal integrity: *Do I make my plans like a worldly man, ready to say Yes and No at once?* Again the question expects a negative answer. To act *like a worldly man* (lit. 'according to [the] flesh') would in this context imply a readiness to renege on commitments if they no longer suited their author, and that with little concern for other parties involved. He would change his 'Yes' to a 'No' without any compunction if it so suited him. Paul's question is meant to evoke from his readers an emphatic denial that their apostle would act in such a way.

18. *As surely as God is faithful, our word to you has not been Yes and No.* This sentence constitutes an assertion under oath[1] by Paul that his word to them was consistent with his firm intentions. He had not said one thing to them while all the time being ready, without any compunction, to do something quite different if it so suited him.

Paul uses oaths quite often in his letters (*cf.* Rom. 1:9; Gal. 1:20; 2 Cor 1:23; 11:10,31; Phil. 1:8; 1 Thes. 2:5, 10) when he wants to defend or lay heavy stress upon the truth of his assertions. This suggests that in the early church Christ's words against swearing in Matthew 5:33–37 were understood as a criticism of the improper use of oaths, rather than their prohibition. According to Matthew 26:63 Christ himself was prepared to be placed under oath when answering the question of the high priest.

19. In the preceding verse Paul asserted the reliability of his word to the Corinthians. He had been concerned to defend his integrity in relation to changes to his travel plans. But it seems Paul felt that if the reliability of his word about travel plans were

[1]Some commentators (*e.g.* Plummer) construe this verse not as an assertion with an oath but as a straightforward statement: 'God is faithful in that our word to you has not been Yes and No.' In this case the sentence becomes an assertion that Paul's reliability rests upon God's faithfulness. However, the majority of scholars (*e.g.* Lietzmann, Hughes, Barrett, Furnish) rightly recognize the presence of an oath formula here. Where Paul uses the expression 'God is faithful' as part of a simple statement it is not followed by a *hoti* clause (Furnish).

being called into question, then the reliability of his gospel message may also be questioned. So here he asserts there is no equivocation in the gospel he preached. *For the Son of God, Jesus Christ, whom we preached among you . . . was not Yes and No, but in him it is always Yes.* There is no changeability in Jesus Christ, the one proclaimed by Paul in his gospel. What this means is further explained in v. 20.

Paul specifically associates with himself in the preaching of the gospel in Corinth both *Silvanus and Timothy.* Silvanus, who may be identified with the Silas of Acts, was one of the leaders of the Jerusalem church chosen to carry the decision of the Jerusalem council to Antioch (Acts 15:22), and the one who became Paul's colleague on the second missionary journey following the dissension between Paul and Barnabas (Acts 15:36–41). When Paul and Silas reached Lystra, Timothy, the son of a Jewish Christian mother and a Greek father, was recruited to join the small missionary team (Acts 16:1–3). Thus when Paul came to Corinth for the first time both these men were associated with him, and joined him in the ministry of the gospel there.

20. *For all the promises of God find their Yes in him.* With these words Paul clarifies what he meant by saying in the preceding verse that in Jesus Christ 'it is always Yes'. The Old Testament contains many promises of God concerning the messianic age. Not one of these will fail to find its fulfilment in Christ. There is no equivocation as far as the fulfilment of the promises of God in Jesus Christ is concerned.

That is why we utter the Amen through him, to the glory of God. The Greek underlying this sentence is difficult to translate and interpret accurately in detail, although its general thrust is clear enough. The RSV translation reflects a background of worship in the early church where ascriptions of praise to God were offered *through him* (Christ) and confirmed by the 'Amen' of the congregation. A similar form is found in many of the ascriptions of praise found in the letters of the New Testament (*e.g.* Rom. 1:25; 9:5; 11:36; 15:33; 16:27; Gal. 1:5; Eph. 3:21; Phil. 4:20; 1 Tim 1:17; 6:16; 2 Tim. 4:18; Heb. 13:21; 1 Pet. 4:11; 5:11; 2 Pet. 3:18; Jude 25; Rev. 1:6; 7:12), a fact which confirms the use of 'Amen' in this way in the early church.

However, the RSV translation does not preserve as well as it might the connection between the first and second parts of the verse which is evident in the original. There it is stressed that it is the same Christ in whom the Yes to the promises of God is found who is also the one 'through whom is the Amen to God'. The thrust of the original appears to be that the 'Amen' is uttered both by Christ and by us, to the glory of God.

It may be observed that it is only as we add our 'Amen' to the promises of God which find their Yes in Christ that those promises become effective in our case, and we may on that account then truly glorify God for his grace to us.

21–22. In these verses we can see why Paul introduced the idea of the unequivocal nature of Christ, the one in whom God's promises find their Yes. For it is in this unequivocal Christ that Paul and his co-workers have been established and commissioned by God as messengers of the gospel, and it is in this Christ also that they have received the seal of the Spirit. Put simply, Paul's answer to those who ascribe fickleness to him because of the changes in his travel plans is that God's work in his life guarantees the trustworthiness of what he says. To explain the nature of this work of God in his life Paul introduces four important expressions.

First, he says: *But it is God who establishes us with you in Christ*. The word 'to establish' (*bebaioō*) is used in a legal sense in the papyri of a guarantee given that certain commitments will be carried out. In the New Testament *bebaioō* is used similarly in connection with the proclamation of the gospel, which is 'confirmed' by miraculous signs or the bestowal of spiritual gifts (Mk. 16:20; 1 Cor. 1:6). When the verb is used of human beings it indicates their strengthening or establishing so that they exhibit certain characteristics. For example, in 1 Corinthians 1:8 Paul writes of believers being established 'guiltless' in the day of the Lord. Here he argues that God has strengthened and established him and his co-workers (as also the Corinthians) to be trustworthy.

Second, Paul says God *has commissioned us*. The verb used is *chriō*, which means to anoint; because anointing was often a rite of commissioning (Ex. 28:41; 1 Sa. 15:1; 1 Ki. 19:16) the RSV rendering *commissioned* is justifiable. However, it does obscure the fact that there was an anointing involved in the commissioning of Paul and his collegues. *Chriō* is found in four other places in the New Testament, once in Hebrews 1:9 ('God, thy God, has anointed thee with the oil of gladness beyond thy comrades') and three times in the writings of Luke (Lk. 4:18; Acts 4:27; 10:38). In the Lucan uses the reference is twice quite explicitly to anointing with the Spirit and arguably it is implied in the third. Given the emphasis on the Spirit in the present context it is best to see here a reference to Paul and his colleagues having been anointed by the Spirit, recognizing that their commission is inextricably bound up with that.

Third, Paul says *he has put his seal upon us*. The verb, 'to put a seal upon' (*sphragizō*) is used in commercial documents found among the papyri of the sealing of letters and sacks so that nobody can tamper with the contents. Used figuratively, as in the New Testament, 'to seal' means to keep secret or stamp with a mark of identification (*cf.* Rev. 7:3–8). Ephesians speaks of Christians being 'sealed with the promised Holy Spirit' (Eph. 1:13; *cf.* 4:30). Here, by the phrase *he has put his seal upon us*, Paul almost certainly means that God has endowed us with the Spirit (whose presence is the identifying mark of every true believer, Rom. 8:9).

Fourth, we read *he has . . . given us his Spirit in our hearts as a guarantee*. The Greek word, *arrabōn*, here translated *guarantee*, is, like *sphragizō*, a commercial term. It is the deposit made by the buyer to the seller as a guarantee that the full amount will be paid over at the proper time. The term is applied figuratively by Paul to the Spirit whom God has given to believers as a guarantee of their full participation in the blessings of the age to come (*cf.* 5:5; Eph. 1:14).

The major thrust of vv. 21–22, then, is that Paul and his colleagues have been established by God as faithful messengers and they have been anointed with his Spirit.[1] But why does Paul

---

[1] A number of scholars argue that the four major expressions introduced by Paul in vv. 21–22 reflect the terminology of early Christian baptismal liturgies. Whether the expressions had baptismal connotations in Paul's day is debatable, but not out of the question, especially in the light of the fact that there was not in the New Testament the separation

make these assertions at this point in his letter? It is to show that the integrity of the apostolic band and the truthfulness of the gospel rests upon nothing less than the work of God. It is the Spirit of God who establishes and anoints them, and whose presence is the authenticating seal upon their mission and message. The implication is that if this work of God in their lives guarantees their trustworthiness in the greater matter of the proclamation of the gospel, then surely it will also render them trustworthy in the lesser matter of their travel plans. Any changes in these will not be the result of mere fickleness, but of genuine unforeseen eventualities.

23–24. Beginning with an oath, *I call God to witness against me*, Paul asserts the purity of his motives, and insists that changes to his travel plans were made bearing in mind the feelings of the Corinthians: *it was to spare you that I refrained from coming to Corinth*. The present context does not tell us from what the Corinthians were spared, but from statements Paul makes elsewhere (13:1–4, 10) it would seem they were spared some sort of disciplinary action which the apostle would have felt compelled to take.

Lest the Corinthians conclude from Paul's allusions to disciplinary action that he exercised some form of spiritual tyranny over them, he adds, *Not that we lord it over your faith; we work with you for your joy.* The role of an apostle (and of all Christian ministers) is that of a servant to the people of God (*cf.* 4:5), not that of a tyrant. But, as v. 23 reveals, serving the people of God does not mean doing only what pleases them. It may involve disciplinary action as well. After all, an apostle (like all Christian ministers), while called to serve the people of God, must do so by carrying out the desires of his master. Verse 23 also contains a most attractive description of the purpose of Christian ministry: to work alongside people to increase their joy!

The reason Paul gives here why he does not lord it over their faith is found in the words: *for you stand firm in your faith.* It is true that the Corinthians came to faith through Paul's ministry, but their faith was their own, and rests upon the power of God

---

between the rite of baptism, belief and reception of the Spirit that some see today. *Cf.* Acts 2:38; 1 Cor. 12:13; Eph. 1:13. *Cf.* also J. D. G. Dunn, *Baptism in the Holy Spirit* (SCM, 1970), pp. 131–134.

(*cf.* 1 Cor. 2:5; 15:1–2, 11). Because of their faith, believers have their own standing before God (Rom. 5:1–2; 11:20), and in this respect they are subject to no-one else (Rom. 14:4).

2:1. *For I made up my mind not to make you another painful visit.* In 1 Corinthians 16:5–7 Paul had informed his readers that he intended to visit them after passing through Macedonia. Subsequently he changed his plans so as to visit Corinth first on his way to Macedonia, and then again on his way back, thereby giving the Corinthians 'a double pleasure' (1:15–16). Paul apparently made the first of these promised visits, and because it turned out to be so painful for both the Corinthians and himself he aborted the return visit and wrote them the 'severe' letter instead. Some hints as to the nature of the pain experienced when Paul made the first of the promised visits are contained in the following verses.

2. *For if I cause you pain, who is there to make me glad but the one whom I have pained*? Paul asks who there would be to make him glad if when he made the second of these promised visits he caused the Corinthians (*you*, plural) further pain. He answers his own question by saying that only *the one* (singular) he has pained could make him glad again. Most commentators identify *the one* of the second part of the verse with the *you* of the first part. This is done either by regarding *the one* as a representative Corinthian, or, as in the case of the translators of the NIV, by simply replacing *the one* with 'you'.

An alternative approach is to identify *the one* of this verse with the 'one' of vv. 5–8. In this case the pain caused to *the one* would be the pain of realizing that disciplinary action had been demanded of the congregation against him by Paul. The pain caused to the Corinthians (*you*) would be the rebuke implied by Paul's (renewed) demand for disciplinary action, something they had been reluctant to carry through even when their apostle had been caused pain (*cf.* v. 3). This interpretation yields good sense. Paul caused pain to both the offender and the Corinthian congregation by his demand for disciplinary action. There can be no more joy in his relationship with the Corinthians until the offender has been brought to repentance and restored to fellowship. Then the one whom Paul has pained will make him glad. (See Introduction, pp. 41–45, for a suggested identification for the offender.)

3. *And I wrote as I did.* This refers to the writing of the 'severe' letter after the apostle's return from the 'painful' visit (see Introduction, pp. 21–22). Paul wrote rebuking the Corinthians because they had not come to his defence when he was maligned by 'the one who caused pain', demanding that they punish this individual and making it clear that he expected their obedience in this matter (*cf.* vv. 6, 9).

Paul's hope in writing was *so that when I came I might not suffer pain from those who should have made me rejoice, i.e.* he expected his letter to cause his readers to take the necessary steps to remove the source of friction which existed between them and their apostle. During the 'painful' visit Paul had been caused mental anguish by the offending individual, while the Corinthians, who should have made him rejoice, apparently stood by and did nothing. The 'severe' letter was intended to ensure that this would not happen again.

If the first part of the verse shows the purpose of the 'severe' letter, the second part indicates the confidence with which it was written: *For I felt sure of all of you, that my joy would be the joy of you all.* Though the 'severe' letter was certain to cause pain to Paul's readers, nevertheless he wrote it in the confidence that they would rejoice to see their apostle joyful once more. So Paul could tackle the thorny problem of the punishment of 'the one who caused pain', confident of the basic goodwill of the Corinthians towards him at this stage.

4. *For I wrote you out of much affliction and anguish of heart and with many tears.* The reference to the *much affliction* out of which Paul wrote may be either another way of speaking of the *anguish of heart* which he felt at the time or an allusion to the affliction in Asia to which he refers in 1:8–9. If the latter, then Paul's situation would have been poignant indeed. While in despair of life itself because of persecution in Asia he was further burdened with *anguish of heart* over the situation in Corinth. In that case we can appreciate why the letter was written *with many tears.*

Not to cause you pain but to let you know the abundant love that I have for you. The 'tearful' letter must have contained some sort of rebuke to the Corinthians (*cf.* 7:8–9), but Paul assures them here that his intention was not to cause pain but to let them know his love for them. He showed this, not by glossing over a bad situation but by confronting it and demanding (again) that the Corinthians take action. It takes real love to confront a difficult situation rather than side-stepping it.

B. Forgiveness for the Offender (2:5–11)

Paul's 'severe' letter proved to be effective in that the Corinthians did take strong disciplinary action against the offender. Having heard of the strong action taken, Paul was both relieved (*cf.* 7:6–13) and concerned. His concern now was that Satan might gain the advantage if the offender were to be overwhelmed by excessive sorrow, so he urged his readers to turn and reaffirm their love to the offender.

5. Obviously Paul's words, *But if any one has caused pain, he has caused it not to me,* must not be taken on their own to mean he is denying that he suffered any wrong. They must be taken with the words which follow, *but in some measure – not to put it too severely – to you all,* and the whole then shows Paul at pains to stress that the wrong done had affected the Corinthians as well as himself. In fact, had the wrong done affected only the apostle we might well ask why he did not follow his own advice given in 1 Corinthians 6:7 and simply suffer the wrong. However it was the congregation as a whole, as well as Paul, that had been affected. (Introduction, pp. 41–45, make suggestions regarding the nature of the harm done.)

6. Turning from the injury done, to the punishment carried out against the offender, Paul says, *For such a one this punishment by the majority is enough.* The word translated *punishment* (*epitimia*) is used only here in the New Testament, but in extra-biblical writings it is used of the imposition of either legal penalties or commercial sanctions. Its use here approximates to the former sense and suggests that the congregation had acted formally and judicially against the offender. The word translated *majority* (*pleionōn*) could be also construed 'the rest', in which case the punishment of the offending member would have been determined by a unanimous decision of the rest of the congregation, not simply by a majority. In whatever way the punishment was decided and carried out, Paul was now convinced that it is enough.

7–8. Because he regarded the punishment as sufficient (and presumably because the offender had been brought to repentance), Paul says, *so you should rather turn to forgive and comfort him.* Although the punishment of the offender was deserved, it brought Paul no joy (*cf.* v. 2), it was restoration for which he longed. And if the church did not turn and forgive, there would be the danger that the offender *may be overwhelmed by excessive sorrow.* The verb 'to overwhelm' (*katapinō*) was also used of animals who 'devour' their prey, and of waves or waters which 'swallow up' objects and people. Paul is afraid that the offender, if not forgiven, may 'drown' in his sorrow, and adds: *So I beg you to reaffirm your love for him.* The Greek word translated *to reaffirm* (*kyrōsai*) was used in the papyri to denote the confirming of a sale or the ratification of an appointment. The confirmation of love for which Paul calls, then, appears to be some formal act by the congregation, in the same way that the imposition of punishment in the first place appears to have been formal and judicial.

9–11. Paul now shifts his attention from the offender to the Corinthians themselves. It is true that the 'severe' letter's purpose was to demand disciplinary action against the offender, but this demand was intended also to test the Corinthians' obedience: *For this is why I wrote, that I might test you and know whether you are obedient in everything.* What Paul expected was not obedience to him personally, but obedience to the gospel and its implications. It is significant that throughout his letters Paul consistently bases his ethical demands on the first principles of the gospel, not upon his personal authority. It is to the gospel and its implications that believers must be obedient.

Any one whom you forgive, I also forgive. Paul calls upon his readers to forgive the offender (vv. 6–7) and here assures them: 'to whom you forgive anything, I also [forgive that]' (this is the literal rendering). Perhaps the apostle says this to allay any fears that he might not approve the reinstatement of one who had hurt him so badly.

What I have forgiven, if I have forgiven anything, has been for your sake in the presence of Christ. Three matters call for comment. First, Paul appears to be playing down the extent of his hurt when having said, *What I have forgiven*, he adds, *if I have forgiven anything.* There is no question that he had something to forgive, as the general thrust of 2:5–11 and 7:8–13 reveals. Second, Paul stresses that he has forgiven the offence *for your sake.* This may show that the apostle realized his own forgiveness was needed before the Corinthians themselves would feel free to effect reconciliation with the offender. His forgiveness then would be for their sake in that it opened the way for this reconciliation and thereby the restoration of a sense of well-being in the church. Third, the expression *in the presence of Christ* (lit. 'in [the] face of Christ') is difficult, and could be construed in a number of ways. It could be taken as an oath formula, in which case Paul would be saying: 'As I stand in the presence of Christ, I have forgiven the offence.' Alternatively, it could mean his forgiveness has the approval of Christ. In this case the translation would run: 'What I have forgiven has been forgiven before the face of Christ that looks down with approval.' Finally, the expression could reflect that at the time of writing the apostle had not had opportunity to express his forgiveness face to face with the individual, but nevertheless he had already, before the face of Christ, forgiven the offence.

In all this Paul was concerned *to keep Satan from gaining the advantage over us* (lit. 'that we be not taken advantage of by Satan'). A possible interpretation of this statement is that Satan would be allowed to take advantage of the situation and keep the church weak if there were no reconciliation. However, a more specific interpretation is possible and preferable. The Greek word *pleonekteō* ('to take advantage of') is found in four other places in the New Testament – all in Paul's letters (2 Cor. 7:2; 12:17–18; 1 Thes. 4:6). All of the other uses in 2 Corinthians (and arguably so for that in 1 Thessalonians) denote a taking advantage of people in the sense of defrauding them of something which belongs to them. It seems most likely, therefore, that what Paul has in mind in this verse is the possibility that Satan might take advantage of the situation and defraud the congregation of one of its members permanently. So, being *not ignorant of his designs*, Paul urges the Corinthians to reaffirm their love for the offender to forestall such a possibility. Later in the Epistle (see commentary on 11:3, 14–15) we will see that Paul recognizes an active role on the part of Satan to undermine the faith, devotion and good order of the church.

C. *Waiting for Titus* (2:12–13)

According to the reconstruction of events adopted in this commentary (see Introduction, pp. 21–22), it was some time after Paul returned to Ephesus, following the 'painful' visit to Corinth and after he had written the 'severe' letter, that he made his way north to Troas. In Paul's day Troas was an important sea port and commercial centre.

12. *When I came to Troas to preach the gospel of Christ, a door was opened for me in the Lord.* Paul's primary purpose in coming to Troas was *to preach the gospel of Christ*, and, as he himself testifies, he found *a door was opened* for him there. In 1 Corinthians 16:9 Paul used the metaphor of the open door to describe the opportunity he had for 'effective work' in Ephesus. We know that as a result of his labours there not only was a church founded in Ephesus, but the gospel was taken to other cities in the region (*e.g.* Colossae and Laodicea, and probably to the rest of the cities of the seven churches in Asia mentioned in Rev. 2 – 3; *cf.* Acts 19:10). When Paul describes the opportunity he found in Troas as 'a door opened' for him in the Lord, it suggests that it was of similar potential to that in Ephesus.

13. *But my mind could not rest because I did not find my brother Titus there.* Titus is here mentioned for the first time in the Corinthian correspondence. Paul spoke of him in Galatians 2:1–3 as one whom he took to Jerusalem, and who, 'though he was a Greek', was not compelled to be circumcised. Apart from this we know nothing of Titus' background, it being doubtful whether he can be identified with the Titius Justus of Acts 18:7.

However, as 2 Corinthians itself reveals, Titus played a crucial role in relations between Paul and the church at Corinth. One of the Pastoral Epistles is addressed to Titus, who was then active in Crete and responsible for setting up elders in the churches there (Tit. 1:5).

Paul says that because he did not find Titus in Troas he *took leave of them and went on to Macedonia.* The fact that Paul was prepared to leave behind so great an 'open door' in Troas only serves to underline the unrest he felt because he had not made contact with Titus. The relief Paul experienced when he finally met up with Titus in Macedonia is described in 7:5–16. From this passage we may infer that in Troas Paul was deeply concerned whether Titus would be well received on his errand to Corinth, and whether the church there would respond positively to the demands of his 'severe' letter.

Paul returns to these matters in 7:5ff., but before that there is a long digression (2:14 – 7:4) in which he speaks about the nature of his ministry and how he was upheld in it during very distressing times.

D. Led in Triumph (2:14–17)

What Paul has been saying up until this point in the letter could be taken as a rather depressing account of his ministry. He has spoken of affliction in Asia, criticisms of his integrity, the pain experienced in Corinth because of the offender, and his inability to settle to missionary work in Troas. As if to balance this somewhat depressing account, Paul in these verses strikes a positive note, describing how God always and in every place enabled him to carry on an effective ministry despite the difficulties.

14. Despite all the difficulties of his mission Paul is able to say, *But thanks be to God, who in Christ always leads us in triumph.* The words *leads us in triumph* translate *thriambeuonti hēmas,* the exact meaning of which has been the subject of much debate (see Additional Note, pp. 88–89). The viewpoint adopted in this commentary is that *thriambeuonti hēmas* is best understood to mean that God leads Paul and his co-workers as victorious soldiers in a triumphal procession. Such an interpretation allows vv. 14–17 to function as a counterbalance to the preceding sections where Paul dwells upon the difficulties and sufferings involved in the apostolic mission. It does not support a 'triumphalist' approach to ministry, but sees ministry as victory through suffering, *i.e.* that despite the difficulties, God ensures the effectiveness of the ministry of Paul and his colleagues. This is a major theme running through the whole of 2 Corinthians.

Paul describes the effectiveness of their ministry with the words: *and through us [God] spreads the fragrance of the knowledge of him everywhere.* The imagery of the triumphal procession (during which incense was burnt to the gods and the fragrance of which wafted over the spectators as well as those in the procession) appears to be carried into this part of v. 14 and into vv. 15–16.[1] The fragrance spread abroad through Paul's ministry was *the knowledge of him*, *i.e.* the knowledge of God which is reflected in the face of Christ (*cf.* 4:6), whom Paul proclaims in his gospel.

15–16. *For we are the aroma of Christ to God.* Paul can describe himself in these terms because by the preaching of God's word (v. 17) he spreads abroad the fragrance of the knowledge of Christ. Paul extends the metaphor to describe the two possible responses to gospel preaching by adding the words, *among those who are being saved and among those who are perishing.* The smell of incense burnt to the gods in a Roman triumphal procession would have had different connotations for different people. For the victorious general and his soldiers, and for the welcoming crowds, the aroma would be associated with the joy of victory. But for the prisoners of war the aroma could only have been associated with the fate of slavery or death which awaited them. In like fashion, then, the preaching of the gospel would be *a fragrance from life to life* for those who believed, but *a fragrance*

---

[1]Barrett has argued that the imagery is drawn rather from the world of sacrifice (the smell of the burnt offerings or incense ascending to the nostrils of the deity). He draws attention to the words 'we are an aroma of Christ to God (*tō theō*)' in v. 15, arguing that the 'aroma' is intended primarily for God, not human beings. However, as Furnish points out, the *fragrance* or aroma in the present context is thought of primarily as something affecting human beings, not God. Also, the words *tō theō* could be translated 'for God', thus yielding a translation: 'we are an aroma of Christ for God', *i.e.* an aroma for God 'among those who are being saved and among those who are perishing'.

from death to death for those who refused to obey it. The triumphal procession background also makes it possible to suggest the significance of Paul's reference to his being an aroma of Christ *to God*. In the Roman victory procession the incense was offered to the gods, even though it was the people who smelt its aroma. So likewise, while Paul is primarily concerned here with the response of the people to the proclamation of the gospel, nevertheless he realizes that the proclamation of Christ is well-pleasing to God, it is the aroma of Christ to God.[1]

The heavy responsibilities of such a ministry force the apostle to ask, *Who is sufficient for these things?* It is not until 3:5 that we find Paul's answer: 'Not that we are competent of ourselves . . . our competence is from God'.

17. *For we are not, like so many, peddlers of God's word.* Paul implies that the heavy burden of responsibility which he feels results from the fact that he refuses to act like so many others and simply 'peddle' the word of God.[2] The verb used in the statement *we are not . . . peddlers* is *kapēleuō*, whose literal meaning was 'to trade in' or 'to peddle'. Because of the tricks of petty traders, who would adulterate their wine with water or use false weights, the word came to have negative connotations. Paul's meaning here then is that he felt the burden of responsibility of gospel preaching so greatly because he refused to tamper with God's word (*cf.* 4:2) and remove its offence so that like others he might peddle it for personal gain. Later Paul will write about Jewish Christian intruders who came to prey upon the Corinth-

[1] Another possible approach to the interpretation of these verses is suggested by T. W. Manson ('2 Cor. 2:14–17: Suggestion towards an Exegesis', *Studia Paulina*, ed. J. N. Sevenster and W. C. van Unnik (Bohn, 1953), pp. 155–162). He cites rabbinic sources in which the Torah acts both as an elixir of life (for Israel) and a deadly poison (for Gentile nations). It is with this background that Paul speaks of Christ as an aroma which has similarly diverse effects on those who believe or disbelieve the gospel.

[2] In chs. 10 – 13 Paul speaks of certain individuals who were passing themselves off as true apostles. Paul himself called them 'false apostles' and 'deceitful workmen', and implied that they were in fact servants of Satan (*cf.* 11:12–15). They were men who prided themselves on their Jewish credentials (11:21b–22), and who persuaded the Corinthians to accept a different gospel (11:1–6). Later in Paul's career there were Jewish-Christian preachers who took advantage of his imprisonment to preach in such a way as to cause him dismay (Phil. 1:15–17). It is probably people like these to whom Paul refers when he speaks of *peddlers of God's word*. Their influence had already been felt in Corinth when Paul wrote chs. 1 – 7 and it reached a peak by the time chs. 10 – 13 were written.

ians (11:20). Quite possibily these men were already operating in the background at Corinth when chs. 1 – 7 were being written, and it may well be that Paul is alluding to them when he speaks of *peddlers of God's word*. Then contrasting himself and his colleagues to such people, Paul says: *as men of sincerity, as commissioned by God, in the sight of God we speak in Christ*. An apostle is one who is *commissioned by God*, and must therefore carry out his mission *in the sight of God*, and finally render an account of himself to God (*cf*. 5:10–11).

Additional Note: The Meaning of Thriambeuonti Hēmas in 2:14

The word *thriambeuō* is found only twice in the New Testament (here and in Col. 2:15), not at all in the LXX, but a number of times in extra-biblical writings (see LSJ, MM, BAGD *ad loc.*). Four major interpretations of *thriambeuō* followed by an accusative object have been suggested. (a) To cause someone to triumph. This is the rendering of the AV, but it has no lexical support and has been universally abandoned by modern interpreters. (b) To put someone on show or display. This view has been recently advanced by R. P. Egan,[1] who rejects any association of *thriambeuō* with the Roman triumphal procession, and argues that Paul wishes to stress the idea of openness or visibility by the use of the verb. (c) To lead someone as a captive in a triumphal procession. This has the best lexical support, is the rendering of the NEB and GNB, and is adopted by Hughes and L. Williamson Jr,[2] and is essentially the view adopted by P. Marshall,[3] though the latter does argue that Paul's main intention in using the verb was to depict himself as a figure of shame. The problem with this approach is that the notion of a captive in a Roman procession, especially where the stress is upon the captive as a figure of shame, does not provide the necessary counterbalance to the preceding sections where Paul dwells on the difficulties he has experienced. (d) To lead someone as a soldier in a triumphal procession. This does not have clear lexical support in extra-biblical texts, but it does seem to fit best

---

[1]'Lexical Evidence on Two Pauline Passages', *NovT* 19 (1977), pp. 34–62.
[2]'Led in Triumph' *Int* 22 (1968), pp. 317–332.
[3]'A Metaphor of Social Shame: *Thriambeuein* in 2 Cor. 2:14', *NovT* 25 (1983), pp. 302–317.

with the flow of Paul's thought in the context. It is the interpretation underlying the JB translation, and the choice of Allo, Héring, Barrett and Bruce. It does enable good sense to be made of the aroma/fragrance imagery of vv. 14b–16, *i.e.* by seeing in these, allusions to the incense burnt in Roman triumphal processions (for which there is evidence, despite Egan's denial of the same). It is this fourth option which is adopted in this commentary.

E. *Letters of Recommendation* (3:1–3)

Paul has a lot to say one way or another about the commendation of servants of God in this Epistle (see also 4:2; 5:12; 6:4; 10:12, 18; 12:11). In this section he speaks about letters of recommendation, claiming that in the case of the Corinthians at least he did not need to either produce one for them or receive one from them. It is not that Paul disapproves of letters of recommendation, in fact he himself provided commendations for others in his own Epistles (*cf.* Rom. 16:1; 1 Cor. 16:10–11; Phil. 2:19–24). It is rather that as founding apostle of the Corinthian church he feels no letter of recommendation is needed to prove the authenticity of his apostleship to that church, and also the fact that he has successfully planted the church in Corinth can be seen by others as proof of this apostleship, so that he does not need a letter of recommendation from them either.

But why does Paul raise the question of a letter of recommendation at all? We have to assume that the fact that he did not bring such a letter with him to Corinth had been used as a basis of criticism by someone in the church. Quite likely it was the offender (the one who caused pain, 2:5; who did wrong, 7:12) who, in mounting his personal attack against Paul, criticized the apostle's lack of such a letter. In so doing the offender probably received moral support at least from the 'false apostles' who had already infiltrated the church and were themselves to oppose Paul so vehemently later on (as reflected in chs. 10 – 13).

1. *Are we beginning to commend ourselves again?* Paul is very sensitive about the matter of self-commendation (*cf.* 5:12; 10:18). He has spoken in his own defence once already in the Epistle (1:12–14), and is obviously reluctant to do so again. But criticism that he did not bring letters of recommendation forces him to say something. So he asks, *Do we need, as some do, letters of recommendation to you, or from you?* Others had come to Corinth with letters (*e.g.* Apollos, *cf.* Acts 18:24–28) because they needed them. It is absurd that anyone should require Paul to bring such letters to the Corinthian church when he was its founding apostle. Thus Paul's question (introduced by the Greek negative particle, *mē*) expects an emphatic 'No' as an answer.

2. *You yourselves are our letter of recommendation.* The very existence of the Corinthian church testified to the effectiveness and authenticity of Paul's ministry. They were his letter of recommendation. This letter, says Paul, is *written on your hearts, to be known and read by all men.*[1] The work of God in their hearts through the agency of the apostle had effected a change in their lives and allegiance. This very change constituted a 'living letter' that could be known and read by everyone .

3. *You show that you are a letter from Christ.* If the Corinthians are Paul's letter of recommendation, the author of that letter is Christ. Thus Paul claims that no-one less than the exalted Lord has produced this letter for him. But while Christ is the author of the letter, Paul says it was *delivered by us.* The word *delivered* is a translation of *diakonētheisa*, which literally means 'ministered' or 'serviced'. Within a metaphor of letter writing (as here) where an author and a scribe are envisaged, a better rendering would be 'enscribed'. So Paul sees the Corinthians as a 'living letter' dictated by Christ, but 'enscribed' by Paul through the apostolic ministry of gospel proclamation. Paul takes the analogy one step further when he says this scribal work was carried out *not with ink but with the Spirit of the living God.* His ministry was

[1]Other ancient manuscripts support a reading of 'our' instead of *your*. In fact the former has the stronger manuscript support. However, many commentators adopt the latter because it fits better in the context, despite its weaker attestation.

If the stronger reading, 'our', is adopted then the *letter* would be carried in the hearts of Paul and his co-workers, and presumably consisted of the knowledge of what God had done in the lives of the Corinthians through the preaching of the gospel. This Paul could appeal to whenever his credentials were questioned. However, this view is hard to reconcile with the statements of v. 2a (*you yourselves are our letter of recommendation*) and v. 3 (which proponents of the view must construe to mean that the hearts on which the letter is written are those of Paul and his fellow missionaries).

empowered by the Spirit of God so that any changes wrought in the lives of his hearers were effected by the Spirit (Rom. 15:17–19; 1 Cor. 2:4–5). At the end of the verse, while furthering his argument, Paul varies the metaphor by saying this letter writing was carried out *not on tablets of stone but on tablets of human hearts*. Here Paul leaves behind the contrast between the work of a scribe using pen and ink and the work of an apostle ministering in the power of the Spirit, and introduces another contrast, that between writing on tablets of stone and on human hearts. This latter contrast is clearly an allusion to the prophetic description of the new covenant (*cf.* Je. 31:31–34; Ezk. 36:24–32) under which God would write his law on human hearts. The allusion paves the way for Paul's description of himself and his co-workers as ministers of the new covenant (vv. 4–6) and for the extended comparison and contrast between ministry under the old and new covenants (vv. 7–18).

It is worth noting just what an exalted view of ministry is implied by vv. 1–3. Paul and his colleagues were privileged to be the agents by whom 'living letters' from the exalted Christ were enscribed in the hearts of men and women. For this ministry the apostles were entrusted with the precious 'ink' of the Spirit. By the grace of God, the results effected became letters authenticating and commending the very ministry by which they were produced.

F. Ministers of the New Covenant (3:4–6)

It is here that Paul answers the question he asked in 2:16 ('Who is sufficient for these things?') by showing that his competence as a minister of the new covenant comes from God.

4. *Such is the confidence that we have through Christ toward God.* This looks forward to what is to be said in vv. 5–6. Paul's confidence is based on the fact that God himself makes his servants competent to carry out the tasks he assigns to them, and this he does by bestowing upon them his Spirit through Christ. Confidence or boldness was one of the distinguishing marks of early preachers of the gospel (*cf.* Acts 4:13, 29, 31; 28:31; Eph. 6:19; Phil. 1:20). Elsewhere Paul speaks of confidence as the effect of the Spirit's presence in the believer, a confidence which is the opposite to fear and timidity (Rom. 8:15–17; *cf.* 1 Tim: 3:13; 2 Tim. 1:7).

5. *Not that we are competent of ourselves to claim anything as coming from us.* Paul's confidence in the matter of ministerial competence is not self-confidence, rather he insists *our competence is from God.* This does not reflect an exaggerated humility on the part of the apostle, but rather a sober recognition of the facts of the matter. Spiritual work can be accomplished only by the power of God released through the preaching of the gospel (*cf.* Rom. 15:17–19; 1 Cor. 1:18 – 2:5).

6. Paul further describes his confidence by saying that it is God *who has made us competent to be ministers of a new covenant.* The expression *new covenant* is found in only one other place in Paul's writings, *i.e.* in 1 Corinthians 11:25, where it forms part of the Lord's Supper tradition which Paul says he received ('This cup is the new covenant in my blood'). This use of the term by Paul makes it plain that he, like the writer to the Hebrews (*cf.* Heb. 9:15–28), saw the death of Christ as that which established the new covenant. However, what Paul stresses in the present context is that the ministry of the new covenant is one which is *not in a written code but in the Spirit* (lit. 'not of letter but of Spirit'). This has been interpreted in the past as a ministry which does not focus upon the literal meaning of the Old Testament ('letter'), but on its real underlying intention ('spirit'). But such an interpretation fails to recognize that in this chapter it is the law of Moses ('carved in letters on stone', v. 7) and the Holy Spirit (v. 8) which Paul contrasts as the primary features by which the ministries under the old and new covenants are to be distinguished.

Paul, after describing his ministry as one not of the written code but of the Holy Spirit, highlights the difference involved by adding *for the written code kills, but the Spirit gives life.* But how can Paul say that the written code kills? The answer seems to be that the written code (the law) kills when it is used improperly, *i.e.* as a set of rules to be observed in order to establish one's own righteousness (*cf.* Rom. 3:20; 10:1–4). To use the law in this way inevitably leads to death, for no-one can satisfy its demands, and therefore all come under its condemnation. So a ministry of the written code in this sense is a ministry of death. However, the ministry of the Spirit is quite different. It is a ministry of the new covenant under which sins are forgiven and remembered no more, and people are motivated and enabled by the Spirit to do what the improper application of the law could never achieve (cf. Je. 31:31–34; Ezk. 36:25–27; Rom. 8:3–4).

It needs to be stressed that when Paul contrasts the written code which kills and the Spirit who gives life, no downgrading of the role of Scripture in Christian life and ministry is involved. The written code which kills refers to the law of Moses used improperly as a means to establish one's righteousness before God. Scripture, and in particular the gospel it enshrines, is the primary instrument by which the Holy Spirit mediates life to God's people.

G. Two Ministries Compared and Contrasted (3:7–18)

In 3:6 Paul spoke of his ministry under the new covenant of the Spirit and contrasted it with the ministry under the old covenant. In 3:7–18 the apostle, by means of an exposition of Exodus 34:29–32 and then of 34:33–35, further compares and contrasts the ministries of the new and old covenants so as to demonstrate the superiority of the former. Paul's primary purpose in so doing is to highlight the glorious character of the ministry with which he has been entrusted and so explain why, despite so many difficulties, he does not lose heart (cf. 4:1).

The fact that Paul pursues this purpose by comparing the superior splendour of the ministry of the new covenant with the lesser splendour of the ministry of the old covenant may indicate an underlying apologetic and even polemic intention as well. If those whose opposition to Paul is reflected so vividly in chs. 10 – 13 had already begun to exercise some influence in Corinth by the time Paul wrote chs. 1 – 7, then an apologetic or polemic undertone in our present passage is understandable. If these people who stressed their Jewish connections (cf. 11:21b–22) were already causing trouble, then Paul's exposition of Exodus 34:29–32 and 34:33–35 which shows the inferiority of the splendour accompanying the ministry of Moses may have been written to counteract an overemphasis on these things.

The passage 3:7–18 falls into two sections. The first, vv. 7–11, is an exposition of Exodus 34:29–32 (which tells of the glory that attended the giving of the law, a glory reflected in the shining face of Moses which struck fear into the hearts of the Israelites). Paul recognizes that the old covenant was accompanied by splendour, but using a rabbinic method of exegesis (from the lesser to the greater) he argues that the new covenant is accompanied by far greater splendour. The superiority of new covenant is argued on three counts: (a) the ministry of the Spirit is more splendid than the ministry of death, (b) the ministry of righteousness is more splendid than that of condemnation, and (c) the permanent ministry is more splendid than that which fades away.

The second section, vv. 12–18, is an exposition of Exodus 34:33–35 (which tells how Moses veiled his face after communicating God's law to the Israelites so that they would no longer have to look upon its brightness). Paul interprets this as an attempt to conceal from the Israelites the fading nature of the splendour which accompanied the old covenant. He also sees in the veiling of Moses' face something analogous to the 'veil' which lay over the minds of many of his Jewish contemporaries who could not properly understand the law of Moses when it was read in their synagogues. Believers, by contrast, are those who with unveiled faces behold the glory of the Lord.

1. Exposition of Exodus 34:29–32 (3:7–11)

7–8. These verses contain the first of three counts on which Paul argues the superiority of the new covenant. He begins by acknowledging the splendour which accompanied the old covenant: *Now if the dispensation of death, carved in letters on stone, came with such splendour that the Israelites could not look at Moses' face because of its brightness, fading as this was.* The reference is to Exodus 34:29–32, which describes Moses' descent from the mount with the two tables of the law in his hands, and the fear that was struck into the hearts of the Israelites by the brightness of his face.

Paul describes the law *carved in letters on stone* as *the dispensation* [lit. 'ministry'] *of death.* This is best understood in the light of

Romans 7:10, where the apostle says, 'the very commandment which promised life proved to be death to me'. Although Leviticus 18:5 may promise life to those who keep the law, Paul knew that no-one does so in fact, and that the law can only pronounce the verdict of death over the transgressor.

Will not the dispensation of the Spirit be attended with greater splendour? Unlike the law *carved in letters on stone*, which could not enable a person to fulfil its own demands, the Spirit given under the new covenant actually causes people to walk in the way of God's commandments (*cf.* Ezk. 36:27; Rom. 8:3–4). For this reason *the dispensation of the Spirit* is far more splendid than *the dispensation of death*.

9. *For if there was splendour in the dispensation of condemnation, the dispensation of righteousness must far exceed it in splendour.* This is the apostle's second argument from the lesser to the greater to demonstrate the more splendid character of the new covenant. Here the old covenant is called *the dispensation of condemnation*, reflecting again the fact that the law operating under it can only condemn those who fail to meet its demands. The new covenant is called *the dispensation of righteousness* because under its provisions those who are certainly guilty of transgressions are nevertheless accounted righteous by God (*cf.* Rom. 3:21–26). Once again the new covenant is shown to be more splendid than the old, for under the new covenant the grace of God is seen far more clearly.[1]

10. *Indeed, in this case, what once had splendour has come to have no splendour at all, because of the splendour that surpasses it.* The whole point of vv. 7–11 is focused in this statement. Such is the surpassing splendour of the new covenant of which Paul has been made a minister that the old covenant of which Moses was minister, though certainly attended by a splendour of its own (Ex. 34:29–32), has now by comparison come to have no splendour at all.

---

[1]Some have argued that the doctrine of justification by faith, far from being central in Paul's gospel, was only an idea introduced by the apostle for polemic purposes when he was opposing the Judaizers. It is noteworthy then that here in 2 Cor. 3, where Paul's primary concern is to highlight the glory of the ministry entrusted to him, the motif of justification comes to the fore once again.

11. *For if what faded away came with splendour, what is permanent must have much more splendour.* This is the third of Paul's arguments from the lesser to the greater in this context. The old covenant is here described as that which *faded away* (NIV, 'was fading away', is better). It is important to recognize that Paul does not imply that the law itself was fading away, but that it was the ministry of the law that was fading away. The law as the expression of the will of God for human conduct is still valid. In fact Paul says the purpose of God in bringing in the new covenant of the Spirit was precisely that the righteous demands of the law might be fulfilled in those who walk by the Spirit (Rom. 8:4). However, the time of the ministry of the law has come to an end (*cf.* Rom. 10:4; Gal. 3:19–25).

The new covenant is described as *what is permanent*, and in this respect it is superior to what *faded away*. The new covenant of the Spirit is not to be superseded by another covenant as was the covenant of the law. Because of its permanence it is far more splendid than what proved to be transitory.

2. Exposition of Exodus 34:33–35 (3:12–18)

In this exposition Paul stresses two matters: first, the boldness of his own ministry, which he contrasts with that of Moses, who covered his face with a veil; and second, his own beholding the glory of God with 'unveiled face', which he contrasts with the blindness of his Jewish contemporaries, over whose minds a veil still lay when the law of Moses was read.

12–13. *Since we have such a hope, we are very bold.* This statement is connected with what precedes in v. 11, where the permanence of the new covenant was emphasized. Paul's hope relates to the permanent character of the new covenant of which he is a minister. He has no fear that this covenant will be superseded, and for that reason he can be *very bold* in his ministry. It is in this respect that he declares he is *not like Moses, who put a veil over his face so that the Israelites might not see the end of the fading splendour.* Paul could be bold because he ministered under the provisions of a permanent covenant, whereas Moses lacked boldness because the covenant under which he ministered, and its splendour, were fading away.

Exodus 34:33–35, which forms the basis of Paul's exposition here, gives no indication that the reason Moses veiled his face was *so that the Israelites might not see the end of the fading splendour*. The apostle seems to have drawn two inferences of his own from the text: first, that the brightness of Moses' face did fade after a short while;[1] and second, that the reason Moses veiled his face was to conceal the end of the fading splendour from the Israelites. Paul saw in the fading brightness a symbol of the transitory character of the old covenant, and inferred that Moses, lacking boldness because he was the minister of a fading covenant, veiled his face so that the Israelites might not see its end.[2]

14. *But their minds were hardened.* The purpose of these words appears to be to correct any impression that Moses was to blame for the Israelites' inability to behold the splendour of the old covenant reflected in his face. Moses may have veiled his face, but it was the Israelites' minds that were hardened (*cf.* Ps. 95:8; Heb. 3:8, 15; 4:7). Rabbinic writings of *c.* AD 150 say that it was the effects of Israel's sin in making the golden calf while Moses was on the mount which resulted in their being unable through fear to look upon the brightness of Moses' face (Str-B 3, p. 515).

For to this day, when they read the old covenant, that same veil remains unlifted. The hardness of mind of the Israelites of Moses' day reminds Paul of the hardness of mind of the Jews of his own day, and he finds in the idea of the veil a way of describing that hardness. Just as the veil prevented the ancient Israelites from seeing the brightness of Moses' face, so too *the same veil*, as it were, remained unlifted when the Jews of his own day read the Old Testament. They could not see that the old covenant had come to an end and the new had already been inaugurated.

Because only through Christ is it taken away. It is *only through* [lit.

---

[1] Later Jewish writings say that this brightness persisted on Moses' face till the time of his death, and thereafter even remained with him in the grave (Str-B 3, p. 515).

[2] The word used is *telos*, which can mean 'end' either in the sense of 'terminus' or in the sense of 'goal'. Some scholars argue for the latter, saying the glory reflected on the face of Moses was the glory of the (pre-existent) Christ, the goal of the old dispensation, but the flow of Paul's thought here demands the former, as recognized by most commentators.

'in'] *Christ* that the veil over people's minds is removed.[1] When people become believers in Christ, they experience at the same time the removal of the veil of ignorance and unbelief which previously prevented them from understanding the true meaning of the Old Testament, *i.e.* its witness to Jesus Christ and the end of the old covenant which his coming brought about.

15–16. What was said in v. 14 is reiterated in v. 15: *Yes, to this day whenever Moses is read a veil lies over their minds,* and then in v. 16 the exposition is taken another step forward: *but when a man turns to the Lord the veil is removed.* This is an adaptation of Exodus 34:34 ('whenever Moses went in before the Lord to speak with him, he took the veil off'). After Moses descended the mount and after he had communicated God's message to the Israelites, he veiled his face so they would no longer have to look upon its brightness. However, when he went in before the Lord he removed the veil and replaced it again only when he came out to the people. Paul applies this to his Jewish contemporaries by saying that if any one of them turns to the Lord the veil over his mind will be removed.

Normally when Paul uses the word *Lord* it refers to Christ. But here, where he is adapting the LXX reading of Exodus 34:34, the title must be understood to denote God. We may add that for Paul it is now only through Christ that a person comes to God, for the glory of God now shines in the face of Christ (*cf.* 4:4, 6), nevertheless in the present context the title *Lord* denotes God.

17. *Now the Lord is the Spirit.* These words have given rise to much debate. If *the Lord* is taken to refer to Christ, then it may be asked whether Christ is equated with the Spirit – with all the implications such an identification would have for the doctrine

---

[1]Assuming that when Paul says *only through Christ is it taken away*, 'it' refers to the veil. Other commentators suggest that 'it' refers to the old dispensation which is annulled by Christ. In favour of the former it can be argued that the veil is the subject of v. 14a and therefore presumably the subject of v. 14b as well, and also that throughout vv. 14–16 the veil is the main subject of Paul's reflection. In favour of the latter it is argued that in the wider context (vv. 7ff.) it is the old dispensation that is being annulled, and that should inform the exegesis of v. 14a. The same verb *katargeō* ('to annul') is used in both places. If Paul meant to say the veil was taken away he would have used the verb *periaireō* ('to take away') as he does in v. 16.

of the Trinity. However, the meaning of the statement can be determined only by seeing it in the wider context of Paul's argument in this chapter.

It needs to be remembered that Paul's main concern in chapter 3 is to highlight the greater splendour of the new covenant of the Spirit (*cf.* vv. 3, 6, 8, 18) which he contrasts with the lesser splendour of the old covenant of the law. Paul's Jewish contemporaries related to God through the law, but believers relate to God through the Spirit. Further, it must be recalled that in v. 16 'the Lord' refers to God, not Christ, and therefore the same words in v. 17 are to be understood in the same way. The thrust of the two verses then is that when people turn to God the veil over their minds is removed, and they realize that the time of the old covenant of the law has come to an end and that of the new covenant of the Spirit has begun. So when under the new covenant they turn to the Lord they experience him as the Spirit. The expression *the Lord is the Spirit* is not a one-to-one identification, but rather a way of saying that under the new covenant the Lord is *to us* the Spirit.

And where the Spirit of the Lord is, there is freedom. This statement too must be understood within the overall context of chapter 3, where the new covenant of the Spirit is contrasted with the old covenant of the law. Under the new covenant, where the Spirit is the operative power, there is freedom. Under the old covenant, where the law reigns, there is bondage.

When people live under the old covenant in the way some of Paul's contemporaries did (seeking acceptance before God by works of law), there is no freedom. The demands of the law cannot be fulfilled and therefore they stand under its condemnation. But under the covenant of the Spirit there is liberty. There is no more remembrance of sins (Rom. 4:6–8), and no condemnation of the sinner (Rom. 8:1). The Spirit himself bears witness with our spirits that we are children of God (Rom. 8:15–16), and walking by the Spirit the righteous demands of the law are fulfilled in us (Rom. 8:3–4). Such liberty engenders boldness, and so in vv. 12–13 Paul can say he is 'very bold' (in his dealings with the Corinthians), unlike Moses, who lacked that boldness (towards the Israelites).

18. *And we all, with unveiled face, beholding the glory of the Lord.*
Paul takes up again his exposition of Exodus 34:33–35 (in which
we are told how Moses removed his veil when he went in before
the Lord). While Moses may have lacked boldness before the
Israelites and so veiled his face (v. 13), when he went in before
the Lord he did so with confidence and freedom symbolized by
the removal of the veil.[1] Like Moses, then, Paul and all believers
approach God in confidence and freedom *with unveiled face*, and
like Moses also they behold *the glory of the Lord*. To express the
latter Paul uses the middle participle *katoptrizomenoi*. The middle
form of the verb *katoptrizō* generally means 'to look at oneself or
something as in a mirror', although there is evidence to show it
could also be used to mean 'to reflect as in a mirror'. However,
the idea of beholding fits the context better. In Exodus 34:33–35,
which forms the basis of Paul's exposition here, we are told that
it was when Moses went in before the Lord that his face was
unveiled, and at that time he was beholding, rather than reflecting, the glory of the Lord. Further, Paul's idea of *being changed
into his likeness from one degree of glory to another* (v. 18b) is better
understood to occur while believers are beholding rather than
reflecting the glory of God. Finally, in 4:6 it is certainly the
beholding of the glory of God that Paul has in mind.

If we were to ask Paul in what way believers behold the glory
of God, his answer would be that they do so as the 'veils' are
removed from their minds so that the truth of the gospel is no
longer hidden from them. Thus it is in 'the light of the gospel'
that they behold 'the glory of Christ, who is the likeness of
God', and they see 'the light of the knowledge of the glory of
God in the face of Christ' (4:3–6).

*And we all . . . are being changed into his likeness from one degree of
glory to another.* It is important to note that the changing into his
likeness takes place not at one point of time, but as an extended
process. The verb *metamorphoumetha* ('we are being changed') is
in the present tense, indicating the continuous nature of the
change, while the words *from one degree of glory to another* stress
its progressive nature. The verb *metamorphoō* is found in three

---

[1] W. C. van Unnik ('"With unveiled face", an exegesis of 2 Corinthians iii 12–18', *NovT* 6
(1963), p. 161) provides evidence that in early rabbinic texts '"to cover the face" is a sign of
shame and mourning; "to uncover the head" means confidence and freedom'.

other places only in the New Testament. It is used to describe Jesus' transfiguration in Matthew 17:2 and Mark 9:2, and Paul uses it in Romans 12:2 to denote moral transformation ('Do not be conformed to this world but be transformed by the renewal of your mind').

Paul speaks often of the transformation of believers in other passages, though words other than *metamorphoō* are employed. In some cases he has in mind the future transformation of believers' bodies to be like Christ's glorious body (1 Cor. 15:51–52; Phil. 3:21). In other cases it is clearly a present moral transformation that is in view (Rom. 6:1–4; 2 Cor. 5:17; Gal. 6:15). The Old Testament prophets who spoke beforehand of the new covenant certainly anticipated a moral transformation of those who were to experience its blessings (Je. 31:33; Ezk. 36:25–27), and Paul saw this expectation fulfilled in the lives of his converts (1 Cor. 6:9–11; 2 Cor. 3:3). These last references, together with Romans 12:2 cited above, provide the clue to Paul's meaning in the present context. The continuous and progressive transformation by which believers are changed *from one degree of glory to another* is the moral transformation which is taking place in their lives so that they approximate more and more to the likeness of God expressed so perfectly in the life of Jesus Christ.

For this comes from the Lord who is the Spirit. The reference to *the Lord who is the Spirit* may be taken to mean God, who under the new covenant is present, and experienced by believers, as the Spirit (see commentary on v. 17). The Spirit's activity is the major characteristic of the new covenant and the transformation of believers is wholly attributable to his work in their lives (*cf.* Rom. 8:1–7).

H. The Conduct of Paul's Ministry (4:1–6)

In 3:7–18 Paul outlined something of the splendour of the ministry which had been entrusted to him. It was a ministry of the Spirit which brings life, righteousness and transformation of character to those who believe the gospel. In 4:1–6 Paul tells how, in the light of the great privilege of having such a ministry, he conducts himself and proclaims the gospel. He also tells why the minds of some are still blinded to his gospel, and concludes by explaining the content of his gospel – Christ as Lord – and by affirming that the glory of God shines in the face of the Christ he proclaims.

1. *Therefore, having this ministry.* With these words the readers' attention is referred back to the ministry of the new covenant whose splendour Paul has depicted in 3:7–18. The apostle was very conscious that he had this ministry only *by the mercy of God*, for he never forgot that he was formerly a persecutor of the church of God (*cf.* 1 Cor. 15:9–10; 1 Tim. 1:12–16). The awareness of the great privilege involved caused the apostle not to *lose heart*, despite the many difficulties and sufferings he experienced in the carrying out of that ministry.

2. Because of the greatness of the ministry entrusted to him Paul *renounced disgraceful, underhanded ways.* What this meant is spelt out both negatively and positively in the rest of the verse.

Negatively Paul says *we refuse to practise cunning.* He uses the word *cunning* (*panourgia*) again in 11:3, where he speaks of 'the serpent [who] deceived Eve by his cunning'. Paul asserts that there was no attempt to deceive by cunning in his preaching of the gospel, *or to tamper with God's word.* The verb translated *to tamper with* (*doloō*) is found only here in the New Testament. Its use in the papyri in relation to the dilution of wine suggests that Paul had in mind the corruption of the word of God by mingling it with alien ideas (see commentary on 2:17).

Positively he claims *by the open statement of the truth we would commend ourselves to every man's conscience in the sight of God.* The contrast between practising cunning and the open statement, and between a word of God that has been tampered with and the truth, is clear. By his straightforward presentation of the truth Paul commends himself *to every man's conscience.* For the apostle the conscience is that human faculty by which a person approves or disapproves his or her actions (those intended as well as those already performed) and also the actions of others (see commentary on 1:12). Thus by the straightforward nature of his ministry Paul invites the approval of everyone, convinced that when true to their own consciences they will be forced to acknowledge that he has acted with integrity. The final words, *in the sight of God*, remind us that the apostle, while concerned that the conduct of his ministry should commend itself to people's consciences, is ultimately concerned to minister only in a way that finds God's approval. In 1 Corinthians 4:3–4 he goes so far as to say, 'with me it is a very small thing that I should be judged by you or by any human court . . . It is the Lord who judges me.'

3–4. It is difficult to know why Paul, having just spoken about his open statement of the truth, immediately goes on to discuss its hiddenness: *and even if our gospel is veiled*. Possibly he had come under criticism because his gospel had been rejected by so many (especially those of his own nation, *cf.* Acts 13:44–45; 17:5–9; 18:5–6, 12–31; 19:8–9). If he is responding to such criticism, then his answer is that the hiddenness of the gospel is due to the condition of the hearers: *it is veiled only to those who are perishing. In their case the god of this world has blinded the minds of the unbelievers.* The problem is to be located not in Paul's proclamation but in the minds of those who reject it, minds which have been blinded by the god of this world. In ch. 3 Paul spoke of the veil over the minds of his Jewish contemporaries which prevented them from understanding their own Scriptures. It is quite likely that the words *it is veiled only to those who are perishing* in the present context also refer primarily to them. This would certainly fit in with the suggestion that Paul was responding to criticisms that even the majority of his own fellow nationals would not accept his gospel. However, it is clear from other references in 2 Corinthians that the apostle in no way saw the activity of the god of this world (=Satan) as restricted to the Jews (*cf.* 2:11; 11:3, 14).

In each place where Satan (or as here, *the god of this world*) is mentioned in 2 Corinthians he is seen to be actively seeking to hinder the work of God. However, it must be remembered that Satan can carry out such a function only with divine permission, and the blindness of mind which he is allowed to impose can at any time be penetrated by a blaze of light if God so wills. This, of course, was Paul's own experience. In his blindness he persecuted God's church until such time as it pleased God to reveal his Son to him (*cf.* Acts 9:1–19; Gal. 1:13–17).

To keep them from seeing the light of the gospel of the glory of Christ, who is the likeness of God. This is one of three places in the Corinthian correspondence where Paul reveals something of the content of the gospel which he preached (*cf.* also 1 Cor. 1:17–18, 23; 15:3–4). Paul stresses that the gospel concerns *the glory of Christ, who is the likeness of God.* There may well be an allusion here to the creation of man in Genesis 1:26 ('Let us make man in our image, after our likeness'), especially in the light of the fact that Paul does speak of Christ as the 'last Adam', comparing and contrasting him with the 'first Adam' (1 Cor. 15:45–49). There may also be an allusion here to Israel's wisdom literature, for there Wisdom is personified and her glories celebrated: 'For she is a reflection of eternal light, a spotless mirror of the working of God, and an image of his goodness' (Wisdom of Solomon 7:26). Strengthening the possibility of such an allusion is the fact that elsewhere Paul ascribes to Christ that role in creation which Israel's wisdom literature ascribes to Wisdom (*cf.* Pr. 8:22–31 and Col. 1:15–20). Bringing the two possible allusions together, it has been suggested that for Paul Christ is the likeness of God after the fashion of Adam as far as his humanity is concerned, and after the fashion of Wisdom as far as his transcendence is concerned.

5. *For what we preach is not ourselves, but Jesus Christ as Lord.* This statement could be either apologetic or polemic, possibly even both. It would be apologetic if Paul is responding to criticism that in his preaching he puts himself forward, *i.e.* that he is more concerned to establish his authority as an apostle than to proclaim the gospel. It would be polemic if Paul is implying that, unlike others who put themselves forward in their preaching, he preaches the lordship of Christ. Incidentally, the statement also reveals more of the content of Paul's gospel: the presentation of *Jesus Christ as Lord.* In 1 Corinthians 1:23 Paul says, 'we preach Christ crucified', which, like the preaching of *Jesus Christ as Lord* found here, is a shorthand pointer to the heart of Paul's gospel. In the gospel the lordship of Christ is proclaimed and people are called to give their allegiance to him, but the one to whom they are thus called to submit is also the crucified one, the one who died for them. These two basic elements of the gospel need to be held together, for if they are not the gospel itself is distorted.

With ourselves as your servants for Jesus' sake. Quite contrary to any idea that in his preaching he promotes his own authority and importance, Paul says he regards himself as the servant of those to whom he preaches (*cf.* 1:24). But this must not be misunderstood to mean that they are his masters. Paul acknowledges only one Lord, and it is in obedience to him that he serves humanity.

6. It is the very greatness of the glory of Christ which God has revealed to Paul that ensures he preaches not himself but Jesus Christ as Lord. *For it is the God who said, 'Let light shine out of darkness'.* As it stands this appears to recall Genesis 1:3 ('And God said, "Let there be light"'), and if this is the case then Paul likens the revelation of the glory of God in Christ to the creative act of God whereby the darkness of the primeval world was banished by the light. Thus the darkness of ignorance in which people are held by the god of this world is banished when, by a new creative act, God shines into their hearts the light of the gospel.

There is an alternative and better-attested reading in the Greek manuscripts which has: 'For it is the God who said, "a light shall shine out of darkness"'. In this form it could well allude to the prophecy concerning the land of Zebulun and Naphtali in Isaiah 9:2 ('The people who walked in darkness have seen a great light; those who dwelt in a land of deep darkness, on them has light shined') which is taken up and applied to the ministry of Christ in Matthew 4:15–16 and Luke 1:79.

Who has shone in our hearts to give the light of the knowledge of the glory of God in the face of Christ. Here conversion is understood as illumination, an illumination which reveals the true nature of Christ as the one in whose face the glory of God is seen. Paul's own conversion may well have prompted him to think in this way (Gal. 1:13–17; *cf.* Acts 9:1–9).

Before leaving this passage it is worth noting the very high view of the person of Christ which Paul espouses, and which is implied by the references in vv. 4 ('the likeness/image of God') and 6 (*the glory of God in the face of Christ*). It is true that mankind in general was created in the image of God (*cf.* Gn. 1:26), an image that was subsequently marred by sin and is now being restored by grace (*cf.* 3:18). However, the view of Christ reflected in Paul's words in vv. 4, 6 involves much more than that. Paul's view is most clearly set out in Colossians 1:15–20, where Christ is not only described as the image of God (v. 15) but is also identified as God's agent in creation and providence (vv. 16–17), spoken of as the Lord of the church (v. 18) and said to be the one 'in [whom] all the fullness of God was pleased to dwell' (v. 19).

In holding such an exalted view of Christ, Paul is not alone among the writers of the New Testament. A similarly exalted Christology is to be found, *e.g.*, in John 1:1–4 and Hebrews 1:1–4.

I. *Treasure in Earthen Vessels* (4:7–12)

Having spoken of the glorious light of the gospel in 4:1–6, Paul in 4:7–12 contrasts it with the weakness of those who bear it. This truth is stated as a general principle is v. 7, illustrated in vv. 8–9, restated as a principle in vv. 10–11, and the principle is extended in v. 12.

7. *But we have this treasure in earthen vessels.* Earthenware vessels were a commonplace in virtually every home in the ancient Middle East. They were inexpensive and easily broken. Unlike metal vessels (which could be repaired) or glass ones (which could be melted down and the material reused), once broken, earthenware vessels had to be discarded. They were thus cheap and of little intrinsic value. Paul may have had in mind the small earthenware oil-lamps sold so cheaply in the market-places. If so, 'the light of the gospel' would be the treasure, while the apostles in their frailty would be the earthenware lamps from whom the light was made to shine in the world.

The contrast between the *treasure* and the *earthen vessels* which contain it is intended (*hina*) *to show that the transcendent power belongs to God and not to us*. In 1:9 Paul testified that the affliction he experienced in Asia taught him 'to rely not on ourselves but on God who raises the dead', and in similar vein the frailty of the messengers here shows, not so much to the apostles but rather to the world, that *the transcendent power belongs to God* and not his envoys.

8–9. The general principle enuciated in v. 7 is here illustrated by a series of four paradoxical statements. These reflect the vulnerability of Paul and his co-workers on the one hand and the power of God which sustains them on the other. *We are afflicted in every way, but not crushed; perplexed, but not driven to despair; persecuted, but not forsaken; struck down, but not destroyed.* For the sort of concrete experiences to which these verses allude, see 11:23–33.

10–11. After the illustrations drawn from experience, Paul restates in two couplets the principle enuciated in v. 7. The imagery (the death and life of Jesus) is different, but the principle is the same.

In the first couplet (v. 10) the apostle speaks of *carrying in the body the death [nekrōsin] of Jesus, so that the life of Jesus may also be manifested in our bodies [sōmati]*. In the second (v. 11) he says *we are always being given up to death [thanaton] for Jesus' sake, so that the life of Jesus may be manifested in our mortal flesh [sarki]*. The substitution of *thanaton* and *sarki* for *nekrōsin* and *sōmati* respectively is almost certainly stylistic rather than substantial, and once this is recognized the close parallelism between the two couplets is obvious.

The meaning of Paul's experiencing the death and life of Jesus, as the overall context makes clear, is not to be taken mystically but quite concretely. Caught up in affliction and persecution, Paul was continually exposed to death. In the words of Romans 8:36: 'As it is written, "For thy sake we are being killed all the day long; we are regarded as sheep to be slaughtered."' But as the apostle allows himself to be 'put to death' in this way, he shares the fate of Jesus (*cf.* Col. 1:24), and at the same time finds that the resurrection life of Jesus is manifested in his body (*cf.* 6:9). Thus the one who proclaims the crucified and risen Lord finds that what is proclaimed in his message is also exemplified in his life. On the one hand he is daily subject to forces which lead to death, but on the other he is continually upheld, caused to triumph, and made to be more than a conqueror by the experience of the risen life of Jesus in his mortal body (*cf.* Rom. 8:35–39; 2 Cor. 1:8–10; 2:14; Phil. 3:10; 4:12–13).

12. *So death is at work in us, but life in you.* This summary statement takes the thought one step further. Daily exposure to forces leading to death is Paul's experience, but accompanying that is a continual manifestation of the life of Jesus in the apostle, here not only to sustain him, but to work through him, bringing life to others.

J. The Spirit of Faith (4:13–15)

In these verses Paul tells how, despite the affliction referred to in the previous section, he still operates in a spirit of faith. This faith is strengthened by the knowledge that he will be raised with the Lord Jesus. Including the Corinthians with himself, he says that together they will be brought into the presence of God. All these things are for the Corinthians' sake so that as God's grace extends to more and more of them, there will be an increase in thanksgiving to the glory of God.

13. Paul compares his faith in God to the faith of the psalmist who also maintained faith in the midst of suffering. Paul makes an exact citation from Psalm 115:1 (LXX) when he says: *Since we have the same spirit of faith as he had who wrote, 'I believed, and so I spoke.'* The corresponding reference in our English Bibles, which are based on the Hebrew text, is Psalm 116:10. There is some divergence between the LXX and the Hebrew texts at this point. However, what Paul wishes to stress is quite clear: *we too believe, and so we speak.* Like the psalmist, Paul's faith in God persists despite the sufferings encountered, and in this faith he goes on speaking, *i.e.* he goes on proclaiming God's word (*cf.* 2:17).

14. *Knowing that he who raised the Lord Jesus will raise us also with Jesus.* Paul's faith is strengthened by the knowledge that the God who raised Jesus from the dead will also raise him along with Jesus. In 1 Corinthians 15:20–23 Paul spoke of Jesus' resurrection as the first-fruits which are the sign of the full harvest to follow. God, who gathered the first-fruits, shall surely bring in the full harvest. It is this knowledge which encourages the apostle in the midst of his present difficulties (*cf.* Rom. 8:11, 17).

And bring us with you into his presence. Resurrection is not an end in itself. It is the gateway to immortality in the presence of God. Paul looks forward to the day when through resurrection he will stand with his converts in the presence of God (*cf.* 1:14; Phil. 2:16; 1 Thes. 2:19).

15. Paul says to the Corinthians concerning all his apostolic labours and sufferings, and the faith that sustains him in them, *it is all for your sake, i.e.* that they might experience the grace of God made known through the gospel. But there is a further reason why Paul endures. It is *so that as grace extends to more and more people it may increase thanksgiving, to the glory of God.* We see here then both the penultimate (*for your sake*) and the ultimate (*to the glory of God*) purposes of Paul's apostolic ministry. They are that people should experience the grace of God (penultimate purpose) and that as a result thanksgiving should be increased to the glory of God (ultimate purpose).

K. The Object of Faith (4:16 – 5:10)

1. We do not lose heart (4:16–18)

In 4:1 Paul said that he does not lose heart, because he realized the greatness of the ministry upon which he was embarked. In 4:16–18 he says he does not lose heart, because while afflictions affect the outer man so that it wastes away, his inner man is being renewed every day. And in any case the afflictions are but light and momentary compared with the weight and eternal character of the glory he is to experience as a result. Paul endures afflictions in the present visible world by keeping before him the glories of the yet unseen world.

16. *Though our outer nature is wasting away, our inner nature is being renewed every day.* This wasting away of the outer nature is related to Paul's afflictions (v. 17; *cf.* vv. 8–12). So on the one hand he encounters debilitating persecution which affects his physical body, but on the other he experiences a daily renewal and strengthening in the *inner nature* (*cf.* Eph. 3:16). The expression the *inner nature* is synonymous with the 'heart' for Paul, and denotes the centre of a person, the source of will, emotion, thought and affection. The best commentary on the strengthening of the *inner nature* is found in the prayer of Ephesians 3:14-19. There the *inner nature* is to be strengthened when by the Spirit it is indwelt by Christ and rooted and grounded in the love of God.

Some scholars have inferred from this verse that Paul is adopting a dualistic view of the human constitution, one which regards the *inner nature* (soul) as destined for immortality, but the *outer nature* (body) as that which shall pass away. However, the rest of Paul's writings about personal eschatology make it very clear that he looked for a future existence not as a disembodied soul but as a whole person – with a resurrected body. Paul's longing is not for the freedom of an immortal soul liberated from the shackles of the body, but rather to experience life in the presence of God in a resurrection body (*cf.* 1 Cor. 15:35-38; 2 Cor. 5:1-5).

17-18. Paul further explains the reason why he does not lose heart in the midst of affliction. It is because *this slight momentary affliction is preparing for us an eternal weight of glory beyond all comparison.* Paul's afflictions were of course neither slight nor momentary in themselves. They were the burdensome and virtually constant accompaniment of his ministry. Yet by comparison with the weighty and eternal character of the glory being prepared for him, he saw them as but slight and momentary (*cf.* Rom. 8:17-23). He also sees a connection between the afflictions endured and the glory to be experienced. Verse 17 more literally translated would yield something like: 'For our temporary lightness of affliction is producing for us an eternal weight of glory that is out of all proportion [to the affliction].' The experience of affliction 'is producing' the glory to be revealed. How are we to understand the causal connection between the two? First, it is necessary to realize that such a connection is made also in Romans 8:17 (we are 'fellow heirs with Christ, provided we suffer with him *in order that* we may also be glorified with him'). Second, we need to understand that among Paul's Jewish contemporaries there was a belief that the messianic age would be ushered in by a definite and predetermined measure of afflictions to be experienced by the people of God. These afflictions were known as the birth-pangs of the Messiah (*cf.* Mk. 13:3–8, 17–20, 24–27 and parallels in Mt. 24 and Lk. 21). It is the idea that the afflictions of the last days are the birth pains of the new age that lies behind Paul's statement that the one 'is producing' the other. The clearest statement of this is found in Romans 8:22–23, where Paul speaks of the whole creation, including Christian men and women, 'groaning inwardly' as they wait for the adoption, the redemption of their bodies.

In practice this all means that if Christians are prepared to be identified with Christ in a fallen world and accept whatever sufferings and afflictions they may thus encounter, they will share his glory.

Because we look not to the things that are seen but to the things that are unseen. Paul does not lose heart even though he is exposed to persecution and witnesses the 'wasting away' (v. 16) of his body. This is so, not only because his inner nature is continuously being renewed, but also because his heart is set not upon what is seen but upon what is unseen. When he contrasts the things which are seen with those that are not, he is not contrasting things which are visible with those that are inherently invisible. It is rather a contrast between what is *now* visible and what is *not yet* visible but about to be revealed, *i.e.* at the revelation of Christ and his kingdom at the second coming (*cf.* Rom. 8:24–25; Col. 3:1–4; Heb. 11:1–3).

There is something else about that which is presently unseen but soon to be revealed which further strengthens Paul's resolve not to lose heart. It is that, unlike what may now be seen, which is *transient*, what is presently unseen but soon to be revealed is *eternal*. The present world, including the 'outer nature' of the Christian, is subject to decay, or corruption; the world which is to come, including the glorious resurrection body of believers, is eternal and incorruptible (*cf.* Rom. 8:19–23; Phil. 3:20–21).

2. *The heavenly dwelling* (5:1–10)

This passage is often studied virtually in isolation from the rest of 2 Corinthians because of its obvious importance for understanding Paul's views about life after death. However, in seeking a proper understanding of 5:1–10 it is essential to see it in its context, especially in relation to what immediately precedes it, for in fact 4:16 – 5:10 constitutes one integrated section. It is in the light of the 'wasting away' of the 'outer nature' (4:16) and the fact that 'this slight momentary affliction is preparing for us an eternal weight of glory' (4:17) that Paul proceeds to explain what he looks forward to when 'the earthly tent we live in is destroyed' (5:1).

1. In many ways this verse is the crux of the whole passage. How one interprets this verse determines to a large extent how one understands those which follow. In seeking to understand v. 1 it is important to recognize that the word *for* (*gar*) indicates that what is to follow is closely related to what precedes (*i.e.* the slight momentary affliction which prepares for us an eternal weight of glory).

For we know that if the earthly tent we live in is destroyed. Paul does not use here the usual word for tent (*skēnē*) which is found extensively in the LXX and several times in the New Testament. Rather, he uses the word *skēnos* which is found only twice in the New Testament (here and in v. 4), and only once in the LXX (Wisdom of Solomon 9:15), where it is used figuratively to refer to the human body. It is also used in this manner in the papyri. This strongly suggests that *skēnos* should be understood in the same way here, and this is confirmed by the overall context of 4:16 – 5:10, where Paul is concerned with the 'wasting away' of the 'outer nature', through persecution and suffering which afflict the body. We may conclude that in the first part of the verse, then, he is referring to the final outcome of such a process, *i.e.* the destruction of the body in death. His afflictions could at any time so intensify that they would result in death.

Aware that his *earthly tent* could so easily be destroyed the apostle says that, should this happen, *we have a building from God, a house not made with hands, eternal in the heavens.* While most scholars agree that v. 1a refers to the destruction of the body, there is no such agreement about the meaning of v. 1b. Some have suggested that the words *a building from God* employ temple imagery and recall the accusations made at Jesus' trial: 'We heard him say, "I will destroy this temple that is made with hands, and in three days I will build another, not made with hands"' (Mk. 14:58). Thereupon it is argued that v. 1b refers to a heavenly temple, understood either as the church in heaven, or heaven itself as the dwelling-place of God in which Christians find their eternal habitation. However, such arguments fail to take sufficient account of the fact that Jesus' accusers misunderstood the thrust of his statement, for as the fourth Gospel points out: 'He spoke of the temple of his body. When therefore he was raised from the dead, his disciples remembered that he had said this' (Jn. 2:21–22). The building made without hands was in this case the resurrected body of Jesus himself.

Other scholars interpret the *house not made with hands* of v. 1b as a reference to Jesus' resurrection body, but understood corporately, so that those who believe in him somehow have a share in it. But while it is true that *we have* is in the present tense, it must be remembered that it is part of a conditional sentence (*if the earthly tent we live in is destroyed, we have . . .*) which puts the 'having' of the *building from God* into future time in relation to the destruction of the *earthly tent*. So it is not the resurrected body of Christ presently in heaven nor the believers' sharing in that now that Paul has in mind.

An important factor in determining Paul's meaning is the parallelism existing in this verse. What is *earthly* and threatened with destruction in v. 1a is to be replaced by something corresponding to it which is heavenly and *eternal* in v. 1b. If 'the tent which forms our earthly house' of v. 1a denotes the physical body of the believer, it is reasonable to regard the *building from God, a house not made with hands* as a reference to another body, the resurrection body of the believer.

There is a parallel passage in Romans, a letter written shortly after 2 Corinthians, which lends support to this view. Romans 8:18–24 also deals with the subject of the suffering experienced by believers, comparing it with the glory to be revealed to them. And what the believer looks forward to at the revelation of this glory is the redemption of the *body* (v. 23), clearly a reference to the resurrection body of the believer. Seeing that this passage in Romans treats a similar subject to that dealt with in 2 Corinthians 4:16 – 5:10, and seeing that Romans was written just a short time after 2 Corinthians, it is reasonable to interpret v. 1b in the light of Romans 8:23 and so conclude that the *building from God*, the *house not made with hands*, refers to the resurrection body promised to the believer.

2. *Here indeed we groan, and long to put on our heavenly dwelling.* Once again the parallel in Romans 8:18–24 is helpful, and in this case quite striking. Believers are depicted as groaning (the same verb, *stenazō*, is used) as they wait for their adoption, interpreted as the redemption of their bodies (vv. 23–23). This supports the view that, when he talks about groaning and longing to put on the *heavenly dwelling* in the present context, Paul is speaking of the same thing.

The main verb in this verse, *stenazomen* (*we groan*), is qualified by the participle, *epipothountes* ('longing'), and so the verse could be rendered: 'for in this [situation] we groan, longing to put on our heavenly dwelling'. What is being described is essentially a positive longing to put on a *heavenly dwelling*. While afflictions experienced by the apostle may have caused him to *groan* and sharpened his longing, this all resulted in a strong desire for what God had promised rather than a preoccupation with the afflictions themselves – something which would have been quite uncharacteristic of the apostle as we see him in his letters.

3. *So that by putting it on we may not be found naked.* Consistent with the line of interpretation adopted, the nakedness which Paul expects to avoid when he puts on the heavenly dwelling is the nakedness of a disembodied soul. Paul, as a Jew, would regard existence as a disembodied soul as something to be eschewed. The promised heavenly body will save him from that. It may be that in emphasizing the future embodied state he is countering any Gnostic ideas of salvation (the release of the soul from the prison of the body) which may have been of some influence in Corinth.

4. *For while we are still in this tent, we sigh with anxiety.* Referring now to the present situation in which *we are still in this tent*, *i.e.* being in the physical body and exposed to the afflictions which come upon it, Paul says *we sigh with anxiety* (*stenazomen baroumenoi*). A more literal translation, 'we groan, being weighed down' better captures Paul's meaning. He does not so much *sigh with anxiety* (RSV), as groan because he is weighed down by afflictions experienced in his body.

Not that we would be unclothed. Although the apostle groans, being burdened by sufferings and persecutions which afflict the body, he does not therefore seek escape into a permanent disembodied state. He longs for a new and better embodiment. What he wants is then described with the use of two metaphors. First, the metaphor of putting on extra clothing to cover that already being worn (*we would be further clothed*). Second, the metaphor of one thing being devoured by another so that the one ceases to exist as it was, but is taken into and transformed in the other (*what is mortal may be swallowed up by life*).

In this way Paul clearly shows that it is not release from bodily existence for which he longs, but rather for a bodily existence which is permanent and heavenly. In the categories of Romans 8:23, it is the redemption of the body for which he hopes, or in the terms of Philippians 3:21, for the transformation of his body to be like Christ's glorious body.

5. Having stated the nature of his hope for the future, Paul picks up again the idea introduced already in 4:17 and reminds his readers that *He who has prepared us for this very thing is God*. It is not a vain or empty hope which the apostle entertains, rather it is based upon the known fact that God himself has prepared him for such a future. It must not be overlooked that, in the light of 4:16–17, part of the process of preparation for the glorious future is participation in present suffering (*cf.* Rom 8:17). But this idea must be complemented by that found in Romans 8:28–30, where God's election, calling and justification of sinners form the basis upon which he prepares his children for glory.

Paul's hope rests not only upon the objective knowledge that it is God who is preparing him for a glorious future but also upon the subjective experience of the Spirit which he enjoys. The God who prepares is also the God *who has given us the Spirit as a guarantee*. It was by the Spirit that Christ was raised from the dead with his resurrection body. The same Spirit has been given to Christians as a guarantee that they too shall in their turn be raised up and clothed with a resurrection body. (For an explanation of the concept of the guarantee (*arrabōn*), see commentary on 1:22.)

It is worth noting that up to this point, by the use of various images, Paul has spoken of the destruction of the physical body being compensated for by the provision of the resurrection body, and that he has done so without any reference to the possibility that the former may take place without the latter following immediately. It is in vv. 6–9 that he grapples with this possibility, very probably in the light of his own increasing awareness that he personally might experience the destruction of the body before the general resurrection.

6–7. From the time Paul began in 2:14ff. to explain how, despite many difficulties, he remains confident in God, he has again and again affirmed this confidence and the fact that he does not lose heart (*cf.* 2:14; 3:4, 12; 4:1, 16), and here in v. 6 he picks up the theme again: *So we are always of good courage.* Yet while affirming this Paul confesses that the present situation does leave something to be desired: *we know that while we are at home in the body we are away from the Lord.* What this means can be ascertained from the parenthesis the apostle provides in v. 7 before returning to the main stream of his thought in v. 8. In parenthesis he says, *for we walk by faith, not by sight.* This suggests that to be *at home in the body* means that God is not accessible to our sight (and in that sense we are *away from the Lord*), but is accessible to us only *by faith* (*cf.* Jn. 20:29).

8. *We are of good courage.* With these words Paul takes up the train of thought he was pursuing before the parenthesis. But here, despite the assertion that he is of good courage, he proceeds to confess his desire for a better situation: *we would rather be away from the body and at home with the Lord.* As the parenthesis of v. 7 threw light backward upon the meaning of v. 6, so too it throws light forward upon the statement in v. 8. To be *away from the body* means to be *at home with the Lord* in the sense that then the Lord will be accessible to sight, and no longer accessible only to faith. In the words of 1 John 3:2, 'we shall see him as he is'.

In v. 8 Paul seems to recognize that although he does not wish to experience a disembodied state he will have to do so if he dies before the parousia. But this verse expresses his conviction that even if this should be his lot for a time, it would be more preferable than remaining 'in the body' and so 'away from the Lord' (v. 6). Paul says elsewhere, 'My desire is to depart and be with Christ, for that is far better' (Phil. 1:23).

9. Paul does not provide any clues as to what he may have thought the nature of the disembodied state might be. What he does in v. 9, however, is to stress something which is more important than speculation about that: *So whether we are at home or away, we make it our aim to please him.* How long he will continue to live at home in the body or whether he will soon die and be away from the body are matters which he cannot determine. But what he must determine is *how* he will live. Paul determines that it will be his aim in life to please the Lord.

10. *For we must all appear before the judgment seat of Christ.* The apostle is determined to live in a way pleasing to the Lord because he knows that all believers must *appear before the judgment seat of Christ.* The word used here for *judgment seat* is *bēma.* Among the ruins of ancient Corinth there still remains an impressive stone structure known as the *bēma* (see Introduction, p. 16, for more details). According to Acts 18:12–17 Paul was brought before the *bēma* ('tribunal') by angry Corinthian Jews who made accusations against him before the proconsul, Gallio. However, Gallio refused to sit in judgment in Jewish matters and drove Paul's accusers from the *bēma.* Both Paul and his readers knew what being brought before the judgment seat in Corinth meant. What Paul is saying here is that we need to order our lives in the light of the fact that each one of us shall be brought *before the judgment seat of Christ* (cf. Rom 14:10).

So that each one may receive good or evil, according to what he has done in the body. There is no question of a person's acceptance before God depending upon what he has done in the body. In his letter to the Romans Paul makes it abundantly clear that no human being shall be justified in God's sight on the basis of what he or she has done, 'since all have sinned and fall short of the glory of God' (Rom. 3:23). It was for this reason that God made a new way for people to be justified in his sight apart from works (*cf.* Rom. 3:21–26).

What then does Paul have in mind here when he speaks of receiving *good or evil* according to what a person *has done in the body*? It is a recognition that God will evaluate the lives and ministries of his children and reward those who have acted faithfully, while those who have not will suffer the loss of any reward. In 1 Corinthians 3:10–15 Paul applies this to the work of those who found and build up churches. He says, 'the Day will disclose it . . . and the fire will test what sort of work each one has done. If the work which any man has built on the foundation survives, he will receive a reward. If any man's work is burned up, he will suffer loss, though he himself will be saved' (vv. 13–15).

It is important to note that it is what a person *has done in the body* that will be evaluated at the judgment seat of Christ. In the present context, where Paul has been speaking of living 'at home in the body' and 'away from the body', what a person does *in the body* can refer only to what he or she does in this life. All this means that what believers do in this life has serious implications. They are accountable to the Lord for their actions, and will be rewarded or suffer loss accordingly. It is this awareness which Paul carries forward into the next section, where he speaks of 'knowing the fear of the Lord'.

L. *The Ministry of Reconciliation* (5:11 – 7:4)

In this central section of the letter Paul appeals to the Corinthians to be reconciled to God and to open their hearts to their apostle. He clears the ground for these appeals by first responding to criticisms of the style of his ministry (5:11–15), and then by stating the theological basis upon which reconciliation rests (5:16–21). Paul then makes the appeals (6:1–13; 7:2–4), and intersperses between them a call for holy living (6:14 – 7:1).

1. Response to criticism (5:11–15)
Paul responds to criticism of the style of his ministry by relating it first to the judgment of God (v.11) and later to the love of Christ (vv. 14–15).

11. *Therefore, knowing the fear of the Lord, we persuade men.* The word *therefore* indicates that what Paul is about to say follows on from what he said in v. 10 about appearing before the judgment seat of Christ. Paul is not 'afraid' of the Lord, but he does have a 'reverential awe' of him and recognizes that his whole life and ministry will come under God's scrutiny. It is with this awareness that he persuades men.

There are two possible ways to understand Paul's reference to persuading men. According to the first, the apostle is saying the awareness of his accountability to God motivates him to be diligent in his efforts to persuade men, *i.e.* to bring about in them the obedience of faith, as he was commissioned to do. What would have been involved in such persuasion can be glimpsed from a number of references in Paul's writings (*cf.* 1 Cor. 2:1–5; 2 Cor. 10:5; Col. 1:28) and also the testimony of Luke in Acts (Acts 9:20–22; 13:16–43; 17:22–34; 19:8–10; 26:24–29; 28:23). He sought to remove intellectual barriers, to overcome prejudice and ignorance, to convince by argument and testimony, and by the straightforward proclamation of the gospel.

According to the second, Paul, anticipating the defence of the style of his ministry which is to follow, stresses that the persuasion he practised was free from all dubious methods, being carried out with a proper fear of the Lord, who would countenance nothing less than full integrity in his messengers. It is perhaps significant that in the only other place Paul uses the verb 'to persuade' (*peithō*) where other persons are the objects of the persuasion, it carries a negative connotation: 'Am I now seeking the favour [*peithō*] of men, or of God? Or am I trying to please men?' (Gal. 1:10). What seems to be indicated in that use of the verb is a persuasion by adulterating the gospel so that he might please his hearers. In the light of this, v. 11 would be seen as Paul's concession that he practises persuasion but with the implied assertion that his is not a persuasion which sacrifices the truth in order to please men. His persuasion is quite straightforward, carried out with a proper fear of the Lord.

This second interpretation receives some support from the words which follow: *but what we are is known to God*. Paul's motives and actions lie open before God, who sees there is no deception involved in his attempts to persuade men. *And I hope it is known also to your conscience*. Here he appeals to the conscience of his readers (*cf.* 4:2) in the hope that they too will recognize his integrity when they listen, not to the criticisms of others, but to the testimony of their own consciences (see commentary on 1:12 for an explanation of Paul's understanding of the role of the conscience).

12. *We are not commending ourselves to you again*. Paul is very sensitive about self-commendation (*cf.* 3:1; 10:18) and it is quite likely that some of the criticism directed against him was related to this. So he denies that, in defending the straightforward character of the persuasion he practises, he is indulging in self-commendation. Rather, what he is doing is *giving you cause to be proud of us, so that you may be able to answer those who pride themselves on a man's position and not on his heart*. Paul is aware that there are those present in Corinth who are critical of his motives and methods, and he makes this defence of his integrity so that his converts may be able to deal with the criticisms of those men. He wants his readers to be able to feel justly proud of the way in which their spiritual father conducts himself, and so be able to answer his detractors.

The detractors who lurk behind the scenes in the Corinthian correspondence Paul describes as *those who pride themselves on a man's position and not on his heart*. From hints provided in both chs. 1–7 and the later chs. 10–13 we can see the sort of outward matters upon which these men prided themselves. These include the letters of recommendation they carried (3:1), their Jewish ancestry (11:22), their ecstatic visionary experiences (12:1) and the apostolic signs they performed (12:11–13). Paul implies that for them such outward matters were more important than the condition of a person's heart, which is what God sees.

13. *For if we are beside ourselves, it is for God.* There are two possible ways in which this could be taken. First, it could be Paul's response to charges that he was mad. Such charges were certainly made later in his career, and they had also been made against his master. Jesus was accused of being mad because of his unflagging zeal in ministry (Mk. 3:21) and because his teaching offended his hearers (Jn. 10:20). This latter reason underlay the charge of madness that Festus made against Paul (Acts 26:22–24), which charge, of course, Paul rejected: 'I am not mad, most excellent Festus, but I am speaking the sober truth' (Acts 26:25).

Second, it could be Paul's response to those in Corinth who denied that his ministry was truly spiritual because he gave no evidence of ecstatic experience. To this Paul would reply, *For if we are beside ourselves* (*exestēmen*), *it is for God.* This is the only place where Paul uses the verb *existēmi*, but the cognate noun *ekstasis* ('trance, ecstasy') is used in Acts 22:17, where Paul describes a visionary experience which he had in the Jerusalem temple. In the light of this parallel, Paul's statement in the present context could be paraphrased: 'For if we do experience ecstasy, that is something between us and God.'

If we are in our right mind, it is for you. If we adopt the first of the alternatives above, then Paul is saying, 'Even if [as some say] we are mad, that is but the result of our faithfulness to God in preaching a pure gospel, but if we are in our right mind [as we are], then that is for your sake [who benefit from the sober truth we speak].' On the second alternative Paul is saying, 'If we do experience ecstasy, then that is something between us and God [not something to be displayed before others as proof of the spiritual charater of our ministry], but if we are in our right mind [and use reasonable, intelligible speech], that is for your benefit.'

14. Still by way of explanation and defence of the conduct of his ministry, Paul now says, *For the love of Christ controls us.* There is a parallel use of the verb translated *controls* (*synechei*) in Philippians 1:23, where Paul, facing the possibilities of departure to be with Christ through death or a longer life and further ministry, says, 'I am hard pressed (*synechomai*) between the two.' He felt the pressure of two alternatives so that he was motivated on the one hand to do one thing, but on the other hand to do the opposite. This illustrates the basic meaning of *synechō*, which is 'to press together, constrain'. It is the pressure applied not so much to control as to cause action. It is motivational rather than directional force. The verb here in v. 14 is in the present tense, which emphasizes the continuous nature of the pressure upon Paul. The source of the pressure is *the love of Christ*. This can be construed either as Paul's love for Christ (objective genitive), or Christ's love for Paul (subjective genitive). In the light of what follows (vv. 14b–15) the second option is to be preferred. It is Paul's recognition of Christ's love shown in his death for all which acts as the motivation for the apostle's ministry.

The love of Christ which so deeply influenced the apostle that he gave his whole life in unflagging zeal to his service must be something quite exceptional. Paul was so affected, he says, *because we are convinced that one has died for all*. It was not some vague idea of Christ's goodwill that moved him, but rather the fact that *one has died for all*. The verb *has died* (*apethanen*) is in the aorist tense, pointing back to the historic event of the cross. But it was not the bare fact of Christ's death on the cross that moved Paul, it was the death of Christ understood in a particular way. It was his death *for all* (*hyper pantōn*). There has been a lot of debate whether this *hyper* should be understood to mean 'instead of' (*i.e.* Christ dying 'in place of' all) or 'for the sake of' (*i.e.* Christ dying 'for the benefit of' all, understood to mean something different from 'instead of' all). Against the former it has been argued that if Paul had meant to say Christ died 'instead of' all he would have used the Greek preposition *anti* which more clearly expresses that idea. It is true that *anti* expresses the idea unambiguously, but it must be remembered that while *hyper* need not denote 'instead of', it may do so.

The matter cannot be settled by consideration of this text in isolation. Other Pauline texts bearing upon the subject must be allowed to guide us. For example, in Galatians 3:13 Paul says, 'Christ redeemed us from the curse of the law, having become a curse for (*hyper*) us – for it is written, "Cursed be every one who hangs on a tree."'' In that context Christ clearly endures God's curse instead of us. There was absolutely no reason for him to endure God's curse otherwise. So on the tree, *i.e.* in his death upon the cross, he bore the curse of God instead of us. It is not unlikely, therefore, that in the present context *one has died for (hyper) all* means that Christ died instead of the 'all'.[1] The interpretation preserves the logical connection with what follows: *therefore all have died*. If Christ did not die instead of the 'all', then the 'all' cannot be said to have died (the meaning of 'all' is discussed along with the meaning of 'world' in the commentary on v. 19, where the latter is found).

It is the exceptional character of Christ's love, understood as that which moved him to die in our place, which alone accounts satisfactorily for its great motivational power in Paul's life. It is just that function which the affirmation has in the present context. Paul will give some further clues concerning the significance of Christ's death in vv. 18–21, but for the moment his main concern is with its motivational power, and that concern carries over into v. 15.

15. In this verse Paul states the purpose of Christ's death in so far as the lives of those who benefit from it are concerned. Stating it first negatively he says, *And he died for all, that those who live might live no longer for themselves,* and then putting it positively, *but for him who for their sake died and was raised*. The possibility that those who have benefited from Christ's death and resurrection should revert to living for themselves is ever present, and was the path actually taken by a number of Paul's associates (Phil. 2:21; 2 Tim. 4:10). What kept Paul on the right path, and will keep us there too, is an awareness of the exceptional character of Christ's love for us. We love him and desire to live for him as we realize that he loved us and gave himself for us (Gal. 2:20).

The scope of the 'all' in this verse is discussed along with the meaning of the other universal expression, 'the world', in the commentary on v. 19 (in which the latter is found).

[1] This is the way *hyper* is construed here by both BAGD, *ad loc.*, and H. Riesenfeld, *TDNT* 8, pp. 509–510.

As noted above, in this whole section (5:11–15) Paul is responding to criticisms of the style of his ministry. In response he has claimed that his motives and actions lie open before God, who sees there is no deception involved in the conduct of his ministry. Further, if he does experience ecstasy, that is something between himself and God, but when he uses intelligible speech, that is for the benefit of his hearers. He argues that he could not do otherwise than serve Christ, striving for the utmost integrity, for the very love of Christ controls him now. He is convinced that Christ died in his stead, and now he wants to live for him. So we see in 5:11–15 the two poles of Paul's motivation for ministry. On the one hand he is aware of accountability and so has a healthy fear (v. 11), and on the other he knows of the great love of Christ and so could not do otherwise than live for the one who died and rose for him (v. 14).

2. God's reconciling act in Christ (5:16–21)

This section takes its point of departure from the effect of Christ's death and resurrection upon believers – they have died in Christ and live in him. One result of all this is that Paul and his colleagues have a completely new outlook. As part of the new creation being effected by God in Christ, their old attitudes have passed away. All this they owe to God and his reconciling activity towards the world. The message concerning this reconciliation is entrusted to Paul and his colleagues, through whom, as ambassadors for Christ, God makes his appeal to men and women that they be reconciled to him. The means by which God has effected reconciliation is by making Christ to be sin that sinners might become the righteousness of God in him.

16. *From now on, therefore, we regard no one from a human point of view.* From the time Paul realized the significance of the death of Christ – 'one has died for all; therefore all have died' (v. 14) – the love of Christ for him expressed therein had been the motivating power of his life, and not only so, but had also changed his whole outlook. He could no longer regard others *from a human point of view.* Things which once had been regarded as important were now seen to have no real value at all (*cf.* Phil. 3:4–8). He can no longer pride himself 'on a man's position', only his standing before God, which is a gift of grace (*cf.* v. 12). He confesses that he *once regarded Christ from a human point of view*. In his pre-conversion days he judged Christ using human criteria and came to the wrong conclusion, but after God had been pleased to reveal his Son to him, he had to say *we regard him thus no longer*, *i.e.* no longer from a mistaken human point of view.

This verse, with its reference to regarding Christ *from a human point of view* (lit. 'according to [the] flesh') has been used as a proof text by those who argue that Paul showed little interest in the historical Jesus (Christ after the flesh) but focused attention upon the Christ of faith. However, such a view can claim no support from this verse because Paul is talking about a way of knowing ('according to the flesh'), not about a particular phase of Christ's existence (Christ after the flesh = the historical Jesus). What Paul is saying is that previously he had a completely inadequate knowledge of Christ – one based on a human point of view – but now his understanding of Christ is no longer limited in that way. We should look to the way Paul regarded Christ before and after his conversation to appreciate the contrast of viewpoints spoken of here. Before his conversion he would have regarded him as a false Christ, whose followers ought to be stamped out. Afterwards he knew Jesus was God's Christ, the one who was to make all things new, and to whom all men must be called to respond in the obedience of faith.

17. Something of the great significance of Christ is expressed when Paul says of the person who belongs to him, *Therefore, if any one is in Christ, he is a new creation* (lit. 'so that, if anyone in Christ, a new creation'). The thrust of this statement is that when a person is *in Christ*, he or she is part of the new creation. God's plan of salvation, while primarily concerned with humanity, encompasses the whole created order (Rom. 8:21). When a person is *in Christ* he or she has become already part of the new creation so that it may be said, *the old has passed away, behold, the new has come.* This participation in the new creation is reflected in the changed outlook of which v. 16 spoke and in a new holiness of life (*cf.* 1 Cor. 6:9–11), and will culminate in the renewal of the whole person by resurrection to immortality in the new created order at the parousia (*cf*. Is. 65:17; 66:22; Rom. 8:19–23).

It is true, of course, that for the time being the old still persists and the new has not yet fully come (*cf*. Rom. 8:18–25; Gal. 5:15–26). However, in our present passage it is the newness of life in Christ now which is being stressed, rather than the limitations and the tension involved in participating in the new creation while still living as part of the old.

18. Paul here underlines the fact that *All this is from God, who through Christ reconciled us to himself*. The heart of Paul's gospel is Christ crucified as Lord, but the framework of that message is decidedly theocratic. The great plan of salvation by which all creation is to be redeemed is God's, and he it is who through Christ reconciled us to himself. Wherever the language of reconciliation is found in the New Testament, God is always the subject of the reconciling activity. There is no hint that Christ is the gracious one who must overcome unwillingness on God's part to be reconciled with sinful humanity. It is God himself who initiates and effects the reconciliation through Christ. On the other hand this does not mean that there existed no obstacle on God's part that had to be overcome before reconciliation could be effected with humanity. God's wrath, revealed from heaven against the wickedness of humanity, had to be dealt with (*cf*. Rom. 1:18; 5:9–11). What is stressed in the present passage is the amazing grace of God revealed when he himself took the initiative in Christ to remove the obstacle to reconciliation existing on his part. It is only on this basis that there exists a gospel of reconciliation by which humanity can now be called to be reconciled to God.

It is important to note that in one sense reconciliation has been accomplished already. God through Christ has already *reconciled* (the aorist participle is used) us to himself. He has broken down the tremendous barrier which alienated us from him. What that barrier was and how it was broken down Paul describes in vv. 19, 21. However, before doing that he fore-shadows in the words *and gave us the ministry of reconciliation* the fact that the reconciling process is in another sense still incomplete. The preaching of reconciliation has to be carried out and people must hear the call to be reconciled to God. Unless they respond to that call they cannot actually experience the reconciliation.

19. The ministry of reconciliation is primarily the proclamation of what God has done, and this Paul reiterates with the words, *that is, in Christ God was reconciling the world to himself, not counting their trespasses against them.* Consistent with Paul's shift of focus from his own experience of reconciliation to the message he proclaims to the world, the object of God's reconciling activity is no longer simply 'us' (v. 18), but *the world* and *them.* The barrier which alienated people from God (and God from them) is identified, *i.e. their trespasses.* The reconciliation which God effected in Christ is the removal of this barrier by his *not counting their trespasses against them.* The basis upon which this non-reckoning of sins was made possible is indicated in v. 21.

The non-counting of people's trespasses against them (in which the reconcilation consists) is expressed by Paul in Romans 4:8 by citing Psalm 32:2: 'blessed is the man against whom the Lord will not reckon his sin'. This blessing, Paul goes on to explain, is not restricted to Jews ('the circumcised') but is pronounced over all who believe, including Gentiles ('the uncircumcised) (Rom. 4:9–12). It is probably in this way that we should interpret the universal expressions *the world* (in this verse) and 'all' (v. 14). It hardly applies to the created order, as the trespasses involved are those of humanity, and it is difficult to see it applying extensively to every individual human being, because elsewhere Paul clearly implies that the sins of unbelievers are and shall be counted against them (*cf.* Rom. 1:18–32; 2:5–11; Eph. 5:3–6; Col. 3:5–6).

And entrusting to us the message of reconciliation. God has not only reconciled *the world* to himself, he has also commissioned messengers to proclaim that good news. All who heed the call to repentance and faith will experience for themselves the joy of their reconciliation with God.

20. Because God entrusted him with the message of reconciliation (v. 19) Paul is able to say, *So we are ambassadors for Christ, God making his appeal through us.* The Greek verb *presbeuō*, which Paul uses in the expression *we are ambassadors*, meant essentially 'to be older or the eldest', but came to be used in connection with functions for which the wisdom of age was a necessary prerequisite. In the political sphere it was used of an ambassador who represented his nation, while in the religious sphere it was used figuratively (*e.g.* by Philo when speaking of the angels or Moses as God's emissaries). The striking thing about Paul's ambassadorship is its relation to God's activity as the reconciler. The God who reconciled the world to himself through the death of his Son, now actually appeals to the world, through his ambassadors, to be reconciled to him.

We beseech you on behalf of Christ, be reconciled to God. This may very well reflect the language of Paul's evangelistic preaching, but here the appeal is directed to members of the Corinthian church. Paul can hardly mean by this that his readers had not yet responded to the gospel, for they had accepted the message he himself had brought to them. However, Paul's apostolic authority and gospel had been called into question in Corinth, and in succeeding passages he is to entreat his converts not to accept the grace of God in vain (6:1–3) and to open their hearts to their apostle (6:11–13; 7:2–4). It is perhaps by way of preparation for these appeals that Paul employs the language of evangelistic preaching here in v. 20.

21. Before proceeding to his appeal to the Corinthians in 6:1–13, for which he prepared the way in v. 20, Paul makes a highly compressed but extremely profound statement concerning the work of Christ: *For our sake he made him to be sin who knew no sin.* This is the way Paul (in this letter) describes the basis upon which God reconciled us to himself. From this statement we get some idea why the cross, as the expression of the love of God in Christ, had such great motivating power in the apostle's life.

Consistent with the witness of the rest of the New Testament (*cf.* Mt. 27:4,24; Lk. 23:47; Jn. 8:46; Heb. 4:15; 1 Pet. 1:19; 2:22), Paul describes Christ as one *who knew no sin.* There may be an allusion here to the Suffering Servant of Isaiah ('he had done no violence, and there was no deceit in his mouth', Is. 53:9), but be that as it may, what Paul stresses is that God made this sinless one *to be sin* for our sake. Various interpretations have been suggested for this profound statement: (a) Christ was made a sinner, (b) Christ was made a sin-offering, (c) Christ was made to bear the consequences of our sins. The first suggestion is rightly rejected out of hand. The second can be supported by appeal to Paul's use of sacrificial terminology elsewhere to bring out the significance of Christ's death (*e.g.* Rom. 3:25; 1 Cor. 5:7). It has also been pointed out that in Leviticus 4:24 and 5:12 (LXX) the same word, 'sin' (*hamartia*), is used to mean 'sin-offering'. However, with only one possible exception (Rom. 8:3), the word is never used in this way in the New Testament, and it is doubtful whether it carries that meaning here. The understanding of Christ's death as a sacrifice for sin is certainly Pauline, but it is probably not the best way of understanding the present statement. The third suggestion then is to be preferred and is supported by the fact that Paul in Galatians 3:13 interprets the work of Christ in terms of his bearing the consequences of our sins: 'Christ redeemed us from the curse of the law, having become a curse for us – for it is written, "Cursed be every one who hangs on tree" '.

This interpretation is further supported by the fact that the statement, *he made him to be sin who knew no sin* (v. 21a) is balanced in antithetical parallelism by the words, *so that in him we might become the righteousness of God*. We must construe the former in such a way that the latter is understood as its antithetical counterpart.

In seeking to understand what it means to be *the righteousness of God*, we receive assistance from certain other passages where Paul touches upon the same subject (Rom. 3:21–26; Phil. 3:7–9). *The righteousness of God*, understood as that which believers have or become, is the gift of a right relationship with God based upon the fact that he has adjudicated in their favour by refusing, because of the death of Christ in their place, to take account of their sins.

If becoming *the righteousness of God* means God has adjudicated in our favour and put us in right relationship with himself, then to become sin, being the antithetical counterpart of this, will mean that God has adjudicated against Christ (because he took upon himself the burden of our sins, *cf.* Is. 53:4–6, 12) with the result that his relationship with God was (momentarily, but terribly beyond all human comprehension) severed. If this interpretation is correct, then we can perhaps begin to understand something of the agony of Gethsemane ('Father, if thou art willing, remove this cup from me; nevertheless not my will, but thine, be done', Lk. 22:42) and the awful cry of dereliction from the cross ('My God, my God, why hast thou forsaken me?', Mt. 27:46). We obviously stand at the brink of a great mystery and our understanding of it can be only minimal.

3. An appeal for reconciliation (6:1–13)
Paul, having spoken in the previous chapter of the reconciling activity of God and his own role as a messenger of reconciliation, now in 6:1–13 enacts that role for the benefit of his readers. He exhorts them not to receive the grace of God in vain (vv. 1–2) and appeals to them to open their hearts and so be fully reconciled to their apostle (vv. 11–13). Between the exhortation and the appeal Paul makes another defence of his ministry (vv. 3–10).

1. *Working together with him, then.* Following the theologically profound parenthesis of 5:21, Paul picks up again the theme of 5:20 – his appeal to the Corinthians that they be reconciled to God. The expression *working together with him* translates one Greek word, *synergountes* ('working together with'). The RSV rightly provides the word *him* in translation, indicating that it is God with whom Paul works, and this is made even more explicit in the NIV ('As God's fellow-workers . . .'). Although the party with whom Paul works could conceivably be understood as one or more of his colleagues, the context here (5:20) supports the RSV and NIV renderings.

We entreat you not to accept the grace of God in vain. In 5:20 God is said to have made his appeal through Paul, but in this verse the apostle himself makes the appeal as one working together with God. These are but two different ways of expressing the one reality of divine involvement in Paul's ministry. *The grace of God* may be understood as all that was proclaimed in the 'message of reconciliation' (5:19), what God in his love has wrought through Christ and offers through the preaching of the gospel. Paul's readers had accepted his gospel and experienced something of the grace of God of which it speaks. Now he exhorts them to make sure their acceptance is not in vain. It is unlikely that Paul implies their acceptance may have been only superficial (like seed sown on rocky ground). It is more likely that he has in mind how easily these people are influenced by others, whether by the offender who made the personal attack against Paul (2:5; 7:12) or the critics of the apostle who were already lurking in the background in Corinth. He does not want the lives of those who made a good response to the gospel to be marred now by entertaining criticisms of that gospel and the one who brought it to them.

2. To underline the gravity and urgency of his appeal Paul introduces, with the words, *For he says*, a verbatim quotation from Isaiah 49:8 (LXX): *At the acceptable time I have listened to you, and helped you on the day of salvation.* In their original context these words are addressed to the Servant of the Lord and applied to the time of Israel's release from exile in Babylon. Paul makes his own application: *Behold, now is the acceptable time; behold, now is the day of salvation.* If the time of the exiles' return was a day of salvation, then the time when God has acted in Christ to reconcile the world to himself is the day of salvation *par excellence*. However, the idea of the day of salvation is not exhausted by what is already present, for Paul and other New Testament writers looked forward to the parousia of Christ as the great day on which salvation would be consummated (*cf.* Rom. 13:11; 1 Thes. 5:8–9; Heb. 9:28; 1 Pet. 1:5).

3–4a. *We put no obstacle in any one's way.* Paul has exhorted his readers 'not to accept the grace of God in vain', and here insists that his own conduct as God's messenger does not constitute a stumbling-block which might hinder the proper acceptance of God's grace by others. What he means is clarified by what follows: *so that no fault may be found with our* [lit. 'the'] *ministry*. If fault could be found in his ministry, and there were in Corinth those only too prepared to find it, then presumably that could be used as an excuse to reject his message. Therefore Paul says, *but as servants of God we commend ourselves in every way.* What is involved here is not primarily personal commendation, something which the apostle eschewed (3:1; 5:12), but the commendation of a ministry. In vv. 4b–10 we see what Paul means by *in every way*.

4b–5. *Through great endurance.* This appears to be the general heading for nine factors Paul adduces to commend his ministry. These comprise three sets of three. The first set, *afflictions, hardships, calamities*, is expressed in general terms, the second represents particular examples, *beatings, imprisonments, tumults*, while the third speaks of hardships voluntarily undertaken, *labours, watching, hunger*. Chapter 11 and the account of Paul's ministry in Acts provide the best commentary on these verses. Two of the factors call for explanation. By *tumults* Paul means 'civil disorders' or 'riots' (*cf.* Acts 13:50; 14:19; 16:19; 19:29), and *watching* refers to wakefulness or sleepless nights (*cf.* 11:27) probably due to the pressures of travel, ministry and his concern for the churches.

It may seem strange that Paul should appeal to such hardships to commend his ministry. But underlying the appeal is the recognition that the true servant of God is the Suffering Servant, and that he who is the loyal follower of Christ will share his fate: 'A disciple is not above his teacher, nor a servant above his master' (Mt. 10:24; *cf.* Acts 20:19).

6–7. Proceeding with his commendation, Paul speaks of moral integrity and the 'weapons' employed. Thus he commends his ministry *by purity* [or 'sincerity'], *knowledge, forbearance, kindness, the Holy Spirit* [the dynamic of Paul's ministry derived from the Spirit], *genuine love, truthful speech* [lit. 'word of truth', possibly the gospel], *and the power of God* [*cf.* 1 Cor. 2:5]; *with the weapons of righteousness for the right hand and for the left*.

Ministry *with the weapons (hoplōn) of righteousness for the right hand and for the left* has been variously interpreted: a ministry that is (a) ready for an attack from any quarter, (b) armed with weapons of offence (a sword for the right hand) and defence (a shield for the left), (c) carried out both in prosperity (the right hand) and adversity (the left hand). This sort of military metaphor is used in other passages in Paul's writings, and a consideration of these throws light on its use here. In 10:3–5 Paul speaks of 'the weapons (*hopla*) of our warfare' which are not worldly but 'have divine power to destroy strongholds'. These strongholds are 'arguments and every proud obstacle to the knowledge of God', and the purpose of their destruction is to 'take every thought captive to obey Christ'. What we see here is the offensive weapon of gospel presentation and argumentation (*cf.*, *e.g.*, Acts 19:8–10) whereby the power of God is released to bring about the overthrow of false arguments and folly and bring people to the obedience of faith.

In Romans 13:12 Paul writes: 'the night is far spent, the day is at hand. Let us then cast off the works of darkness and put on the armour [*hopla*, lit. 'weapons'] of light'. The exhortation forms part of a call for godly living in contrast to revelling and drunkenness *etc.*, so the expression 'armour of light' here stands for Christian character and behaviour.

In Ephesians 6:10–20 the various items of the Roman soldier's equipment form the basis of a description of the Christian's 'armour'. Paul says, 'put on the whole armour [*panoplian*] of God'. The word *panoplian* was used of the equipment of a heavily armed soldier. While the actual Greek word used is different (*i.e.* not *hopla*), the underlying military metaphor is the same. The items of armour listed are mostly defensive (*e.g.* breastplate, shield, helmet – *cf.* 1 Thes. 5:8, where some similar items are listed), but include one offensive weapon, 'the sword of the Spirit', which symbolizes 'the word of God'. The presentation of the gospel is the only means known and used by Paul to confront the 'principalities and powers' which oppose the progress of the gospel.

In the light of all this it is best to adopt the interpretation of weapons *for the right hand and for the left* which sees here a reference to weapons of both offence and defence.

8–10. Paul further commends his ministry by setting forth nine antitheses. In each case one part of the antithesis represents an evaluation of his ministry 'from a human point of view', and the other part, the true view of one 'in Christ'. Thus he commends his ministry *in honour and dishonour, in ill repute and good repute*. Those who judge from a human point of view (outsiders, or perhaps his critics in Corinth) hold him in dishonour and ill repute, but those who no longer view things from a human point of view hold him in honour and good repute. *We are treated as impostors, and yet are true.* Those who criticized Paul because he did not not carry letters of recommendation (3:1–3) may have regarded him as an imposter, but those with godly discernment would recognize that he was a true apostle. *As unkown, and yet well known.* By the world and by his critics Paul was regarded as a nobody, he was not 'recognized', but those who no longer judged according to worldly standards recognized his apostolate and to them he was well known.[1] *As dying, and behold we live; as punished, and yet not killed.* Judged by worldly standards Paul's career was a miserable one. He was continually exposed to the danger of death, punished by angry mobs and civil authorities, but God delivered him again and again (see 1:8–10 for the most recent deliverance) so that contrary to all expectation, behold he lives, and is not killed. *As sorrowful, yet always rejoicing.* This antithesis is closely related to the previous two. In all his troubles Paul appeared a sorrowful sight to those who regarded him from a human point of view, but the truth was that by the grace of God he was always rejoicing (*cf.* Acts 16:19–26). *As poor, yet making many rich; as having nothing, and yet possessing everything.* It was a commonplace in Paul's day, *e.g.* among Cynic and Stoic philosophers, to speak of having nothing materially, but possessing everything in a higher sense. Paul's *having nothing* would be the result in part of his refusing either to accept support from the Corinthians (11:7–9), or to 'peddle' the gospel for financial gain (2:17). Nevertheless he regarded himself as truly rich because he was already experiencing as a sort of first-fruits the spiritual blessings of the age to come. And further, he rejoiced that, though materially poor, he could make many rich by enabling them to share in the spiritual blessings through Christ.

The purpose of Paul's long commendation (vv. 3–10) is to show that no fault was to be found in his ministry, and thereby

---

[1] The present passive participle here rendered *well known* is *epiginōskomenoi* from the verb *epiginōskō* which Paul uses in 1 Cor. 16:18, where he urges the Corinthians to 'recognize' certain Christian fellow workers.

to clear the ground for an appeal to the Corinthians for a full reconciliation with their apostle. Having done this, Paul proceeds immediately to his appeal (vv. 11–13).

11. *Our mouth is open to you, Corinthians.* The similar expression, 'he opened his mouth [and taught them]' is often used of Jesus in the Gospels (*e.g.* Mt. 5:2; 13:35) and reflects a common Hebraic idiom meaning simply 'he spoke'. However, Paul's expression, *Our mouth is open to you*, is a Greek idiom denoting candour, or straightforward speech. By adding, *our heart is wide*, Paul affirms that there is plenty of room for the Corinthians in his affections.

12. *You are not restricted by us.* The Greek underlying this translation contains the idea that the Corinthians are not restricted to a narrow place in Paul's affections. The apostle then adds, *but you are restricted in your own affections.* The constraints existing in their relationship with Paul are the result of their own affections having been squeezed, as it were, into a narrow place. They have allowed the events of the past and the criticisms levelled against their apostle to restrict the breadth of their affection for him.

13. *In return – I speak as to children – widen your hearts also.* The pastoral concern of a spiritual father is reflected in this verse expecially. Those whom he addressed as 'Corinthians' in v. 11, are here addressed as *children* (*cf.* 1 Cor. 4:14–15). When Paul says, *In return . . . widen your hearts also*', he is appealing to his beloved children to respond to his own open-heartedness towards them (v. 11) by showing the same to him. He longs for their reciprocal affection.

4. A call for holy living (6:14 – 7:1)

This passage poses many problems for the reader because its connection with what precedes and follows it is not obvious. The question as to whether it is to be regarded as a later interpolation has been discussed in the Introduction (pp. 37–40). There it was concluded that the interpolation theory raises greater problems than it solves, for it is extremely difficult to explain, on that theory, *why* anyone would introduce such a passage at this place. If in fact it is not a later interpolation we have two tasks before us: to understand the message of 6:14 – 7:1 itself, and to relate it somehow to the rest of the letter, especially its immediate context.

To understand the passage itself we need first to recognize its structure. It consists of (a) an introductory exhortation not to be mismated with unbelievers (6:14a), (b) five rhetorical questions which bring out the necessity of heeding this exhortation (6:14b–16a), (c) an affirmation of believers' unique relationship with God (6:16b), (d) a number of quotations from the Old Testament which highlight the privilege involved in this relationship and reiterate the content of the exhortation (6:16c–18), and (e) a concluding call to cleanse oneself from defilement and make holiness perfect.

14a. *Do not be mismated with unbelievers.* The expression *be mismated (ginesthe heterozygountes)* contains the idea of being unevenly yoked. The verb *heterozygeō* is found only here in the New Testament, but is used in the LXX at Leviticus 19:19 as part of a prohibition on yoking different types of animals together.[1] It is used by Philo and Josephus in the same way. The concept, but not the word, is found in Deuteronomy 22:10. Using language reminiscent of these prohibitions, Paul exhorts his readers not to enter into 'partnerships' with unbelievers. But what sort of partnerships did he have in mind? Were they marriage partnerships (*cf.* 1 Cor. 7:39), or was it the more general notion of partnership in pagan practices (*cf.* 1 Cor. 10:14–22)? In the light of what follows (vv. 15–16) the latter seems more likely.

14b–16a. The opening exhortation of v. 14a is here backed up by five rhetorical questions which underline its importance. *For what partnership have righteousness and iniquity? Or what fellowship has light with darkness?* The contrasts between righteousness and iniquity, light and darkness contained in these first two ques-

---

[1] The Hebrew text of Lv. 19:19 on which our English versions are based contains a prohibition, not of yoking, but of breeding different species of animals.

tions are found frequently in the Dead Sea Scrolls also (*e.g. The Hymns* 1:26–27; *The War Rule* 3:19). The word *Belial*, found in the third question (*What accord has Christ with Belial?*), is also found frequently in the Dead Sea Scrolls (*e.g. The War Rule* 1:1, 5, 13, 15; 4:2; 11:8) and in the intertestamental literature (*e.g. Testament of Levi* 3:3). In these writings Belial is a name given to the chief of demons, or Satan. (In the AV the expression 'sons of Belial' or the like is found in a number of places in the Old Testament, *e.g.* Dt. 13:13; Jdg. 19:22; 1 Sa. 2:12; 1 Ki. 21:10, 13, but such expressions are not found in the RSV, where the rendering 'base fellows' is used instead.)

In Colossians 1:12–14 Paul depicts salvation as the deliverance of believers from the dominion of darkness into the kingdom of God's Son, where they share in the inheritance of the saints in light. Thus those who have been transferred into the kingdom of Christ and light can have no fellowship with Satan and the dominion of darknesss. In 1 Corinthians 10:14–22 Paul speaks of participation in pagan worship as fellowship with demons, and his question, *What accord has Christ with Belial?*, probably reflects concern in the same area. In this case his fourth rhetorical question, *Or what has a believer in common with an unbeliever?*, would be best interpreted also in relation to worship, and the call for separation which this whole passage makes should then be related not to the day to day contacts that believers have with unbelievers (*cf.* 1 Cor. 5:9–10), but to the matter of pagan worship.

What agreement has the temple of God with idols? This final question with its worship imagery offers extra support for the view that the earlier questions reinforce a call to have no involvement in pagan worship. When Paul speaks here of *the temple of God* the background imagery is that of the Jerusalem shrine, but in the foreground is the Christian community as God's temple. This is confirmed by the affirmation which follows in v. 16b.

16b. *For we are the temple of the living God.* Having emphasized the incompatibility of 'the temple of God' and idols (v. 16a), Paul with this affirmation shows why the Christian community must not become involved in pagan worship: it is because its members constitute *the temple of the living God.*

In 1 Corinthians Paul speaks of both the individual Christian's body (1 Cor. 6:16–20) and the Christian community as a whole (1 Cor. 3:16–17) as God's temple. It is the latter sense which he employs here. The expression *the living God* is also used frequently by the apostle (*cf.* Rom. 9:26; 2 Cor. 3:3; 1 Thes. 1:9; 1 Tim. 3:15; 4:10). Its background is the Old Testament contrast between the living God of Israel and the lifeless idols of pagan nations. In the present context the same contrast is implied. Elsewhere Paul states clearly that idols in themselves are nothing, the danger of idolatry being that the involvement with demonic powers active therein provokes the Lord to jealousy (1 Cor. 8:4–6; 10:19–22).

16c–18. The series of Old Testament quotations contained in these verses is introduced by the formula, *as God said*. In their original context God was in fact the speaker in each case, and the people of Israel were those addressed. Paul applies these words of God to the Christian community in Corinth.

I will live in them and move among them, and I will be their God, and they shall be my people. There is no exact counterpart in the LXX or the Hebrew Bible. Paul's 'quotation' appears to be a free one, and possibly draws upon both Leviticus 26:11–12 and Ezekiel 37:26–27. However, the promises contained here are repeated again and again in the Old Testament (*cf.*, *e.g.* Ex. 25:8; 29:45; Je. 31:1) and are taken up in Revelation to express the final bliss of the redeemed: 'Behold, the dwelling of God is with men. He will dwell with them, and they shall be his people, and God himself will be with them' (Rev. 21:3). The people of God enjoy no greater privilege than that of belonging to him and having him dwell with them. In the Old Testament period God made himself present in tabernacle and temple. Since Pentecost he dwells with his people in a far more intimate way through his Spirit, and this is a foretaste of the final bliss of which Revelation 21:3 speaks.

In the light of the great privileges of the people of God expressed in the passages cited in v. 16, Paul reiterates in v. 17 the exhortation to have nothing to do with paganism, and does so by making use of another passage from the Old Testament. *Therefore come out from them, and be separate from them, says the Lord, and touch nothing unclean.* In substance this is taken from

Isaiah 52:11, where the primary appeal is for the Jewish exiles in Babylon to leave their pagan place of exile and return to Judea and Jerusalem. In like manner Paul appeals to the Corinthians to separate themselves from paganism in Corinth.

To encourage his readers to make this stand, Paul brings forward more quotations to show how God welcomes those who turn to him. First there is a brief quotation from Ezekiel 20:34 (LXX): *then I will welcome you.* The primary reference of the text was to the exiles returning from Babylon, but again Paul makes an application of a text to the Corinthians who are being called to abandon compromise with paganism. There follows an adaptation of 2 Samuel 7:8, 14 (LXX): *and I will be a father to you, and you shall be my sons and daughters, says the Lord Almighty.* This promise, originally addressed to King David, Paul adapts by substituting the second person plural pronouns (*you*) and adding the words *and daughters.* As it stands in the present context the quotation further emphasizes the immense privilege of belonging to God's people. What greater incentive could there be to abandon all idolatrous practices than knowing there was a welcome from the Lord Almighty who will treat them as his children?

7:1. *Since we have these promises, beloved, let us cleanse ourselves from every defilement of body and spirit.* In the light of the great promises he has set forth in 6:16c–18 Paul reiterates his call for holy living. The term *beloved* reveals Paul's affection for the Corinthians, and the use of the hortatory subjunctive (*let us cleanse*) and the first person plural reflexive pronoun (*ourselves*) shows how he includes himself and his colleagues with his readers as those who must fulfil the exhortation.

The word *defilement* (*molysmos*) is found only here in the New Testament and only three times in the LXX. In all cases it denotes religious defilement. Paul's reference to *defilement of body and spirit* may imply either simply that the 'whole person' can be affected adversely by idolatrous practices, or more specifically that both a person's body (external) and spirit (internal) can be defiled. The latter alternative may be illustrated by 1 Corinthians 6:15–18, where the apostle describes a person's sexual involvement with a prostitute as a sin 'against his own body' (sacred prostitution was part of pagan worship in Corinth), and by 1 Corinthians 10:19–21, where participation in idolatrous worship involves partnership with demons, *i.e.* defilement of spirit. To cleanse oneself from such defilement would mean abandoning any participation in pagan worship.

Paul's call for holy living finishes on a positive note: *and make holiness perfect in the fear of God*. He uses the noun *holiness* (*hagiōsynē*) in Romans 1:4, where he speaks of 'the Spirit of holiness' by whom Christ was designated Son of God with power, and also in 1 Thessalonians 3:13, where it comes as part of a benediction: 'so that he [God] may establish your hearts unblamable in holiness'. In the present passage Paul exhorts his readers to make their holiness perfect. For them that would involve abandoning all compromise with idolatry. This break they would have to effect themselves, but in this, as in all growth in holiness, they could depend upon God's grace mediated through the Spirit of holiness.

The fear of God, like 'the fear of the Lord' in 5:11 (see commentary on that verse) is to be understood not as terror but as 'reverential awe'.

The whole passage, 6:14 – 7:1, then, constitutes a call and encouragement for Christians to have nothing to do with pagan worship, but rather to *make holiness perfect in the fear of God*. The difficult question remains as to why, if it is not an interpolation, the passage is included by Paul at this point in the letter. Various suggestions have been made (see Introduction, pp. 39–40), the least unsatisfactory of which seem to be: (a) that Paul, deeply concerned to re-establish fellowship with the Corinthians (*cf.* 6:11–13; 7:2–4), nevertheless reminds them that full restoration of fellowship can be achieved only if they cease all involvement with pagan worship, and (b) that Paul was warning his readers that if they were to join the opposition to him and his gospel, such action would be tantamount to siding with Satan/Belial. He calls on them to avoid any such liaison and to be reconciled with their true apostle instead. It is of course possible that Paul has jumped from one subject to another and then back again, and that there is *no* logical connection. Most people who write letters do this occasionally, and we should allow that Paul might have done so here.

5. A further appeal for reconciliation (7:2–4)
Here, following the section calling for no compromise with paganism (6:14 – 7:1), Paul renews his appeal to the Corinthians to open their hearts to their apostle, thus taking up again what he said earlier in 6:11–13.

2. *Open your hearts to us* (lit. 'make room for us'). The verb form is aorist imperative, indicating that Paul was looking for some specific action, rather than simply making a general exhortation, which in turn suggests that Paul believed there was still some reticence on the part of the Corinthians to make room in their hearts for him. In the earlier appeal (6:11–13) he stressed that his own heart was opened wide towards them and that the remaining restriction in the relationship was on their side.

To support this renewed appeal Paul asserts his integrity on three levels. In each case the aorist tense is employed, indicating that he has in mind the particular occasions of his past visits to Corinth and the way he conducted himself then. First, Paul asserts, *we have wronged no one*. What had happened in the relationship, of course, is that Paul had been wronged (*cf.* 7:12) and not vice versa. Second, he says, *we have corrupted no one*. The verb, 'to corrupt' (*phtheirō*), is used three times in the Corinthian correspondence. In 1 Corinthians 3:17 Paul uses it after speaking of the building of the church on the foundation of Christ by various ministers, all of whose work is to be tested. He warns that anyone who 'destroys' (*phtheirei*) 'God's temple', that person God will 'destroy' (*phtheirei*). In 1 Corinthians 15:33 Paul speaks of bad company which 'ruins' (*phtheirousin*) good morals (a parallel use to this is found in Ephesians 4:22 where the 'old nature' is said to be 'corrupt' (*phtheiromenon*) through deceitful lusts). In all probability, therefore, Paul's meaning in our present context is that he has caused the church no harm, his teaching and example have not corrupted it or encouraged immoral behaviour. Third, Paul assures his readers, *we have taken advantage of (pleonekteō) no-one*. This is one of four places where the verb 'to take advantage of' is used by Paul in this Epistle. In 2:11 the idea is that the congregation will be taken advantage of by Satan if he is allowed to rob it of one of its members. In 12:17 and in 12:18 it is used with the idea of taking advantage of people for financial gain, and it is in this way that we are to understand the present use. Paul claims personal integrity in financial matters. He has not used his position for personal gain.

3. *I do not say this to condemn you.* Paul may have felt that the strong defence of his own integrity in v. 2 might be taken to imply a questioning of the Corinthians' integrity. If so, these words would constitute an immediate denial of such an attitude on his part. On the contrary, his real attitude towards them is much more positive: *for I said before that you are in our hearts* (*cf.* 6:11), *to die together and to live together.* In the papyri the expression 'to live together and to die together' is found where mutual friendship and loyalty are extolled. The idea is that those involved have a friendship that will be sustained throughout life and will keep them together even if death is involved (*cf.* Mk. 14:31). In his affirmation of friendship Paul reverses the order, *i.e.* not to live and die, but to die and live together, and this reflects a fundamental Christian outlook. It is by dying that we live; it is by suffering that we are prepared for glory. The idea originated with Jesus himself (*cf.* Mk. 8:34–36; Jn. 12:24–26) and is found frequently in the writings of Paul (*cf.* Rom. 6:8; 8:17, 36–39; 2 Cor. 4:8–12, 16–18; 2 Tim. 2:11). When Paul says the Corinthians are in his heart *to die together and to live together* it is in recognition of the fact that to be a Christian was to expose oneself to suffering and possible death, but to do so was also to put oneself in the way of experiencing the daily renewal and the manifestation of the life of Christ within. And by this process a person is prepared for eternal life and glory (*cf.* Rom. 8:18; 2 Cor. 4:17). It is the recognition of this fact also which enables us to make sense of Paul's words at the end of the next verse ('With all our affliction, I am overjoyed').

4. Despite the fact that Paul felt there may still have been some reticence on the part of the Corinthians to embrace him fully in their affections, he nevertheless felt and expresses great confidence in them: *I have great confidence in you; I have great pride in you.* This expression of confidence and pride, repeated in vv. 14, 16, indicates that despite the attack made upon his integrity by the offender (*cf.* v. 12 and Introduction, pp. 41–45), at this point he still believed strongly in the basic loyalty of the Corinthians towards him. It only needed to be released from the restrictions brought about by painful past events and the criticisms they had entertained concerning his integrity. When Paul says, *I am filled with comfort. With all our affliction, I am overjoyed*, it is almost certainly a reflection of the great relief and joy he experienced when he heard of the steps taken by the Corinthians in obedience to the demands he made in the 'severe' letter. They had demonstrated their loyalty to the apostle, so he is able to say, *I am overjoyed*, despite all the affliction (*cf.* v. 5, which indicates that Paul was still embroiled in affliction when he wrote these words).

M. Paul's Joy after a Crisis Resolved (7:5–16)

In this section Paul returns to the account of his travels which was broken off at 2:13 to include the long treatment of the nature, integrity and divine enabling of his ministry (2:14 – 7:4). He now picks up the threads dropped at 2:13, and in the rest of ch. 7 completes the account of his travels and concerns in relation to the Corinthian crisis. He recounts the great relief he experienced when he finally met up with Titus in Macedonia and received the good report of affairs in Corinth which he brought (vv. 5–7). He tells how in the light of the events reported by Titus he no longer regrets the writing of the 'severe' letter, though shortly after sending that letter he had regretted having done so. His change of attitude had been brought about by seeing the positive benefits now resulting from that letter (vv. 8–13). Finally Paul tells how he is relieved by the good reports also because the confidence he had expressed to Titus about the Corinthians has proved to be justified.

5. In 2:12–13, before the long diversion concerning ministry, Paul told the Corinthians that when he came to Troas to meet Titus as previously arranged, he did not find his colleague there. What he did find was a great open door for evangelism in that city, but because of his anxiety and longing for news from Titus he was unable to take up the evangelistic opportunity presenting itself. So he left Troas and went on to Macedonia.

Here in v. 5 Paul tells how having arrived in Macedonia he found himself embroiled in troubles again. *For even when we came into Macedonia, our bodies had no rest*. The word translated *bodies* is *sarx* (lit. 'flesh'), and it is worth noting that this word, which in the Pauline letters is used predominately with a negative connotation, has here a neutral sense, denoting simply the whole person. This is confirmed by the parallel statement which follows: *we were afflicted at every turn*. Paul goes on to describe the affliction as *fighting without and fear within*. The *fighting without* may possibly refer to Paul's sharing the persecution in which the Macedonian churches were immersed (*cf*. 8:1–2). However, the word 'fightings' (*machai*), where found elsewhere in the New Testament (2 Tim. 2:23; Tit. 3:9; Jas. 4:1), applies only to quarrels and disputes, so Paul's 'fightings' may have been heated disputations with either unbelievers (*cf*. Acts 17:5–14) or Christian opponents (*cf*. Phil. 3:2) in Macedonia. The *fear within* could refer either to fear of persecution (during his first visit to Corinth Paul had on one occasion been in danger of being reduced to silence through fear, *cf*. Acts 18:9) or alternatively to fear about the spiritual losses that would be incurred if the Corinthians did not react positively to his 'severe' letter (evidence that Paul experienced this sort of fear can be seen in 11:3 and Gal. 4:11). Whatever the exact nature of the *fighting without and fear within*, Paul was obviously in a state of some distress as he awaited Titus' arrival in Macedonia.

6–7. *But God, who comforts the downcast*. Paul knew this comfort not only in the sense of verbal encouragement but also in that God intervened to alleviate his situation (1:3–11; *cf*. Is. 49:13), assured him of his protection (*cf*. Acts 18:9–10) and when necessary provided the grace to endure (*cf*. 12:7–10). In the distress in which he found himself in Macedonia Paul says, *God . . . comforted us by the coming of Titus*. The very meeting with Titus, so long delayed but finally achieved, brought great relief to the apostle, but as he goes on to say the relief he experienced was brought about *not only by his coming but also by the comfort with which he was comforted in you*. When Titus set out for Corinth as Paul's envoy after the apostle's own 'painful' visit, he would have done so with a good deal of apprehension, despite Paul's expressions of confidence in his converts. When he arrived and found how they had responded to Paul's 'severe' letter, and how they received him, he was greatly relieved and comforted (*cf.* 7:13b–16). When Paul received news of Titus' relief he too was comforted, but he was comforted even more and made to rejoice by what he calls *your longing, your mourning, your zeal for me* (see commentary on v. 11, where the nature of this response is spelt out in greater detail).

8–9. Paul tells of the regret he felt over the writing of the 'severe' letter because it caused such pain to his readers. Yet in the light of the response it evoked he can say, *even if I made you sorry with my letter, I do not regret it (though I did regret it)*. The reason why he felt regret no longer is that the grief caused by the letter was *only for a while*. He hastens to add that he found no pleasure in causing grief through that letter: *As it is, I rejoice, not because you were grieved* (*cf.* 2:3–4). The only pleasure he derived was from the positive response of the Corinthians: *I rejoice . . . because you were grieved into repenting*. The grief they experienced was not a useless remorse without any corresponding action to rectify the situation. It was a *godly grief* leading to repentance, which brought positive results so that they *suffered no loss* by the receipt of Paul's 'severe' letter. What loss Paul thought they might have experienced is not specified. However, he uses the same verb (*zēmioō*) in 1 Corinthians 3:15 of the person who suffers loss of reward if his or her works do not pass God's test on the last day. Paul may have felt that the Corinthians' positive response to his 'severe' letter had saved them from such a loss.

10. Paul contrasts godly grief with worldly grief. The first *produces a repentance that leads to salvation and brings no regret*, the second *produces death*. The difference between godly grief and worldly grief is that the first issues in repentance while the second ends with remorse. Godly grief which issues in repentance (*i.e.* a change of mind and heart and a willingness to change behaviour) when coupled with faith in God leads to salvation. Involved, then, is the joy of the Lord and therefore no regrets. On the other hand, worldly grief does not progress beyond remorse. There are deep regrets over what has happened, but there is no accompanying change of mind and heart, nor any willingness to change behaviour, nor any faith in God. The result is not salvation, but death (*cf.* Rom. 6:15–23).

Biblical examples of godly grief can be seen in the cases of David (2 Sa. 12:13; Ps. 51), Peter (Mk. 14:72) and Paul himself (Acts 9:1–22), while examples of worldly grief are to be found in the cases of Esau (Gn. 27:1–40; Heb. 12:15–17) and Judas (Mt. 27:3–5). It is worth noting that Paul acted to head off the possibility of mere worldly grief in the case of the 'offender', when in 2:7 he urged his readers to reaffirm their love to him so that he might not be overcome with grief and so be lost to the church (see commentary on 2:5–11).

11. Paul reminds his readers of the outworking of this godly grief in their case: *For see what earnestness this godly grief has produced in you, what eagerness to clear yourselves, what indignation, what alarm, what longing, what zeal, what punishment!* The *indignation* was probably directed towards the 'offender' who was at the centre of the trouble (*cf.* 2:5; 7:12). The *alarm* (lit. 'fear') may have been their fear of God because they realized they had not accorded his apostle proper respect, while the *longing* Paul speaks of was probably a desire for restoration of fellowship with him. Thus Paul's 'severe' letter awakened in his readers a deep sense of shame and repentance over the deterioration in the relationship with their apostle and the state of affairs in their church. The result was energetic and zealous action to clear themselves, restore fellowship with Paul and discipline the 'offender'. And so when Paul heard of this he was able to assure them: *At every point you have proved yourselves guiltless in the matter*. It seems then that while the congregation as a whole may not have sprung to the apostle's defence when he was maligned in their presence by the 'offender', and while they had been lax in responding to earlier calls to discipline him, nevertheless they themselves were not involved in the maligning. In that matter at least they proved to be guiltless when they finally acted to discipline the offender.

12–13a. Because of such a positive response on the part of the Corinthians to the 'severe' letter Paul is now able to say to them that his real motive in writing was not simply to get action taken against the 'offender' (*not on account of the one who did the wrong*), nor was it just to have his own position *vis-à-vis* the Corinthians clarified and vindicated (*nor on account of the one who suffered the wrong*), but rather that the Corinthians themselves, by experiencing such godly grief, might realize just how much Paul really meant to them (*in order that your zeal for us might be revealed to you in the sight of God*). That Paul defines the purpose of his 'severe' letter in terms of bringing out the Corinthians' zeal for him *in the sight of God* reflects the fact that they were accountable to God for their action in the whole affair. Paul by his letter had stimulated them to act in a way that is pleasing to God, and that they should have so acted seems to have been the major concern of the apostle, more important to him than his own vindication. And because this has happened Paul concludes: *Therefore we are comforted.*

13b–16. In these verses Paul further explains the reasons for his joy at meeting up with Titus. He rejoiced because Titus' own apprehensions had been dispelled upon his arrival in Corinth and his mind set at rest. He rejoiced too that his confident boasting to Titus about the real attitudes of the Corinthian congregation as a whole, despite their earlier failure to defend their apostle when he was maligned, had been proved true.[1] Paul's pride in them had been justified. He also rejoiced because he saw that Titus' own heart now went out to these Corinthians as he remembered their obedience (to the demands made in Paul's 'severe' letter) and the fear and trembling with which they received him (evidence of the respect in which they held Paul and his apostolic team, evidence in turn that they were guiltless in the matter of personal attacks upon Paul). Paul concludes this major section of the letter with a great expression of confidence in the congregation: *I rejoice, because I have perfect confidence in you.* Such an expression of confidence stands in stark contrast to the way Paul addresses the same people in chs. 10–13 (*cf.* esp. 11:3–4, 19–20), and this is one of the main

---

[1] Subsequent events, reflected in chs. 10 – 13, suggest that either Titus' report or Paul's response to it was prematurely optimistic.

factors which leads many scholars to see in chs. 10 – 13 the remains of a subsequent letter of Paul (see Introduction, pp. 34–35).

III. THE MATTER OF THE COLLECTION (8:1 – 9:15)

Having spoken of his great joy and relief at the news Titus brought of the Corinthians' response to his letter, Paul proceeds to take up with them the matter of the collection which was being made among the Gentile churches to assist the poor Jewish Christians of Judea. These Christians had been hit hard by outbreaks of famine during the reign of the emperor Claudius (AD 41–54) and the largely Gentile church at Antioch (Syria) had responded quickly by sending relief by the hand of Barnabas and Saul (Paul) (Acts 11:27–30). In Galatians 2:10 Paul tells how the leaders of the Jerusalem church, having recognized his apostolate to the Gentiles, urged him to continue remembering the poor, which thing, he said, he was eager to do. By the time Paul wrote 1 Corinthians (c. AD 55) he had already begun canvassing aid from the churches of Galatia, and the Corinthians had heard about it and asked to be allowed to share in this ministry (1 Cor. 16:1–4). And by the time 2 Corinthians was written (c. AD 56) Paul had contacted the Macedonian churches and they had begged him 'for the favour of taking part in the relief of the saints', and he was now using the example of their generosity to stimulate the Corinthians to carry out what they had earlier shown themselves ready to do (8:1–7; cf. 1 Cor. 16:1–4), just as he had used the example of the Corinthians' readiness to motivate the Macedonians (9:1–5).

The significance of the collection for Paul and his mission has been the subject of much comment and discussion.[1] First, the collection is seen to have been a compassionate response to the pressing needs of Judean Christians. Second, it has been noted that the collection was for Paul an important expression of the

[1] K. F. Nickle, *The Collection: A Study in Paul's Theology* (SCM, 1966) is representative of modern approaches and provides a good readable coverage of the main issues involved. See also J. Munck, *Paul and the Salvation of Mankind* (SCM, 1959), pp. 287–305, and the major commentaries by Barrett, Furnish and Martin.

unity of the Jewish and Gentile sections of the church (2 Cor. 8:14–15; cf. Rom. 15:25–27). Third, it has been shown that there are some similarities (and some differences) between the way Paul speaks of the collection and the way in which the Jewish temple tax was administered.[1]

Fourth, and this is more conjectural, it has been suggested that Paul conceived the bearing of the collection to Jerusalem by representatives of the Gentile churches in terms of the Old Testament prophecies of the latter days when the nations and their wealth would flow into Zion (Is. 2:2–3; 60:5–7; Mi. 4:1–2). On this view, Paul hoped this would convince Jewish Christians that God was fulfilling his ancient prophecies, and as this realization dawned upon unbelieving Jews they would become jealous as they saw Gentiles enjoying the blessings of God and this would trigger the repentance of Israel for which Paul longed (Rom. 11:11–14, 25–32). Unfortunately things did not work out as Paul hoped, as his journey to Jerusalem with those bearing the collection (Acts 24:17–21) resulted in a tumult, his arrest and a further hardening of the Jews against the gospel.[2] This suggestion has not been found convincing by the majority of recent commentators, for it constitutes a large superstructure built upon the foundation of inferences from rather limited evidence.

The question as to whether both chs. 8 and 9 were originally connected with chs. 1 – 7 is discussed in the Introduction (pp. 29–31). It was concluded that the evidence in favour of unity is at least as strong, if not stronger, than that against. The connection between chs. 1 – 7 and chs. 8 and 9 can be explained along the following lines. In chs. 1 – 7 Paul responds with great relief and joy to the good news brought by Titus of the turn for the better in the relationship between the Corinthians and himself. He concludes that response (which also contains a long explanation of the nature and integrity of his ministry, and of how God had prospered it despite all his afflictions and anxieties) with an expression of confidence and pride in the Corinthians (7:14–16). Because the relationship was for the time being in a good state, Paul felt he could remind the Corinthians of their earlier earnestness to contribute to the col-

[1]Nickle, *op. cit.*, pp. 74–93.   [2]*Ibid.* pp. 129–142.

lection for the Judean Christians, urging them now to complete what they had previously begun. So although the subject matter of chs. 8 and 9 is quite different from that of chs. 1 – 7, the former can be explained as arising from the latter.

A. The Example of the Macedonians (8:1–6)

In these verses Paul uses the example of the Macedonians' remarkably generous response to the collection appeal to motivate the Corinthians to carry out what they had previously shown themselves ready to do, to provide relief for the saints in Jerusalem.

1–2. Paul begins by making known to his readers *the grace of God which has been shown in the churches of Macedonia*. The Roman province of Macedonia comprised the northern part of Greece wherein were found the Pauline churches at Philippi and Thessalonica, and also possibly a church at Beroea (*cf.* Acts 20:4). The apostle regards the liberality of the Macedonians as the result of God's grace in their lives. God is generous (v. 9; Rom. 5:6–8; 8:31–32; *cf.* Mt. 5:45; 7:11) and where his grace is truly experienced in people's lives the evidence will be a similar love and generosity (*cf.* Mt. 5:43–48; 10:8; Rom. 15:7; Eph. 4:32; 5:1–2; Phil. 2:4–11; Col. 3:12–13; 1 Jn. 4:7–12).

The quite remarkable evidence of God's grace in the churches of Macedonia is shown by the fact that their generosity was exercised in most adverse circumstances. First, it was *in a severe test of affliction*. The birth of the churches in Macedonia was accompanied by much opposition, both to the apostolic team and to the new converts (see the accounts of the mission in Philippi, Thessalonica and Beroea in Acts 16:11 – 17:15), and Paul was still vividly aware of that when he wrote to the churches of Thessalonica and Philippi (1 Thes. 1:6; 2:1–2, 14–16; 3:1–5; 2 Thes. 1:4; Phil. 1:27–30). And the churches of Macedonia were again (or still) embroiled in persecution when Paul wrote to Corinth from Macedonia (2 Cor. 7:5). Second, and equally remarkable, was the fact that the Macedonian churches responded out of *their extreme poverty*. Later in the chapter Paul will talk about the need for equality, one church's abundance supplying another's want (vv. 13–15). The Macedonians were notable in generosity because they responded while being in a condition of great want themselves.

Paul says of the Macedonians that it was *their abundance of joy and their extreme poverty* which *overflowed in a wealth of liberality*. It was the joy of the Macedonians which overflowed in liberality. Jesus told the Twelve when he sent them out on the Galilean mission, 'Freely you have received, freely give' (Mt. 10:8, NIV). The Macedonian Christians knew the joy of being the recipients of God's free giving, and in that joy they gave freely. Because of their own situation, what they gave was probably quite a small amount, but measured against their *extreme poverty* it represented *a wealth of liberality* (*cf.* Mk. 12:41–44).

3–5. Here Paul further explains the nature of the remarkable generosity of the Macedonian churches. *For they gave according to their means, as I can testify.* The expression *according to their means* (*kata dynamin*) is very common in the papyri, especially in marriage contracts where a husband promises to provide food and clothing for his wife 'according to his means'. Paul testifies that the Macedonians have done all that could be expected of them; they have responded to the appeal *according to their means*. But Paul feels forced to add *and beyond their means*. Once again the papyri throw light upon the significance of this sort of expression. 'Beyond one's means' (*para dynamin*) is found in the context of a man's complaint against his wife for whom he has provided beyond what his means really allowed. So Paul says of the Macedonians that they have contributed to the collection for the poor in a way that was over and above anything that could be expected, given their situation.

All this they have done *of their own free will*, even, Paul says, *begging us earnestly for the favour of taking part in the relief of the saints*. Contained in this verse are three key words used by Paul in relation to the collection. (a) *Favour* (*charis*) is used to show that the Macedonians regarded the opportunity to contribute as a favour or privilege. They evidently understood the truth of Jesus' words, 'It is more blessed to give than to receive' (Acts 20:35). (b) *Taking part* (*koinōnia*) indicates that their involvement was seen as participation in a larger entity, *i.e.* an 'ecumenical' act of compassion. (c) *Relief* renders the Greek word *diakonia*, and its use here reflects the fact that contributing to the collection was viewed as Christian 'ministry'. This was a ministry in which the Philippian church at least was involved over a long period of time (Phil. 4:14–20).

Finally, Paul testifies that this outstanding act of generosity was *not as we expected, but first they gave themselves to the Lord and to us by the will of God*. What apparently surprised Paul was that the Macedonians did not only give their money out of compassion for the Judean Christians, but that they also gave themselves first to the Lord and his apostle *by the will of God*. Paul had been appointed an apostle *by the will of God* (1:1) and now he sees his converts in Macedonia dedicating themselves to the Lord and to him. They appear to have recognized Paul's own God-given authority, and their response to his appeal on behalf of the Judean Christians was a recognition of that authority as well as an expression of compassion for those in need.

6. *Accordingly we have urged Titus.* Paul's motivation, in part at least, for reopening the matter of the collection with the Corinthians owes something to the astonishing response of the Macedonians (and his fear of humiliation before them if the Corinthians, of whose readiness to contribute he had boasted, were to be found wanting in the matter, *cf.* 9:1–5). Accordingly he urged Titus *that as he had already made a beginning, he should also complete among you this gracious work.* Verse 10 reveals that some initiatives had been taken in relation to the collection in Corinth 'a year ago'. This probably refers to the initial enquiry made by the Corinthians, and the instructions Paul gave in response (1 Cor. 16:1–4). However, it is unlikely that Titus had been involved at that early stage, because 7:14 suggests that the visit to Corinth from which he had just returned (7:5–7) was his first to the church there. It is more likely, therefore, that it was on his most recent visit that Titus, finding the Corinthians had responded so positively to Paul's 'severe' letter, had begun to work with them on the matter of the collection. In the present context, then, Paul tells his readers that he has urged Titus to complete what he had begun on his most recent visit.

B. Paul Exhorts the Corinthians to Excel (8:7–15)

7–8. If the words of this verse had been found in 1 Corinthians we would suspect the use of satire (*cf.* 1 Cor. 2:14 – 3:4; 6:5), *i.e.* as if Paul were saying, 'If you *think* you excel in everything, then you can excel in this matter as well!' But in the context of a passage connected with chs. 1 – 7, a letter of reconciliation, relief and joy, such satire would be out of place. Paul here acknowledges that the congregation does *excel in everything – in faith, in utterance, in knowledge, in all earnestness, and in your love for us.* (There is a variant reading which has 'in our love for you' instead of *in your love for us*, but the context, where the excellencies of the Corinthians' Christian character are extolled, suggests the latter is to be preferred.) In 1 Corinthians he acknowledged their excellence in utterance and knowledge (1 Cor. 1:4–7), but the earnestness and love for Paul mentioned in the present context are qualities that had been called forth by the 'severe' letter. The closing words of v. 7, *see that you excel in this gracious work also*, are in the form of a command (*hina* plus subjunctive used as an imperative), but Paul goes on to qualify this by adding *I say this not as a command, but to prove by the earnestness of others that your love also is genuine.* Others (*i.e.* the Macedonians) had shown by their astonishingly generous response to the appeal the earnestness of their Christian commitment. When Paul urged the Corinthians to excel in the same area, it was not just a command to be obeyed, but also an encouragement to take the opportunity to demonstrate the genuineness of their own love and commitment. True love never leaves us content to just talk; it has to be expressed in acts of concern (*cf.* Lk. 19:1–10; 1 Jn. 3:16–18).

9. To support his call for love in action Paul cites as an example *the grace of our Lord Jesus Christ.* When Paul speaks of the grace of God, or as here the grace of *our Lord Jesus Christ*, what he means is not an attitude or a gracious disposition but God's love expressed in concrete saving action on behalf of mankind. (And similarly it is a concrete expression of love that Paul expects from his readers.) The nature of Christ's expression of love is stated in the words, *though he was rich, yet for your sake he became* *poor*. It is important, in seeking to understand this statement, that we neither distort the biblical picture of Jesus' experience of poverty nor fail to recognize the nature of the poverty that Paul has in mind here.

As far as Jesus' experience is concerned, it is true that Luke highlights the lowly circumstances of his birth, but this is not an indication of the poverty of the holy family, but rather of the overcrowded conditions in Bethlehem at the time of the census (Lk. 2:7). The offering that Mary made for her purification was that permitted to those who could not afford a lamb (Lk. 2:24; *cf.* Lv. 12:6–8), and this indicates the family were not well off. Jesus was known as 'the carpenter, the son of Mary' (Mk. 6:3), and as a craftsman he would not be numbered among the abject poor. During his Galilean ministry he did remind a would-be disciple that 'Foxes have holes, and birds of the air have nests; but the Son of man has nowhere to lay his head' (Lk. 9:58). However, this must not be taken to mean that as an itinerant preacher Jesus was continually in dire economic circumstances. The indications are that the costs of Jesus' itinerant ministry and the support for his followers were provided by a number of well-off sympathizers who had been the recipients of his healing ministry (Lk. 8:1–3). In addition it was a custom among the Jews to provide hospitality for travelling preachers (*cf.* Mt. 10:9–13) and Jesus enjoyed such hospitality at a number of homes, and especially at that of Mary and Martha (Lk. 10: 38–42; Jn. 12:1–3). On the evidence, then, Jesus was no poorer than most first-century Palestinian Jews, and better off than some (*e.g.* those reduced to beggary). Indeed Jesus and his band of disciples had sufficient money to be able to provide help for those worse off than themselves (*cf.* Jn. 12:3–6; 13:27–29).

Irrespective of the degree of poverty which Jesus may have experienced (and the extent of his poverty can easily be exaggerated), it is not economic poverty of which Paul writes here. It is most likely that what Paul had in mind was the whole drama of redemption, especially the incarnation. The statements from the first chapter of John's Gospel illustrate the self-imposed 'poverty' involved in the incarnation. He who was in the beginning with God and who was God (Jn. 1:1–2) 'became flesh and dwelt among us' (Jn. 1:14). 'He was in the world, and the world

154

was made through him, yet the world knew him not. He came to his own home, and his own people received him not' (Jn. 1:10–11; *cf.* Phil. 2:5–8).

Christ became poor *for your sake*, Paul says, *so that by his poverty you might become rich*. Just as Jesus' poverty is not to be understood in terms of abject want in his incarnate life, so too the riches which he came to make available to believers are not to be understood in terms of material prosperity. It is salvation itself, and the blessings of the new age involved in it, that constitute the riches which Christ by his *poverty* enables believers to enjoy. These riches are experienced both in the present time as a kind of down payment or guarantee, and in full measure at the return of Christ (1 Cor. 1:4–8; 2 Cor. 5:5; Eph. 1:3–14).

We must never forget that it is only *by his poverty* that we may become rich. There was a price to be paid for the blessings we enjoy in Christ. Included in that price was the cost of the incarnation of the pre-existent Son into a fallen world. But, as we know from other passages, the cost of the incarnation, great though it was, was only the beginning. There was also the cost of rejection, ridicule, persecution, betrayal and suffering, all culminating in the agony of Gethsemane and the cross. These things together made up the full price of our salvation (*cf., e.g.* Rom. 3:22b–26; 1 Cor. 5:7; 6:19–20; 15:3; 2 Cor. 5:21; Gal. 3:13–14; 1 Pet. 1:18–20).

10–11. Having cited the example of Christ's self-giving love, Paul urges his readers to show the genuineness of their own love by a concrete act of compassion. *In this matter I give my advice.* Paul's urging does not constitute a command (*cf.* v. 8a). Though the apostle is certainly not averse to making demands which he regards as commands of the Lord to his converts (*cf.* 1 Cor. 14:37–38), nevertheless he sometimes makes a point of distinguishing his own personal advice from such authoritative commands, as he does here (*cf.* 1 Cor. 7:25, 40). Clearly generosity is not something that is subject to command (*cf.* 9:5, 7). *It is best for you now to complete what a year ago you began not only to do but to desire.* While both v. 7 (*hina* plus subjunctive) and v. 24 (imperatival use of participle) have imperatival force, the only actual imperative verb in Paul's entire treatment of the collection in chs. 8 – 9 is found in v. 11. The NIV brings out its imperatival sense well: 'Now finish (*epitelesate*) the work, so that your eager willingness to do it may be matched by your completion of it'. This lets us see what Paul's fundamental concern in these chapters is: to get the Corinthians to finish what they had begun.

Paul says it is best for them to act *now*, because he knew representatives from the Macedonian churches (to whom he had boasted of the Corinthians' readiness) would soon arrive in Corinth. If the Corinthians had not by then carried through in this matter, they would no doubt be embarrassed before the Macedonian Christians (*cf.* 9:1–5), so it would indeed be best for them to complete *now* what they had previously begun.

The reference to what was begun *a year ago* probably relates to the action taken in response to Paul's words in 1 Corinthians 16:1–4. The RSV translations *a year ago* (rendering *apo perysi*) could be misleading. The same expression is used in the papyri to mean 'last year', *i.e.* some time during the previous calendar year. Thus the time reference could be to a point as recent as one month or as long as twenty-three months. In this context, assuming the Corinthians' original initiative in the matter was expressed in their letter to which Paul responded when he wrote 1 Corinthians, the point in time to which *apo perysi* refers will be determined by the period of time we judge to have elapsed between the writing of 1 and 2 Corinthians (see Introduction, pp. 52–53).

We might have expected Paul to speak of 'what they not only began to desire but to do'. However, the order is the reverse of this. Paul speaks of what *you began not only to do but to desire*. This throws emphasis upon the fact that the Corinthians' earlier actions sprang from their own earnest desires, not from any pressure applied by the apostle. But the Corinthians' good intentions had failed to produce results over the past year, so now Paul urges that *your readiness in desiring it may be matched by your completing it out of what you have*. No matter how strong the intentions or desires, they are fruitless unless they are expressed in action.

12. *For if the readiness is there, it is acceptable according to what a man has, not according to what he has not.* That Paul has to explain this to the Corinthians may be an indication that they had not completed what they had begun, because they felt their resources prevented them from raising a suitably large amount (*cf.* Tobit 4:8). The word *acceptable* (*euprosdektos*) is found in three other contexts in Paul's letters. It occurs in Romans 15:16, where it is the Gentiles' acceptability to God that is in view. It is found again in Romans 15:31, where Paul expresses his hope that the collection will be acceptable to the saints (*i.e.* the Judean Christians). And in 2 Corinthians 6:2 it is used of God's acceptable time, his day of salvation. Thus Paul uses *euprosdektos* of acceptability both to God and to human beings. In our present context, where the word is used in an absolute sense, and where no human acceptance is in view, Paul has in mind the acceptability before God of the Corinthians' relief action. Paul assures his readers that when they give according to what they have, that is acceptable or well-pleasing to God. Paul's view is a sane one, in that it takes account of the giver's situation, and does not expect a response which is *according to what he has not.*

13–15. In these verses Paul seeks to prevent any misunderstanding about the collection. The Corinthians must realize that they are not being burdened so that others may live in ease at their expense. Paul argues for an equality among Christians. The relative affluence of the Corinthians at the present time should provide the needs of the poor Judean believers. And in like fashion, if at some future time the positions should be reversed, then *their abundance may supply your want.* It is worth noting that it is from the abundance or surplus of those who are better-off that Paul expects the needs of those who are worse-off to be met. He does not advocate that those who are better-off reduce themselves to poverty also. The reciprocity of giving and receiving is meant to promote an equality. He finds an illustration of this equality in the experience of the exodus community. When God provided manna from heaven each family head was to gather 'an omer apiece, according to the number of the persons whom each of you has in his tent' (Ex. 16:16). As they gathered according to their needs, *'He who gathered much had nothing over, and he who gathered little had no lack'* (*cf.* Ex. 16:18). The needs of all were met, no-one suffered want, no-one had an over-supply. This model illustrates the ideal which Paul sets before his readers. They too should ensure that there is an equality of needs being met among the Christian communities. And for this to occur those enjoying an abundance should meet the needs of those in want.

C. *Commendation of Those who will Receive the Collection* (8:16–24)

Here Paul commends the three brothers who are to come to Corinth to administer the collection. Titus is commended first (vv. 16–17), then the brother famous for his work in the gospel (vv. 18–19) and thirdly the brother 'often tested and found earnest' (v. 22). The passage concludes with a summary commendation of all three (v. 23) and an exhortation that the Corinthians give proof of their love (for Paul) and the truth of his boasting about them (to the Macedonians) when the three brothers arrive (v. 24). Between the commendations of the 'famous' and the 'earnest' brothers Paul digresses briefly to say he is trying to give no opportunity for criticism of the way the collection is being administered (vv. 20–21). It is this concern that probably accounts for the rather full commendations Paul makes. It may also be that Paul, by providing the 'letter of recommendation', is trying to forestall criticisms of the administration of the collection by those in Corinth who previously denigrated him for not bearing such letters (3:1–3).

16–17. *But thanks be to God who puts the same earnest care for you into the heart of Titus.* Paul begins his commendation of Titus with an ascription of thanks to God which reflects his gratitude that his colleague shared the same concern for the Corinthians as he did himself. Paul recognizes that such earnest care has been put into the heart of Titus by God, in the same way as the remarkable generosity of the Macedonians had been the outflow of the grace of God in their lives (vv. 1–2).

For he not only accepted our appeal, but being himself very earnest he is going to you of his own accord. This highlights the concern Titus had for the Corinthians, and therefore constitutes an effective commendation of him to them. Titus, though having only recently returned from Corinth, needed no persuasion from

Paul to make the considerable journey back there again. Being very earnest in his care for the Corinthians, he voluntarily undertook the mission.

18–19. *With him we are sending the brother who is famous among all the churches for his preaching of the gospel.* Literally translated, the second half of this statement would read: 'the brother whose praise in the gospel [is] among all the churches'. The RSV supplies *preaching* and the NIV 'service', which is more general. It is probably better to adopt the more general expression which could include gospel preaching but could also simply denote a ministry generally supportive of the gospel and those who preach it.

And not only that, but he has been appointed by the churches to travel with us in this gracious work which we are carrying on. The second matter Paul stresses in commending this person is his appointment by the churches (he does not tell us which churches). He was their chosen representative for this *gracious work*. It is clear that, whoever this famous early Christian was, he and the churches who appointed him must have shared Paul's view concerning the importance of the collection.

The final words of v. 19 indicate something of the purpose of the collection as far as Paul himself is concerned. It is *for the glory of the Lord and to show our good will*. The collection, taken up among Gentile converts and given to Jewish Christians, was a tangible expression of the reconciliation which God had effected through Christ. By reconciling both Jew and Gentile to himself through the cross, God had at the same time reconciled the two groups to one another. So the collection, as a tangible expression of the new relationship between Gentile converts and Jewish Christians, reflected the grace of God in the lives of those concerned and therefore can be said to be *for the glory of the Lord*. However, the collection was not only for the glory of the Lord but also *to show our good will*. Paul had fought long and hard to preserve the freedom of the gospel for his Gentile converts, and had won the approval of the Jewish mother church for the gospel he preached among the Gentiles (Gal. 2:1–10). It had been agreed that Gentile converts need not submit to circumcision or take upon themselves the yoke of the law (Acts

15:1–35). Because of the two fundamentally different life-styles, it could easily have happened that the Gentile churches would go their own way and have virtually nothing to do with the Jewish churches. When the leaders of the Jerusalem church affirmed the Pauline gospel for the Gentiles they asked Paul to 'remember the poor' (Gal. 2:10). Paul apparently saw this as an important expression of unity between the two very different forms of Christianity, and he was therefore eager to promote a collection among the Gentiles, as this would show the *good will* of both Paul and his churches towards the Jewish Christians.

20–21. Before moving on to the commendation of the third person whom he is sending to Corinth, Paul digresses briefly to explain why so much care is being taken to provide couriers of impeccable credentials to receive the collection and carry it to Jerusalem: *We intend that no one should blame us about this liberal gift which we are administering.* There were opponents of Paul and his gospel who were only too ready to call in question the apostle's motives in financial matters, so that Paul had frequently to defend his integrity (*cf., e.g.* 2:17; 11:7–11; 12:14–18; 1 Thes. 2:3–12; 2 Thes. 3:6–9). The collection was too important for inter-church relations to allow its administration to be frustrated by accusations of impropriety. A *liberal gift, i.e.* a large sum of money, was involved and therefore even greater care than normal had to be taken. Paul further emphasizes the extreme care taken by saying: *for we aim at what is honourable not only in the Lord's sight but also in the sight of men.* Paul's words, which echo those of Proverbs 3:4, show that while the apostle's ultimate concern in this case was that the administration of the collection should be honourable *in the Lord's sight*, it was also very important that it be seen to be honourable *in the sight of men.* The success of the collection depended upon it.

22. Following the brief digression of vv. 20–21, Paul now commends the third member of the group being sent to Corinth. *And with them we are sending our brother whom we have often tested and found earnest in many matters.* It is hard to know why Paul did not name either the person whom he commended in vv. 18–19 or the one he mentions here. The former was famous in all the

churches and presumably would have been known to the Corinthians. The latter was almost certainly known to them also, for
Paul goes on to say that he *is now more earnest than ever because of
his great confidence in you*. It is worth noting how important the
quality of earnestness (or zeal) was to the apostle, both when
commending Christian workers and when exhorting believers
generally. We might place other qualifications higher on our list
of priorities, but for Paul earnestness was among the most
important (*cf., e.g.* Rom. 12:8, 11; 2 Cor. 7:11–12; 8:7–8, 16–17;
Eph. 4:3; 2 Tim. 1:16–17).

23. Paul here sums up his commendation of the three-man
team in such a way as to answer any who might ask, 'Who are
these men?' *As for Titus, he is my partner and fellow worker in your
service.* It is Titus' close association with Paul that is stressed.
This is the only place Paul uses the word 'partner' (*koinōnos*) of a
colleague, but he uses 'fellow worker' (*synergos*) several times, to
denote both male and female colleagues (Rom. 16:3, 9, 21; Phil.
2:25; 4:3; Col. 4:11; Phm. 1, 24). *And as for our brethren, they are
messengers of the churches, the glory of Christ.* In the case of the two
brothers Paul stresses their official capacity as *messengers* [lit.
apostles] *of the churches.* The significance of an apostle (essentially someone charged with a commission) can only be understood when we know by whom he was commissioned and for
what. So, for example, the Twelve were apostles of Christ,
commissioned by him to be witnesses of his resurrection (Lk.
24:44–49; Acts 1:15–26). The two brothers Paul commends were
apostles of the churches, commissioned to represent those
churches and to travel with Paul to Corinth and most likely also
to Jerusalem as bearers of the collection. Paul does not tell us
which churches commissioned these apostles. We might
assume, seeing that Paul was writing from Macedonia, that the
churches referred to and their apostles are Macedonian. However, there are difficulties with this identification if, as we have
assumed, chs. 8 and 9 belong together. In ch. 9 Paul speaks of
the humiliation he and the Corinthians would experience if,
when he comes to Corinth and is accompanied by some Macedonians, they are not ready (9:3–4). If the messengers and the
churches who commissioned them were Macedonian, then the

humiliation of the Corinthians would take place at the arrival of these messengers rather than be averted by it as Paul implies (9:5).

These messengers are further described as *the glory of Christ*. It is difficult to determine what this means. Possibly it is best understood to imply that these men work for the *the glory of Christ* in that they participate in the administration of a collection which is 'for the glory of the Lord' (v. 19).

24. *So give proof, before the churches, of your love and of our boasting about you to these men.* Having spelt out the credentials of the three who are being sent to Corinth, Paul concludes the passage by urging his readers to provide proof (*i.e.* by having their contributions ready) of their love for their apostle, and of the validity of his boasting about their readiness to these men. This proof will be given *before the churches* inasmuch as it is given before their representatives, *i.e.* two of the three being sent by Paul to Corinth.

D. Be Prepared and Avoid Humiliation (9:1–5)

1–2. *Now it is superfluous for me to write to you about the offering for the saints.* In one sense Paul's writing about the collection (as he has done in ch. 8) is superfluous, because the Corinthians had shown their readiness by raising the matter with Paul in the first place (he referred to their enquiry in 1 Cor. 16:1–4). He further underlines that what he has written is superfluous by saying, *for I know your readiness, of which I boast about you to the people of Macedonia.* The content of that boasting is then stated briefly, *saying that Achaia has been ready since last year.* (On *since last year (apo perysi)*, see commentary on 8:10.) The effect of Paul's boasting about the Corinthians' readiness is then recorded: *and your zeal has stirred up most of them (i.e.* most of the Macedonians). It is superfluous to write about the collection to those who have already taken the initiative in the matter and whose zeal for it has been an inspiration to others.

3–4. However, there is a sense in which Paul's writing was not superfluous but necessary. Readiness to give (8:11), or even having made a beginning in setting aside something for the collection (8:10), is not the same as having finished or having everything ready when Paul and the others arrive in Corinth. So Paul writes, *But I am sending the brethren so that our boasting about you may not prove vain in this case, so that you may be ready, as I said you would be.* Brethren here refers to Titus and the two unnamed representatives whom Paul commended in 8:16–24. In boasting about the Corinthians' readiness Paul had stressed not only their willingness but also his confidence that they would have their contributions ready when he came with the others to receive it. But now he is concerned that in the latter respect they may fail. There would be embarrassing consequences if this were to happen. So he is sending the brethren on ahead, he says, *lest if some Macedonians come with me and find that you are not ready, we be humiliated – to say nothing of you – for being so confident.* In fact several Macedonians did come to Corinth, and were included among those those who accompanied Paul from there on his journey to Jerusalem. Three Macedonians are named: Sopater of Beroea, and Aristarchus and Secundus who were Thessalonians (Acts 20:2–6). If when these Macedonians arrived in Corinth they were to have found the Christians there unprepared, Paul's embarrassment would have been acute, exceeded only by the humiliation that would have been experienced by the Corinthians themselves.

5. *So I thought it necessary to urge the brethren to go on to you before me.* To avoid the humiliation, Paul thought it necessary to send Titus and the two brothers (8:16–24) ahead so they could *arrange in advance for this gift you have promised.* Paul wanted to avoid any hasty collection when he himself arrived so that the Corinthians' contribution would appear *not as an exaction but as a willing gift.* The Greek underlying this expression (*hōs eulogian kai mē hōs pleonexian*) may be rendered as here, or as in the NIV: 'as a generous gift, not as one grudgingly given'. In the first case two ways of *securing* a gift are contrasted (relying upon a voluntary offering or extracting a contribution) and in the second case two ways of *giving* (graciously or grudgingly) are highlighted. In the light of vv. 6–7 (where cheerful and reluctant giving are contrasted) the latter option is preferable.

E. An Exhortation to be Generous (9:6–15)

In this section Paul uses agricultural imagery to underscore the point made in v. 5 about a willing gift, and to depict God as the one who enriches his people in every way for generous giving and so to encourage his readers to be generous (vv. 6–10). Then he describes what results he sees issuing from the generous response of the Corinthians which he expects. The needs of the Jewish Christians in Judea will be met, and they will offer thanksgiving to God, recognize the Gentile Christians' obedience to the gospel and the surpassing grace of God at work in them, and so will long for them and pray for them. In short, the outcome will be the enhancement of the unity of the church (vv. 11–14). The section closes with an ascription of thanks to God for *his* 'inexpressible gift', which strikes the same note as that sounded in 8:9.

6. The previous section (vv. 1–5) concluded with Paul's statement that he wanted the Corinthians' contribution 'not as an exaction but as a willing gift'. With this in mind he continues: *The point is this: he who sows sparingly will also reap sparingly, and he who sows bountifully will also reap bountifully.* It is an agricultural truism that, other things being equal, the size of the harvest is always directly proportional to the amount of seed sown (*cf.* Pr. 11:24–25 and Gal. 6:7–9, where the same metaphor is applied not to sowing sparingly or bountifully but to sowing to one's own flesh or to the Spirit). The sowing and reaping in the present context refer to the contribution the Corinthians are to make and the results of that contribution respectively. The bountiful 'reaping' Paul hopes to see as a result of their bountiful 'sowing' is described in vv. 9–14.

7. While Paul is looking for a bountiful contribution from the Corinthians, he stresses that it must be a voluntary gift, not one made simply because he is applying pressure. They must do as they have made up their minds, not reluctantly or under compulsion. Their giving must be in accordance with what they have determined individually in their own hearts. If they give while feeling under compulsion (from Paul), then their contributions will be made reluctantly and the whole purpose of the project (to express the *concern* of the Gentile churches for the needy Jewish churches in Judea) will be negated. It must be a voluntary offering, and to underscore this Paul adds, *for God loves a cheerful giver.* Here he draws upon a rendering of Proverbs 22:8a found in the LXX (but not in the Heb. upon which English translations are based), 'God blesses a cheerful giver' (lit. 'God blesses a cheerful man and a giver'). The need for generosity in giving is stressed in several other places in the Bible (*cf.* Dt. 15:10–11; Mt. 5:43–48; Rom. 12:8). It is not difficult to suggest why God delights in the cheerful giver. He himself is such a giver and desires to see this characteristic restored among those who were created in his image. Christ taught along similar lines (*cf.* Mt. 5:43–48).

8. This verse is replete with comprehensive expressions (and with remarkable paronomasia – the repetition of words having the same stem – in the Greek: *pasan . . . panti pantote pasan . . . pan*) which speak of God's ability to bless his people so that they abound in good works. Paul begins: *And God is able to provide you with every blessing in abundance* (lit. 'And God is able to make all grace abound to you'). In the case of Macedonians, whose response to the collection Paul cited as an example in 8:1–5, the grace of God enabled them to contribute generously out of their poverty. In the case of the Corinthians, whom Paul considered better off at the time (8:14), the grace of God shown to them is to be understood as the blessing of relative affluence. The purpose of God's blessing is then spelt out: *so that you may always have enough of everything and may provide in abundance for every good work.* The meaning of the word (*autarkeia*) translated *enough* or 'sufficiency' had been coloured by its use in ethical discussions from the time of Socrates. In Cynic and Stoic philosophy it was used of the person who was self-sufficient. So Seneca, a Stoic and contemporary of Paul, understood *autarkeia* as that proud independence of outward circumstances and of other people which constituted true happiness.[1] Paul used the word differently. For him *autarkeia* denoted not self-sufficiency but the

---

[1]Sevenster, *Paul and Seneca*, pp. 113–114.

sufficiency provided by God's grace, and as such it made possible not independence of others but the ability to abound in good works towards them. Again the comparison between the Macedonians and the Corinthians is helpful. The Macedonians had been blessed with *autarkeia* (contentment) in their poverty and so were able, even in that situation, to abound in generosity. The Corinthians had been blessed with *autarkeia* (sufficiency) in their relative affluence and so should contribute bountifully.

9. To reinforce his exhortation that the Corinthians contribute bountifully Paul quotes verbatim from Psalm 111:9 (LXX) (ET 112:9): *As it is written, 'He scatters abroad, he gives to the poor; his righteousness endures for ever.'* Psalm 111/112 celebrates the blessedness of the one who fears the Lord and delights in his commandments. Such a person is blessed by God with material prosperity also, and is accordingly generous to the poor. Paul sets forth this God-fearing person as an example of one who abounds in good works (*He scatters abroad, he gives to the poor*), and whose righteousness endures for ever, established by God.

10. The apostle continues the thought of the psalm cited in v. 9 and applies it to the Corinthians. In so doing he cites the text of Isaiah 55:10 (LXX) almost word for word: *He who supplies seed to the sower and bread for food*, and adds that the same one *will supply and multiply your resources and increase the harvest of your righteousness* (*cf.* Ho. 10:12). The word *resources* translates *sporon* (lit. 'seed'). Thus Paul says to his readers that the God who provides seed for the sower will also multiply their 'seed' and increase their *harvest*. In this context the meaning seems to be that God will multiply the material resources of the Corinthians, and as they use them to meet the needs of the Judean Christians he will increase the effect of that righteous deed. The Corinthians by making a monetary gift will sow the 'seed', God will increase the effect of that righteous deed so that it produces a rich *harvest* of unity, love and thanksgiving (*cf.* vv. 12–14).

11. *You will be enriched in every way for great generosity.* The great liberality of the Macedonians was the result of the grace of God at work in them (8:1-2). Paul believed that God would enrich the Corinthians for great generosity as well. The apostle must have known that those with the resources do not always use them with great generosity, so he looked to God to enrich his readers with this grace. Such generosity it is, says Paul, *which through us will produce thanksgiving to God*. By saying *us* he refers to the others appointed to receive and convey the collection to Jerusalem as well as himself. It is through them all that thanksgiving to God will be produced, because they would bring the contributions to those in need.

12. *For the rendering of this service not only supplies the wants of the saints but also overflows in many thanksgivings to God*. The word *service* renders the Greek word *leitourgias*. This word, and its cognate verb *leitourgeō*, was used in non-biblical Greek to denote civil service rendered to the state by one of its citizens, and of service more generally, *e.g.* that of a slave to his or her master. In the LXX the words are used of cultic service to deity, and so also in Hebrews (where the Old Testament cultus and the priestly ministry of Christ are discussed). Paul uses the words outside the present context when speaking of monetary gifts made by Christians (Rom. 15:27; Phil. 2:30) and of their faith (Phil. 2:17). The provision of monetary gifts which Paul describes as 'your service' (*leitourgias*) in Philippians 2:30 is later described as 'a fragrant offering, a sacrifice acceptable and pleasing to God' (Phil. 4:18). The cultic background is very clear. So it seems that Paul regarded Christian giving not only as a service rendered to those in need but also as an act of service to God. It is important to note that for Paul the ultimate purpose of the collection, as of all forms of Christian 'service', is that thanksgiving should overflow from grateful hearts to God.

13. *Under the test of this service, you will glorify God by your obedience* (lit. 'through the test of this ministry glorifying God for your subjection'). The RSV construes this so that the collection is a test which the Corinthians themselves must sustain and thereby glorify God by their obedience. Most other modern versions construe the verse in such a way that the collection is a test which the Corinthians must sustain, but having sustained it they will provide *others* (the Judean Christians?) with a basis upon which to glorify God (NIV: 'Because of the service by which you have proved yourselves, men will praise God for the obedience . . .'; similarly also RV, NEB, GNB, JB) and this is a better approach.[1]

In acknowledging the gospel of Christ, and by the generosity of your contribution . . . Others will glorify God for the obedience of the Corinthians both to the gospel and in their generous giving. People glorify God by acting generously, because it is inspired by him and reflects his own character (*cf.* Mt. 5:43–48; 2 Cor. 8:1–2). The Corinthians' contribution is *for them and for all others. For them* refers to the Judean Christians for whom the collection was being taken up. It is difficult to say who is intended by the words *for all others*. Perhaps it is just a loose reference to any other needy believers who might become recipients of the Gentile collection.

14. *While they long for you and pray for you, because of the surpassing grace of God in you.* Continuing to envisage the effects of the contribution he is sure the Corinthians will make, Paul sees a new bond between Jewish and Gentile Christians being forged. The Jewish believers, seeing the surpassing grace of God effective in the Gentile Christians, will long for them and pray for them. In this way one of the major purposes of the collection as far as Paul is concerned (*i.e.* to promote unity) will have been fulfilled.

15. *Thanks be to God for his inexpressible gift!* This verse strikes the note sounded already in 8:9. There the grace of Christ was shown in his becoming poor for our sakes, that we might become rich. That was God's *inexpressible gift*. The word *inexpressible* (*anekdiēgetos*), which Paul uses here, is found neither in classical Greek nor in the papyri. It appears first in the New

---

[1] The words *by your obedience* in the RSV translate *epi tē hypotagē*. Elsewhere in Paul's writings *epi* with the dative case after verbs like 'to praise', 'to give thanks', 'to rejoice' or 'to glorify' always indicates the ground on which the praise, thanks, *etc.* is expressed. It never indicates the means by which it is expressed. Therefore, in the present context 'praise God *for* the obedience' (NIV, *etc.*) is to be preferred to 'glorify God *by* your obedience' (RSV) and hence the subject of the action is to be understood as others (probably the Judean Christians) and not the Corinthians themselves.

Testament and only in this verse. It seems to be a word which the apostle himself coined to describe the ineffable character of God's gift. Once coined by Paul it was used by Clement of Rome in his letter to the Corinthians (written *c.* AD 95) when writing of God's 'indescribable' judgments, love and power (1 Clement 20:5; 49:4; 61:1). The important thing to note is that for Paul all Christian giving is carried out in the light of God's *inexpressible gift*, and therefore ought to be done with a cheerful heart as an expression of gratitude to God, as well as in demonstration of our concern for, and partnership with, the recipients.

Paul's confidence that the Corinthians would contribute to the collection was finally rewarded. When the apostle wrote Romans during his three month stay in Greece, after the problems reflected in 2 Corinthians had been settled for the time being, he was able to say: 'At present, however, I am going to Jerusalem with aid for the saints. For Macedonia *and Achaia* have been pleased to make some contribution' (Rom. 15:25–26; *cf.* Acts 24:17–21).

B. PAUL RESPONDS TO A NEW CRISIS (10:1 – 13:14)

The reader will notice a marked change in tone when moving from chs. 1 – 9 to chs. 10 – 13. In the former the tone is basically that of relief and comfort, of confidence in God and in the Corinthians, despite the fact Paul felt the need to explain his changed travel plans and stress the integrity of his ministry. The tone of the latter is very different. It is marked by satire and sarcasm, spirited personal defence, reproach directed towards the Corinthians and bitter attack levelled at outsiders who have infiltrated and are now influencing the congregation.

This marked change in tone (among other considerations) has led the majority of recent commentators to view chs. 10 – 13 as probably the greater part, if not the whole, of a letter written prior to chs. 1 – 9 or subsequent to them. Many have concluded that chs. 10 – 13 are best identified as Paul's 'severe' letter written after 1 Corinthians but *before* 2 Corinthians 1 – 9. Others argue that chs. 10 – 13 were written *after* chs. 1 – 9, and possibly constitute the greater part of a fifth letter written by Paul to Corinth. It is the latter view which is adopted as a working hypothesis for the commentary on chs. 10 – 13 provided below. For a fuller discussion of the nature of chs. 10 – 13 and their relation to the rest of the Epistle, see Introduction, pp. 27–35.

In chs. 10 – 13 Paul faces determined opposition. The opponents are Jewish Christians who put themselves forward as apostles of Christ. They highly prized eloquent speech, displays of authority, visions and revelations, and the performance of mighty works as the signs of a true apostle. These men had earlier infiltrated the Corinthian congregation and their criticisms of Paul probably provided some of the 'ammunition' used by the offender (*i.e.* the one who caused pain, 2:5; who did the wrong, 7:12) in his attack against Paul. By writing the 'severe' letter Paul succeeded in moving the church to discipline the offender, and then in his next letter (2 Cor. 1 – 9) urged them to express their love to the now presumably repentant offender and reinstate him lest Satan gain the advantage. In the same letter he called upon the Corinthians to fully open their hearts to him as his own heart was open towards them. Seeing Paul being thus reinstated in the affections of the Corinthians, and his authority re-established among them, the infiltrators mounted their own frontal attack against the validity and integrity of Paul's apostolate. They succeeded in winning over the Corinthian congregation to their point of view and getting them to submit to their authority. Paul, finding his authority usurped and his apostleship called into question, was forced, against his better judgment, to provide a strong personal defence and to mount a vigorous attack against his opponents. The crisis Paul faced in this situation was the most crucial in all his relationships with the Corinthians, and this fact colours both the tone and content of chs. 10 – 13. See Introduction, pp. 45–52, for further discussion of the historical situation in which chs. 10 – 13 were written and of the nature of Paul's opponents in Corinth at that time.

I. THE BODY OF THE RESPONSE (10:1 – 13:10)

Paul's response to the crisis in relationships precipitated by the infiltrators consists of pleas and threats of disciplinary action, personal defence and satirical attack against his opponents, expressions of deep concern about the state of his converts and pointed contrasts between the nature of his own mission and that of his opponents. While obviously reluctant to do so, Paul adds to this his 'fool's speech' in which he parades his apostolic credentials. He cites his impeccable Jewish ancestry, his apostolic sufferings and the visions and revelations he had experienced, and reminds his readers that he had performed 'the signs of a true apostle' among them. He warns them that he is about to make his third visit to Corinth, and says that he will refuse once again to become a financial burden to them, despite criticisms that this is proof either that he does not love his converts or that he is being crafty and intends to take advantage of them by more subtle means. He expresses his concern that when he comes the third time he might find some of them still caught up in immorality, and assures his readers that those who demand proof of his apostolic authority will get what they were asking for when he comes: he will not spare them.

A. An Earnest Entreaty (10:1–6)

Here Paul appeals to the Corinthians so to act that when he comes on his third visit he will not need to take action against them as he is resolved to do against those (his opponents) who question the validity of his apostleship (vv. 1–2). He denies charges that he acts in a worldly fashion, assuring his readers that he conducts his ministry with the weapons of divine power (vv. 3–5). He concludes by informing them that he is standing ready to punish his opponents in Corinth, as soon as their own obedience is complete (v. 6).

1. *I, Paul, myself entreat you.* Great emphasis is placed upon the fact that it is Paul himself (*I, Paul, myself*) who makes the plea – Paul, the founding apostle of the Corinthian church, and his readers' spiritual father (*cf.* 1 Cor. 4:15). He makes his entreaty *by the meekness and gentleness of Christ.* Among the Greeks from classical times onwards *meekness* (*prautēs*) denoted a 'mild and gentle friendliness', a highly prized social virtue, and the opposite of brusqueness or sudden anger. It was regarded as virtuous to show mildness to one's own people and harshness to one's enemies. Mildness on the part of the judge meant sentencing offenders with more leniency than the law prescribed. The meekness to which Paul appeals is that exemplified in the life and ministry of Christ. His meekness was not a condescending softness by which the demands of God's law were lowered. He showed meekness when he dealt gently and compassionately with sinners, but without in any way minimizing their sin (*cf.* Mt. 11:29). It is in the light of this meekness of Christ that the apostle makes his appeal.

The word translated *gentleness* (*epieikeia*) means basically 'suitable' or 'fitting', and when used in a moral sense, 'reasonable' or 'fair'. Applied to rulers it denoted kindness, equity and leniency (*cf.* Acts 24:4). However, in the present context it is part of a hendiadys (the use of two words joined by 'and' to express one idea) and therefore its meaning here is defined by that of *prautēs*, and so is rightly rendered *gentleness* in the RSV.

When Paul appeals to the Corinthians *by the meekness and gentleness of Christ* he is intending that they receive and act upon the content of the appeal which follows in the light of that by which he appeals (*cf.* Rom. 12:1; 15:30; 1 Cor. 1:10). However, before stating the content of his appeal he inserts an ironical reference to criticisms of his behaviour which his readers had entertained – *I who am humble when face to face with you, but bold to you when I am away!* Paul had not acted authoritatively on his second ('painful') visit as he had previously threatened he might (1 Cor. 4:18–21). This was probably the basis upon which his opponents accused him of cowardly and 'unapostolic' behaviour when face to face with the Corinthians, and of being bold only when he was away and at a safe distance (*cf.* 10:10–11).

2. *I beg of you that when I am present I may not have to show boldness.* Paul urges the Corinthians so to act that it will not be necessary for him to show boldness when he comes. He makes this appeal 'by the meekness and gentleness of Christ' because he wants his readers to recognize that his desire not to show boldness can no more be construed as a sign of 'unapostolic' cowardice than can the meekness of Christ be construed as moral weakness. Paul does not wish to show boldness to the Corinthians, he says, *with such confidence as I count on showing against some who suspect us of acting in worldly fashion.* By so saying Paul implies that he is prepared to act boldly when necessary, and is in fact counting on doing so against his opponents who accuse him both of moral cowardice (v. 1b) and of *acting in a worldly fashion* (lit. 'walking according to the flesh'). To walk according to the flesh, as far as Paul's opponents were concerned, probably meant not acting authoritatively (11:20–21), not experiencing visions and revelations (12:1), performing no mighty works (12:11–12) and not being one through whom Christ spoke (13:3). Instead it meant, they would probably have said, carrying on a purely human enterprise using guile and deceit (12:16–18).

Paul responds to the accusation with an extended use of a military metaphor (vv. 3–6). He piles up military (martial) figures – waging war (v. 3b), weapons, warfare, the destruction of strongholds (v. 4), destroying every obstacle (lit. 'every high thing', *i.e.* tower), taking captives (v. 5), and standing at the ready to punish disobedience (*i.e.* to court-martial) (v. 6).

3. *For though we live in the world we are not carrying on a worldly war* (more literally: 'For while we walk in the flesh, we are not waging war according to the flesh'). While acknowledging that he walks *in* the flesh, Paul denies that he wages war *according to* the flesh. 'To walk *in* the flesh' here means to participate in normal human existence with all its limitations. 'To wage war *according* to the flesh' means to carry out ministry with mere human resources without any divine power, with the concomitant tendency to employ doubtful means (*cf.* 1:17; 4:2; 12:16–18).

4. To support the denial that he carries on a 'worldly war' Paul says, *for the weapons of our warfare are not worldly but have divine power to destroy strongholds.* Paul does not in this passage identify his *weapons*, but statements elsewhere in the Corinthian correspondence suggest they consist in the proclamation of the gospel, through which divine power is released (1 Cor. 1:17–25; 2:1–5; 2 Cor. 4:1–6; *cf.* Rom. 1:16).

The word *stronghold* (*ochurōma*) is found only here in the New Testament. It is used in a literal sense in Proverbs 21:22 (LXX), while Philo uses it figuratively of a stronghold prepared by persuasive words against the honour of God (*Confusion of Tongues*, 129). But more important is the fact that the military practice of building strongholds (there was a large one on Acrocorinth) provided the imagery used in Cynic and Stoic philosophers, and in particular by Seneca, a contemporary of Paul, to describe the fortification of the soul by reasonable *arguments* to render it impregnable under the attack of adverse fortune. It is significant that in the next verse Paul speaks of destroying arguments which stand against the inroads of the knowledge of God.

5. *We destroy arguments and every proud obstacle to the knowledge of God.* The military metaphor is evident here. The *arguments* Paul destroys are the 'strongholds' in which people fortify themselves against the invasion of *the knowledge of God* (the gospel). The expression *every proud obstacle* translates *pan hypsōma epairomenon* (lit. 'every high thing lifted up'), which belongs to the world of ancient warfare and denotes a tower or raised rampart. Both the stronghold of v. 4 and the tower (*proud obstacle*) of this verse stand for the intellectual arguments, the reasonings erected by human beings against the gospel. It is by the proclamation of the gospel, however, that God has chosen to release his power by which these very arguments ('the cleverness of the clever', 1 Cor. 1:19) will be destroyed, and by which those who believe will be saved (*cf.* Rom. 1:16; 1 Cor. 1:17–25; 2:1–5; 1 Thes. 1:5; 2:13). It should be added that Paul's proclamation of the gospel, like our Lord's preaching of the kingdom, was not bare declaration, but involved reasoning and arguing with his hearers in an effort to remove false barriers thrown up against the truth (*cf.* Acts 18:4; 19:8–10).

Thus by the proclamation of the gospel Paul can destroy arguments *and take every thought captive to obey Christ*. The imagery is of a stronghold breached and those sheltering behind its walls taken captive. So the apostle's purpose is not only to demolish false arguments but also to bring people's thoughts under the lordship of Christ. His calling as an apostle was 'to bring about the obedience of faith . . . among all the nations' (Rom. 1:5).

6. *Being ready to punish every disobedience, when your obedience is complete.* Paul portrays himself as *being ready* (*en hetoimō echontes* – a term used of military preparedness) *to punish every disobedience*. It is not easy to determine what was the exact nature of the disobedience Paul stood ready to punish. It may have been the breaking of an accord by which the Gentile mission was entrusted to Paul and the Jewish mission to Peter (*cf.* Gal. 2:7–9). Paul may have regarded Achaia as off-limits for the Jewish Christian intruders who aggravated the situation in Corinth. Alternatively, because he had carried out the pioneer evangelism in Corinth, Paul may have believed that this gave him the apostolic authority there, and any others claiming to be apostles ought to be in submission to him in that situation (*cf.* 10:13–16). But in the light of the accusations Paul makes in ch. 11 it is most likely that the disobedience he had in mind was far more serious. It was one which tampered with the truth of the gospel (11:4), and because of that its perpetrators could be called 'false apostles, deceitful workmen', and even servants of Satan (11: 13–15).

If all this be granted, then the complete obedience from the Corinthians for which the apostle waited before taking action against the intruders would be the rejection of the message and claims of those men, and the recognition again of Paul's authority and the truth of his gospel.

B. Paul Responds to Criticisms (10:7–11)

In this passage Paul responds to two criticisms levelled against him by his opponents: first, that he was no true servant of Christ while they themselves were (vv. 7–8), and second, that while his letters were 'weighty and strong', his 'bodily presence [was] weak, and his speech of no account' (vv. 9–11).

7. The first sentence of this verse, *Look at what is before your eyes*, is translated in the RSV as a command, while the NIV translates it as a statement of fact ('You are looking only on the surface of things'). Both are legitimate translations of the original as the verb *blepete* can be construed as either an imperative ('Look!') or an indicative ('You are looking') and even as an interrogative ('Are you looking?'). The imperative rendering of the RSV is to be preferred on the grounds that *blepete* when used elsewhere in Paul's letters is always imperative (1 Cor. 8:9; 10:12, 18; 16:10; Gal. 5:15; Eph. 5:15; Phil. 3:2; Col. 2:8), with only one possible exception (1 Cor. 1:26). The sense of Paul's command is, 'Look at what is patently obvious!

If any one is confident that he is Christ's, let him remind himself that as he is Christ's, so are we. What ought to be patently obvious to Paul's readers is that, even granted for the sake of argument the claims of his opponents to be Christ's (he will deny this later, *cf.* 11:13–15), he himself is equally so.

There has been much debate about the meaning of being *Christ's*. It has been variously understood to mean (a) to be a Christian, (b) to have been a disciple of the earthly Jesus, (c) to be a servant or apostle of Christ, and (d) to be part of Christ (understood along Gnostic lines). The view that it means to be Christ's servant or apostle commends itself most in the light of both 11:23 and the fact that throughout chs. 10 – 13 Paul is defending his apostolate. Paul's claim to be Christ's apostle rested upon his conversion-commissioning experience. And if his colleagues (*e.g.* Timothy, Titus and others) are included in the plural pronoun *we*, then their claim to be servants of Christ probably rested upon the fact that they had been enlisted by Paul to help him fulfil his mandate, though in Timothy's case, at least, there appears to have been some special appointment through prophetic designation (1 Tim. 1:18).

8. *For even if I boast a little too much of our authority.* In vv. 9–11 Paul will claim that what he says (with great authority) in letters is consistent with his actions when present in Corinth. The reference to boasting a little too much of his authority may then be an allusion to the authoritative demands made in his 'severe' letter. But he quickly adds, by way of parenthesis, that his authority is something *which the Lord gave for building you up and not for destroying you*. By *the Lord* here he means Christ, the one who commissioned him as an apostle. The purpose (*eis*) for which the Lord gave him authority is stated both positively (*for building you up*) and negatively (*not for destroying you*). It is pointless to ask how Paul might have used his authority for destroying, because it was not given for that purpose (*cf.* 13:10). If we ask how he used it for building up, the answer suggested by the present passage is that it was by making authoritative demands by letter that his converts live in accordance with the truth of his gospel, even if that meant disciplining one of their members (*cf.* 2:3–4; 7:8–12).

Following the parenthesis, Paul completes what he started to say at the beginning of the verse, *Even if I boast a little too much of our authority . . . I shall not be put to shame*. The clue to understanding this affirmation is to be found in vv. 9–11. Paul is confident that it will emerge that his behaviour when present is completely consistent with his bold use of authority by letter. Accordingly he will be vindicated, rather than put to shame, as far as his boasting of authority is concerned.

It is important to recognize that apostolic authority was of the greatest significance for Paul. He was an ambassador for Christ (5:20), and as such spoke the message entrusted to him with the full authority of his Lord. Because of this Paul expected to be obeyed; anyone who rejected his instructions rejected the word of the Lord (1 Cor. 14:37–38). And because he was entrusted with such authority Paul was careful to distinguish the word of the Lord from his own good advice and from other statements he sometimes felt forced to make (1 Cor. 7:10,25; 2 Cor. 11:17). This authority of Paul was expressed not only in instructions which he expected to be obeyed but also in the dynamic power of God which could be demonstrated (*cf.* 13:2–3). However, having such authority did not exempt the apostle from the experience of weakness, persecution and suffering. In fact the bearer of Christ's authority also shared the experience of Christ's weakness, even while the power of God was at work through him (*cf.* 13:4).

9-10. *I would not seem to be frightening you with letters.* With these words Paul opens up a subject which he knows has been made a basis of criticism against him by his opponents. He has been accused of sending strongly worded letters to Corinth which boast of an authority he does not have. He knows what they have been telling his converts and reproduces it here: *For they say, 'His letters are weighty and strong, but his bodily presence is weak, and his speech of no account.'* While Paul's letters were regarded as intimidating (*weighty and strong*), he himself was deemed to lack signs of authority when actually present in person. The words *his bodily presence is weak* may reflect his opponents' reaction to a physical ailment which was never healed (*cf.* 12:7-9; Gal. 4:15), or his unimpressive physical make-up (*cf. Acts of Paul and Thecla* 3: 'a man of small stature, with a bald head and crooked legs, in a good state of body, with eyebrows meeting and nose somewhat hooked'), or most likely to what they regarded as a lack of a commanding presence because Paul did not provide *displays* of authority and spiritual charismata.

The charge that 'his speech is of no account' was probably made by Paul's opponents either because they disliked his unadorned style of speaking (*cf.* 1 Cor. 2:1-2) or because they could not understand why one claiming to be an apostle of Christ had not spoken boldly in his own defence when attacked by the offender (*cf.* 2:5; 7:12), choosing rather to retire in humiliation and send a strongly worded letter from a safe distance.

11. To those who so criticized him Paul replies, *Let such people understand that what we say by letter when absent, we do when present.* While the apostle may have chosen not to make a show of authority on his second visit, that does not mean he is without it. The one who writes the strong letters is prepared to stand up to his critics when he comes on the third visit. No-one should mistake his efforts to be conciliatory as evidence that he lacks authority.

C. *Boasting within Proper Limits* (10:12-18)

In the previous section Paul had to defend his authority against those who claimed that, while he may write boldly from a distance, his lack of real authority was plain for all to see when he was present in person. In 10:12–18 Paul takes the offensive. He satirizes his opponents who commend themselves (by comparing themselves with one another!). By contrast his own boasting, he says, is carefully measured and based upon the actual work he has done in the sphere of operations assigned to him by the Lord. He concludes, clearly having his opponents in mind, with the statement that 'it is not the man who commends himself that is accepted, but the man whom the Lord commends'.

12. Paul satirizes his opponents when he says, *Not that we venture to class or compare ourselves with some of those who commend themselves.* A popular method used by teachers to attract pupils in Paul's day was to compare themselves with other teachers (*cf. Oxyrhynchus Papyrus*, 2190). Paul says he would not dare to compare himself with his critics! It is the self-commendation of his opponents and the way they go about it that is the particular object of Paul's satire: *But when they measure themselves by one another, and compare themselves with one another, they are without understanding.* We cannot be certain about the criteria they might have employed in this measurement. However, it is likely that they employed the same criteria when comparing themselves with Paul, and there are certain hints in 2 Corinthians concerning what these were. They looked for an authoritative presence and impressive speech (10:1, 10; 11:20–21), the levying of a fee for the message proclaimed (11:7–11), an impeccable Jewish ancestry (11:21b–22), impressive spiritual experiences (12:1–6), the performance of apostolic signs (12:12), and some show of power and authority (11:19–20) to prove that Christ spoke through the person concerned (13:3). The triumphalist nature of these criteria should be noted. There is no room for the expressions of weakness, suffering, persecution and imprisonment which were often Paul's lot, and which Jesus himself said would be the experience of those who followed him. If the approach to the discovery of the criteria followed here is valid, then in the light of the results it is no wonder that Paul should say of these men: *they are without understanding.*

13–14. Having satirized the way his opponents commend themselves, Paul contrasts it with his own measured boasting, which he deliberately restricts to actual work done. *But we will not boast beyond limit, but will keep to the limits God has apportioned us, to reach even to you.* In speaking of the *limits* God has apportioned to him Paul uses the word *kanōn* whose basic meaning is 'a rule' or 'a standard of measurement'. In recently published documents there is evidence for the use of the word to denote services to be rendered within 'a specified geographical area',[1] and the same sense of the word is required here. The *limits* (*kanōn*) God assigned to Paul consist in his service (ministry) of the gospel in Gentile lands (*cf.* Rom. 1:5, 13–14; 15:18–19; Gal. 2:7–8). Included within those limits was his responsibility, he says, *to reach even to you.* The fact that he was within his rights when operating in Corinth seems to have been questioned by his opponents, because Paul immediately asserts, *For we are not overextending ourselves, as though we did not reach you; we were the first to come all the way to you with the gospel of Christ.* Paul bases his right to operate as an apostle in Corinth on two facts: first, God assigned to him the task of evangelizing the nations, and second, he was the first to evangelize Corinth.

15. *We do not boast beyond limit, in other men's labours.* What Paul means by boasting *beyond limit* (*cf.* v. 13) is further clarified in this verse, *i.e.* boasting of the results of the labours of others as if they were the results of one's own. The implication of Paul's claim that *he* does not boast in other men's labours is that his opponents do.

But our hope is that as your faith increases, our field among you may be greatly enlarged (more literally; 'but having hope that, as your faith grows, we shall be magnified among you in accordance with our sphere [of service] for abundance'). This part of v. 15 is very difficult to translate. The RSV and NIV both construe it in the same way to mean that Paul hopes his sphere of service among the Corinthians will be enlarged as their faith grows. Such an

---

[1]G. H. R. Horsley, *New Documents Illustrating Early Christianity. A Review of the Greek Inscriptions and Papyri published in 1976* (The Ancient History Documentary Research Centre, Macquarie University, 1981), pp. 36–45.

enlargement of ministry would both signal the end of the present crisis, leaving Paul free to preach elsewhere, and also provide him with a greatly enlarged support base from which to do so.

16. *So that we may preach the gospel in lands beyond you, without boasting of work already done in another's field.* In Romans, written not long after these chapters were penned, Paul speaks of his ambition to take the gospel to Spain (Rom. 15:24), and we should think of his reference to *lands beyond you* as denoting lands, like Spain, further to the west. Also in Romans Paul expresses his ambition 'to preach the gospel, not where Christ has already been named, lest I should build on another man's foundation' (Rom. 15:20). In the present context the same motivation underlies Paul's desire to preach in *lands beyond* – he wants to preach *without boasting of work already done in another's field*. There is in all this the implication that Paul's opponents, by interfering in Corinth, were doing the very thing which he sought so carefully to avoid.

Before leaving this verse we should note that there remain in the world today both geographical areas and segments within most societies where Christ is not known. There men and women who share Paul's ambition to preach the gospel where Christ has not already been named are still needed.

17. *'Let him who boasts, boast of the Lord.'* Though there may be some room for legitimate pride in work done by the grace of God (*cf.* Rom. 15:17–18), nevertheless the true ground of Christian boasting is the privilege of knowing God himself. Here (and in 1 Cor. 1:31) Paul draws on the teaching of Jeremiah 9:23–24, where the wise, the mighty and the rich are counselled against glorying in their advantages. All who glory are urged to glory in the fact that they know the Lord. Jesus taught the Seventy the same lesson when they came back from their mission rejoicing that they had seen even the demons subject to them (Lk. 10:17–20).

18. The danger is that glorying in success can easily degenerate into self-commendation. Paul reminds his readers (as he reminds himself) that *it is not the man who commends himself that is accepted, but the man whom the Lord commends*. The word translated *accepted* (*dokimos*) carries the idea of approval after testing. Paul uses the word to describe a tried and tested servant of Christ, one whose worth has been proved (Rom. 16:10; *cf.* 2 Tim. 2:15). He uses the cognate verb (*dokimazō*) in reference to the testing of Christian workers (2 Cor. 8:22) and the works of believers (1 Cor. 3:13; Gal. 6:4).

In this verse Paul's eyes are upon the ultimate evaluation of a person's ministry. It matters little what the individual says by way of self-recommendation or what judgments others make. All that matters is the commendation which the Lord himself gives (*cf.* 1 Cor. 4:1–5). This is the rubric under which Paul carried out his apostolic labours, and in the present context it is probably implied that his opponents in Corinth did not. Paul returns again to the theme of passing God's test in 13:5–7.

D. The Corinthians' Gullibility (11:1–6)

In this passage Paul foreshadows the 'fool's speech' (boasting of his apostolic credentials) which is to follow later in this chapter and in the next, and explains that it is his great concern over his readers' gullibility that forces him to make it. He is concerned lest their minds be led astray from devotion to the Christ preached in his gospel by those who question his credentials and proclaim a different gospel.

1. *I wish you would bear with me in a little foolishness*. Paul regards the parading of his credentials which is to follow (11:21b – 12:13) as an act of folly. This is especially so because, as he has just said, 'it is not the man who commends himself that is accepted, but the man whom the Lord commends' (10:18). Yet in the light of the situation in Corinth Paul is forced to set forth his credentials, and that, not as he would have chosen, but in accordance with the criteria favoured by his opponents and apparently now accepted by his converts. So to meet the demands of the situation, Paul 'answers the fool according to his folly'. When he entreats his readers, *Do bear with me!*, it is probably more a sign of his own embarrassment about the whole exercise than a concern that they might see it as inappropriate.

2–3. Paul reveals the deep concern which leads him to indulge in the folly of self-commendation: *I feel a divine jealousy for you* (more literally: 'I am jealous over you with [the] jealousy of God'). As he sees what is occurring in Corinth Paul is deeply moved because he shares the jealousy of God for his people. That the metaphor of marriage is involved here is confirmed by what follows: *for I betrothed you to Christ to present you as a pure bride to her one husband.* Marriage among the Jews of Paul's day involved two separate ceremonies, the betrothal and the nuptial ceremony which consummated the marriage. Usually a year elapsed between the two, but during that period the girl was regarded legally as the man's wife, while socially she remained a virgin. The betrothal contract was binding, and could be broken only by death or a formal written divorce. Unfaithfulness or violation of a betrothed girl was regarded as adultery and punishable as such.[1] These marriage customs provide the background to Paul's statements here.

Paul sees himself as the agent of God through whom his converts were *betrothed* to Christ, and feels under obligation to ensure that they are presented as a *pure* virgin *to her one husband* at the nuptial ceremony when the marriage will be consummated (*i.e.* at the parousia of Christ). In view of recent events in Corinth Paul is forced to say, *But I am afraid that as the serpent deceived Eve by his cunning, your thoughts will be led astray from a sincere and pure devotion to Christ.* To portray the danger he sees Paul compares it with the deception of Eve in the garden ('The serpent beguiled me, and I ate', Gn. 3:13). It is significant that the serpent's 'seduction' of Eve was not sexual, as some rabbinic texts suggest, but rather a beguiling of her mind by denying the truth of what God had said (Gn. 3:1–7). Thus the story of Eve aptly depicts the sort of danger the Corinthians faced, *i.e.* that their *thoughts* will be led astray. The word translated *thoughts* (*noēmata*) is found only six times in the New Testament, every

[1] R. Batey, 'Paul's Bride Image: A Symbol of Realistic Eschatology', *Int* 17 (1963), pp. 176–182.

time in Paul's writings, and five out of the six times in 2 Corinthians. Apart from the present context Paul uses it to describe the 'designs' of Satan (2:11), the hardening or blinding of the 'mind' (3:14; 4:4), the taking captive of every 'thought' to obey Christ (10:5), and the 'mind' that is kept by the peace of God, which passes understanding (Phil. 4:7). In the present passage Paul is concerned with the beguiling of the minds (not the compromise of the morals) of his readers. What he means by this will be revealed in v. 4, but before proceeding to that it is important to stress that Christians' minds are prime targets for the assaults of *the serpent* (which Paul equates with Satan, *cf.* v. 14) which are intended to lead them astray from their devotion to Christ.

4. The Corinthians' minds were being led astray by those who preached another Jesus and a different gospel. Just as Eve was deceived by the serpent which denied the truth of God's word, so Paul's converts' minds were being led astray by those who denied the truth of his gospel and substituted for it another of their own.

For if some one comes and preaches another Jesus than the one we preached. What does Paul mean by *another Jesus*? As noted above in the commentary on 10:12, the criteria for evaluating apostleship that were apparently employed by Paul's opponents were triumphalist in character and left no room for the experience of weakness or suffering. It may well be that in their preaching Paul's opponents stressed the power and glory of Christ to the virtual exclusion of the fact that he had also known weakness, humiliation, persecution, suffering and death. Paul preached Christ *crucified* as Lord, so a proclamation like that outlined above would seem to him to be the preaching of *another Jesus*.

Or if you receive a different spirit from the one you received. If it is legitimate to interpret *another Jesus* along the lines suggested above, then we may apply the same approach to the interpretation of the *different spirit* which Paul says his readers accept readily enough. The Spirit whom the Corinthians received when they responded to the gospel proclaimed by Paul (*cf.* 1 Cor. 2:12; 3:16; 6:19) and with whose power Paul's own ministry was carried out (*cf.* Rom. 15:18–19; 1 Cor. 2:4; 1 Thes. 1:5) was the Spirit who also produced the virtues of love, kindness and gentleness in those whom he indwelt (Gal. 5:22). The spirit in which Paul's opponents operated was authoritarian and over-bearing (11:20), and as far as Paul was concerned drew its inspiration from Satan (11:13–15). If the Corinthians submit to these men, they accept a very different spirit from the one they received when they accepted Paul's gospel.

Or if you accept a different gospel from the one you accepted. Paul uses the same expression, *a different gospel*, when describing the teaching of the Judaizers to which his churches in Galatia were nearly lost (Gal. 1:6–9), and it has been suggested that the *gospel* of Paul's Corinthian opponents may have been the same, *i.e.* a gospel stressing the need for Gentiles not only to believe in Christ but also to take upon themselves the yoke of the law and submit to circumcision if they wanted to be numbered among the true people of God. However, this is unlikely on two counts. First, there is no mention in 2 Corinthians 10 – 13 of demands to keep the law (whether food laws or sabbath and other special day observances) or to undergo circumcision. Second, the emphases we do find in 2 Corinthians 10 – 13 (*e.g.* on skill in speaking, knowledge (11:6), displays of authority (11:20), vis-ions and revelations (12:1) and the performance of apostolic signs (12:12–13)) are not found in Galatians. Therefore it seems better to interpret the *different gospel* in the same way as *another Jesus* and *a different spirit*, *i.e.* as a gospel which stressed the power and glory of Christ and which had little place for Christ *crucified* as Lord.

You submit to it readily enough (lit. 'you bear with it well'). Paul uses the same word here as he did in v. 1. It is no wonder he felt he could ask his readers to bear with him when he knew they were bearing well enough with those who preached a different gospel.

5. *I think that I am not in the least inferior to these superlative apostles.* From expressions of concern, Paul now turns to per-sonal defence. For a discussion of the identity of the *superlative apostles* see Introduction, pp. 45–52. The position adopted in this commentary is that these men are to be identified with those who preached a different gospel (v. 4) and whom Paul calls false apostles and servants of Satan (vv. 14–15). In claiming to be *not* *in the least inferior* to these men Paul is not at the same time conceding that they are his equals. He is just responding to their claims. Later he will make his own claims and assert that he is superior to them (vv. 21b–33).

6. *Even if I am unskilled in speaking, I am not in knowledge.* The first part of this statement can be understood in either of two ways: first, as a straightforward concession that in the use of rhetorical skills in public speaking Paul is inferior to his opponents; and second, as a rhetorical device by which he places himself in an inferior position *vis-à-vis* his opponents even though he knows (and expects his readers to know) that he is in fact superior to them. It is the former alternative which fits the context better, for Paul's purpose seems to be, while conceding superiority in the less important area of rhetorical skills to his opponents, to claim the superiority for himself in the far more important area of knowledge.

By *knowledge* Paul means primarily insight into the mystery of the gospel (*cf.* Col. 1:26–27; Eph. 1:9; 3:1–6), which his opponents have failed to understand properly. Also included are probably an understanding of the gifts bestowed by God upon those who believe (1 Cor. 2:10–13), and what is described as 'the whole counsel of God' (Acts 20:27). Of all this Paul says, *in every way we have made this plain to you in all things*, and undoubtedly he has in mind the eighteen months or more he spent teaching the word of God in Corinth during his first visit to the city (Acts 18:11), as well as the instruction given by letters.

E. *The Matter of Financial Remuneration* (11:7–15)

In these verses Paul responds to criticisms of the practice he adopted during his mission in Corinth of not asking for, or accepting, any financial remuneration from his hearers. Because of this he seems to have come under criticism on two counts. First, the Corinthians probably felt affronted because Paul refused to accept assistance from them, especially when by so doing he was forced to undertake menial work to support himself, work which they regarded as degrading for an apostle (v. 7). Second, this refusal was construed as evidence that Paul did not really love the Corinthians. If he would not accept their money, surely that meant he had no real affection for them (v.11). Despite these criticisms Paul informs his readers that he has no intention of changing his practice, and the reason for this is that he wishes to undercut all claims of his opponents to work on the same basis as he does (v. 12). There follows a strong verbal attack in which Paul dispenses with irony and reveals clearly his opinion of the opponents (vv. 13–15).

7. *Did I commit a sin in abasing myself so that you might be exalted?* According to Acts 18:1–4 Paul worked as a tentmaker to provide for his needs during his first stay in Corinth. By so doing he 'abased' himself, for among the Greeks it was regarded as degrading for a philosopher or itinerant teacher to engage in manual work to supply his needs. No doubt aware of this, Paul asks with ironic exaggeration whether he committed a *sin* by so abasing himself *because I preached God's gospel without cost to you.* Can it be a *sin*, he asks, when for the sake of making the gospel available without cost to you, I abase myself so that you may be exalted?

8. *I robbed other churches by accepting support from them in order to serve you.* The word Paul uses here, *sylaō* ('to rob'), is a strong one. In the papyri it was used with the meaning 'to pillage', and in classical Greek it was used predominantly in a military context meaning 'to strip' (a dead soldier of his armour). Why Paul chose such a strong word is difficult to determine. Perhaps he wanted to bring home to the Corinthians the lengths to which he had gone in making the gospel available to them free of charge, *i.e.* even to the extent of 'robbing' other churches by accepting support from them for work done in Corinth, work from which the donors would receive no benefits.

9. What exactly was involved in 'robbing' other churches Paul spells out here. *And when I was with you and was in want, I did not burden any one, for my needs were supplied by the brethren who came from Macedonia.* The word *supplied* translates the aorist indicative of *prosanaplēroō*, which can mean either simply 'to fill up' or 'to fill up by adding'. In the present context, where the proceeds from Paul's own manual work obviously would have provided some of his needs, the latter sense, 'to fill up by adding' appropriately expresses the function of the gifts brought from Macedonia. From evidence available in Paul's letters it seems that among the Macedonian churches it was the one at Philippi which was the main contributor to the apostle's needs. They repeatedly shared in Paul's ministry by assisting him financially from the time they were converted up until and including the imprisonment during which he wrote Philippians (*cf.* Phil. 1:5; 4:10, 14–18).

So I refrained and will refrain from burdening you in any way. Because Paul's needs were met either by the results of his own manual work or by gifts from the Macedonians he was able to refrain from burdening the Corinthians, and he asserts that he is determined in the future to continue that practice.

10. *As the truth of Christ is in me, this boast of mine shall not be silenced in the regions of Achaia.* The regions of Achaia here denotes the Roman province of Achaia of which Corinth was the major city and administrative centre. Throughout these regions, Paul affirms with an oath, his boast of ministering free of charge will not be silenced. No doubt his opponents would have liked to see it silenced by Paul relenting and accepting financial remuneration, but he was determined that it should not be (*cf.* v. 12).

This policy may have been felt as an affront by the Corinthians, especially having just been told (v. 9), if they had not known before, that while Paul was in their midst he had actually been in need and had accepted help from others while refusing to accept it from them.

There are a number of possible reasons why Paul refused assistance from the Corinthians. First, there was his general ambition to preach the gospel without charge. To preach it was mandatory for him, to preach it without charge was his own choice (*cf.* 1 Cor. 9:15–18). Second, there was his desire not to burden those whom he ministered among, and perhaps we may add that he did not wish to lose his independence by becoming financially obliged to anyone. In Paul's world the acceptance of a benefaction often meant becoming a 'client' of the benefactor, and so sacrificing some of one's independence.

We may wonder, then, why Paul accepted asistance from the Macedonians. Perhaps he felt free to accept gifts from churches who by giving them wished to participate in his ministry in other places. In such cases his ambition to offer the gospel free of charge would not be compromised, and there would be little chance that his benefactors would regard him as their client.

11. Because Paul's opponents could not silence his boasting they tried to undermine his relationship with the Corinthians by suggesting that his refusal to accept their assistance was proof that he did not really love them. Paul was aware of their strategy, so he poses the rhetorical question: *And why? Because I do not love you?* He does not bother to dignify their accusations with a reasoned reply. Instead, calling upon God as his witness, he simply affirms his love for his readers: *God knows I do!*

12. Paul restates the assertion he made in v. 9b, but in slightly different terms: *And what I do I will continue to do, i.e.* refrain from placing any financial burdens upon the Corinthians. In the light of the activity of his opponents in Corinth Paul had an added reason for doing so – *in order to undermine the claim of those who would like to claim that in their boasted mission they work on the same terms as we do.* This part of v. 12 is difficult to translate and interpret, but the RSV rendering captures what is probably Paul's intention here. His opponents, in order to consolidate thoroughly their position in Corinth, wanted to be able to say that they carried out their mission on the same terms as Paul did. However, there was one crucial area in which their terms were different – they wanted financial remuneration from the Corinthians. If they were *bona fide* apostles they need not have been concerned about this distinction, for most other apostles accepted remuneration (1 Cor. 9:3–7), and Paul himself had defended at length the right of Christian workers to do so (1 Cor. 9:7–14). It seems likely that Paul's opponents not only accepted remuneration but greedily extracted it (*cf.* v. 20), and this would have made them particularly sensitive to the odious comparisons which could be drawn between their behaviour and Paul's. They would have been very relieved had Paul discontinued his practice in this matter, but he was for that very reason determined not to, and so to undermine their claims to work on the same terms as him.

13. Paul now dispenses with irony, personal defence and explanations of his policy in money matters, and with striking virulence exposes the true character of his opponents. *For such men are false apostles, deceitful workmen, disguising themselves as apostles of Christ.* Essentially they are deceivers, passing themselves off as apostles of Christ when they were not, and for that reason they deserved the epithet *false apostles*.

14. The deceitfulness of these people does not surprise Paul, *for even Satan disguises himself as an angel of light.* Paul may be thinking here of Genesis 3 and the deceitfulness of the serpent who 'enlightened' Eve. Alternatively there are stories in Jewish pseudepigraphical works in which the devil or Satan appears as an angel to deceive Eve (*Life of Adam and Eve* 9:1 – 11:3; *Apocalypse of Moses* 17:1) and the apostle could be using these as an illustration. Or it may simply be that Paul as a result of his missionary experiences had come to recognize Satan's devices (2:11).

15. Whatever lies behind Paul's statement in v. 14 that Satan disguises himself as an angel of light, the conclusion he draws from it is plain enough. Arguing from the greater to the lesser he says, *So it is not strange if his servants also disguise themselves as servants of righteousness.* Paul's opponents are revealed here as instruments of Satan who disguise themselves as *servants of righteousness.* Satan's attacks on the church are seldom frontal. They are more often subversive, and carried out by those within the church who misguidedly serve his ends. It is precisely this that Paul fears may happen in the Corinthian church as 11:3–4 indicates very clearly.

Of those who serve Satan in Corinth Paul says, *Their end will correspond to their deeds.* In 5:10 Paul reminded his readers that all must appear before the judgment seat of Christ and receive good or evil according to what they have done in the body. In other epistles also, when dealing with those who oppose the truth of God or attack his messengers, Paul asserts that they will face the judgment of God (Rom. 3:8; 1 Cor. 3:17; Phil. 3:19; 2 Tim. 4:14).

F. The Fool's Speech (11:16 – 12:13)

1. Accept me as a fool (11:16–21a)

With this brief section Paul opens his extended 'fool's speech' in which he boasts of his credentials, apostolic trials, visionary experiences and the mighty works he performed. He knows such worldly boasting is foolish, but in the circumstances where his converts have been swayed by the boasting of others, he feels compelled to boast a little himself. So in this opening section Paul asks his readers to bear with him, makes clear that what he is about to say is not said with the Lord's authority, and then with biting irony reminds them that they have been ready enough to bear with other fools, being wise themselves! These others have acted in the most highhanded and pretentious fashion, but, Paul says ironically, 'we were too weak for that!'

16. *I repeat.* Paul had already asked his readers to bear with him 'in a little foolishness' (v. 1), and now following the long diversion of vv. 2–15, he repeats his request in slightly different terms: *let no one think me foolish; but even if you do, accept me as a fool, so that I too may boast a little.* Paul is conscious that the boasting in which he is about to engage is an act of folly, but he does not want the Corinthians to regard him as foolish for doing so. In fact it is only their gullibility *vis-à-vis* the claims of the false apostles which forces Paul to boast at all (12:11). But even if they do perceive his boasting as the act of a fool, let them accept him as such, and listen to his boasting as they have listened to the boasting of the other fools (Paul's opponents) whom they have received.

17–18. These verses are rightly placed in parentheses in the RSV, for they constitute an aside in which Paul makes clear that the boasting in which he is about to indulge is not something he engages in with the Lord's authority. *What I am saying I say not with the Lord's authority but as a fool, in this boastful confidence.* The last phrase can also be translated 'in this matter of boasting', but either way the general thrust of Paul's disclaimer is clear enough. He goes on to indicate what moves him to this act of folly: *since many boast of worldly things, I too will boast.* The words *boast of worldly things* (*kauchōntai kata sarka*, lit. 'boast according to [the] flesh') denote boasting in the way the world does, *i.e.* of human achievement, of power and prestige, and even spiritual experiences, in terms which do not take into account what is pleasing to God. It is because *many* (his opponents) boast according to the flesh, and because his converts have been won over by such boasting, that Paul feels forced to indulge in it too for their sakes, even though he is painfully aware that such boasting is pure folly.

19. Following the parenthesis of vv. 17–18, Paul returns to his request that if the Corinthians regard him as a fool they should accept him as such and bear a little boasting from him (*cf.* v. 1). Thus, making further use of irony, he says, *For you gladly bear with fools, being wise yourselves!* As far as Paul is concerned the fools they bear gladly are the intruders, his opponents. So, as the Corinthians have demonstrated how gladly they bear with those fools, he asks that, if they regard him as a fool, to bear with him as well. The expression *being wise yourselves* is probably a cutting allusion the Corinthians' tendency to pride themselves on their own wisdom (*cf.* 1 Cor. 3:18–20; 4:10; 6:5; 8:1–7; 13:2).

20. *For you bear it if a man makes slaves of you.* Unlike Paul, who saw his role as working with people for their joy, not lording it over their faith (1:24), the intruders did bring those they influenced under their 'lordship'. Paul exposes the despicable display of authoritarianism of his opponents, as well as the misplaced forbearance of the Corinthians, by piling up in close succession four expressions which depict the nature of the Corinthians' enslavement. You accept it, he says, if a man *preys upon you, or takes advantage of you, or puts on airs, or strikes you in the face. Preys upon* (*katesthiei*, lit. 'consumes') probably refers to the intruders' greedy demands for remuneration. The verb translated *takes advantage of* (*lambanei*, lit. 'takes') is used by Paul again in 12:16 where he writes, 'But granting that I myself did not burden you, I was crafty, you say, and got the better of (*elabon*) you by guile.' This illuminates the unusual use of the verb *lambanō* in the present context: the Corinthians were 'taken in' or 'fleeced' by Paul's opponents. *Puts on airs* (*epairetai*) signifies a presumptuous lifting up of one's self. Paul uses the same verb in 10:5 when referring to 'every proud obstacle to [lit. 'every high thing lifted up against'] the knowledge of God'. In the expression *strikes you in the face* Paul uses the verb *derō* which meant 'to flay' or 'to skin' an animal, and more commonly 'to beat'. Paul uses the word in 1 Corinthians 9:26 where it bears the more common sense 'to beat' ('I do not box as one *beating* the air'), and this is probably how it should be understood in the present context as well. If this is the case it would indicate that his opponents had become so inflated in their own opinions that they would actually strike across the face those whom they had brought under their authority.

21a. Paul concludes this paragraph with another statement filled with scathing sarcasm: *To my shame, I must say, we were too weak for that!* The Corinthians had entertained the criticisms of Paul's opponents that he was weak (10:10). Paul now throws that back at them, saying in effect, 'Yes, I am ashamed to say, we were too weak to make such a despicable display of overbearing authoritarianism as that provided by those intruders!'

2. *Paul's Jewish ancestry and apostolic trials* (11:21b–33)

In this section Paul responds to his opponents' claims to impeccable Jewish ancestry and to be the servants of Christ. He concedes these for the sake of argument (even though he denied the latter in vv. 13–15), but asserts that his own Jewish credentials are just as good, and claims that he is a better servant of Christ (vv. 21b–23a). Then to reinforce his claim to be a better servant of Christ, Paul provides a list of his apostolic trials (vv. 23b–29) which may be divided into four sections: (a) vv. 23b–25, imprisonments, beatings and being near death, including a detailed explanation of what these involved, (b) v. 26, frequent journeys, with a description of the dangers of travel, (c) v. 27, toil and hardship, with an account of the privations involved in these, and (d) vv. 28–29, anxiety for all the churches, with an example of what caused it. Finally he narrates the story of his ignominious flight from Damascus as a further illustration of his 'weakness' as an apostle (vv. 30–33).

21b–23a. Paul begins his 'fool's speech' proper with the words, *But whatever any one dares to boast of – I am speaking as a fool – I also dare to boast of that.* The apostle will take up in turn those things of which his opponents boast: their Jewish pedigree and their being servants of Christ (vv. 22–23), visions and revelations experienced (12:1), and the performance of mighty works (12:12). Then he will indulge in a little boasting of his own to show that he is in no way inferior in any of these areas. Both here (vv. 21b, 23a) and in three other places in the speech (11:30; 12:1,11) Paul shows how uneasy he is about boasting – *I am speaking as a fool.*

Are they Hebrews? So am I! The designation *Hebrews* may be understood in two ways. First, it was used to denote ethnic purity as in the expression 'a Hebrew born of Hebrews' (Phil. 3:5), and second, it was employed to distinguish Aramaic-speaking Jews who generally lived in Palestine (Hebrews) from Greek-speaking Jews generally of the dispersion (Hellenists) (*cf.* Acts 6:1). However, this second distinction was not as clear cut as it might seem, for as the inscription, '[Syn]agogue of the Hebr[ews]', found in Corinth (see Introduction, p. 15) shows, even Jews of the dispersion referred to themselves as 'Hebrews'. In the present context it is best to see Paul claiming that he has the same pure Jewish ancestry as that claimed by his opponents. Whether they were Palestinian or Hellenistic Jews cannot be determined from these verses.

Are they Israelites? So am I. It is difficult to know whether in Paul's mind *Israelites* were distinguished from *Hebrews.* However, seeing that proselytes were admitted into Israel but could never, of course, claim to be Hebrews (born of Hebrews), the term 'Israelite' should probably be taken to denote the religious and social aspects of being a Jew.

Are they descendants of Abraham? So am I. It is quite difficult to see what distinction, if any, is intended between the terms *Israelites* and *descendants of Abraham*, especially since Paul himself uses the terms as synonyms in Romans 11:1. One suggestion is that if *Hebrews* is to be understood ethnically, and *Israelites* religiously and socially, then *descendants of Abraham* should be understood theologically and related to God's call and promises to Abraham's offspring.

While there are difficulties in discerning the precise nuances of these three terms, Paul's main thrust is clear. Whatever boasting his opponents indulge in as far as their Jewish connection is concerned, Paul may boast of the same.

Are they servants of Christ? I am a better one – I am talking like a madman. Responding to his opponents' claims regarding Jewish ancestry, Paul simply claimed to be their equal, but here, with rhetorical heightening, Paul responds to their claim to be servants of Christ by saying that he is a better one. He is prepared, for the sake of argument here, to concede what he elsewhere (vv. 13–15) denies, *i.e.* that they are servants of Christ, because he will show that he is more than their equal anyhow. By saying, *I am talking like a madman*, Paul reveals again his reluctance to be involved at all in this 'fool's speech'. The very comparing of one servant of Christ with others is something he had already warned the Corinthians against (1 Cor. 1:11–16; 3:4–9, 21–22; 4:1), and now through the force of new circumstances he is engaging in that very practice himself.

23b–25. This first section of the trials list opens with the words, *With far greater labours, far more imprisonments, with countless beatings, and often near death.* The *far greater labours* probably refers to the strenuous exertions of Paul in his missionary work, exertions far greater than those of his opponents, and even of the other apostles (*cf.* 1 Cor. 15:10). Acts records only one imprisonment before the time these chapters were written, the overnight stay in the prison at Philippi (Acts 16:19–40). Paul's brief reference to far more imprisonments reminds us both that he experienced far more trials than Acts records, and how limited our knowledge of his missionary career really is, even with the Acts account to draw upon.

What is meant by the *countless beatings, and often near death* is revealed in vv. 24–25. *Five times I have received at the hands of the Jews the forty lashes less one.* Jesus warned his disciples that they would be flogged in the synagogues (Mt. 10:17; Mk. 13:9), and Paul in his pre-conversion days actually instigated such floggings (Acts 22:20; 26:11). Having been converted to the faith he once opposed, he himself had, by the time he wrote these words, been subject five times to judicial floggings in synagogues. This reveals indirectly that, despite much opposition, Paul did not give up his connection with Judaism or the synagogue and lose himself in the Gentile world. Deuteronomy 25:1–3 specifies that punishment by beating must not exceed forty strokes, and as a hedge around the law the Jews of Paul's day limited the number to forty less one, lest by an error in counting the prescribed number be exceeded and the law be broken.

Three times I have been beaten with rods. The one such incident we know of took place in Philippi (Acts 16:22–23). In fact it was illegal for a magistrate to have a Roman citizen (as Paul was) beaten, though from this incident and some recorded in other ancient literature it is clear that the law was not always observed. It is probably for this reason that Paul, writing shortly after this incident, speaks of being 'shamefully treated at Philippi' (1 Thes. 2:2), and for this reason also the magistrates came to apologize to Paul for what they had done (Acts 16:38–39).

Once I was stoned. Stoning could be either a Jewish judicial execution (*cf.* Lv. 24:14,16) or an act of mob violence. The latter was the case in Lystra where Paul was stoned and left for dead (Acts 14:19).

Three times I have been shipwrecked; a night and a day I have been adrift at sea. From Acts we know of only one shipwreck in which Paul was involved, and that took place after this letter was written. However, Acts records nine sea voyages which the apostle made prior to this time, and there were almost certainly others. There were then plenty of voyages during which Paul could have suffered shipwrecks. Being adrift for *a night and a day* at sea must have brought the apostle face to face with death, as had his stoning at Lystra.

26. *On frequent journeys.* With these words the second section of Paul's trials list begins, and what follows sheds light upon the dangers he faced on his many journeys. These include dangers from *rivers*, *robbers*, his *own people* (the Jews) and the *Gentiles*, as well as dangers *in the city*, *in the wilderness*, *at sea*, and *from false* *brethren*. The latter probably refers to fellow Christians who opposed Paul and his gospel (*cf.* Gal. 2:4), and here, most likely, Paul has in mind especially those who opposed him in Corinth.

27. The third section of the trials list bears the heading, *in toil and hardship*, and once again a general description is followed by specific examples. *Through many a sleepless night*. If this meant sleeplessness because of anxiety it would probably have been included in v. 28, where Paul speaks of the pressure of his anxiety over the churches. But as it is included among examples of toil and hardship, the sleepless nights are better taken to be due either to his preaching and teaching into the early hours (*cf.* Acts 20:7–12,31), when those who had to labour during the day would be free to listen, or to the occasions when he had to ply his trade at night so as to support himself when he used the daylight hours for missionary activity (2 Thes. 3:7–8). *In hunger and thirst, often without food, in cold and exposure*. Despite income from manual work and gifts from the Macedonians, there were times when Paul suffered want (Phil. 4:10–13) and must have gone without food, drink and adequate clothing (*cf.* Rom. 8:35; 1 Cor. 4:11; 2 Tim. 4:13).

28–29. This fourth section of the trials list differs from the previous three in that it deals with subjective rather than objective matters, *And, apart from other things, there is the daily pressure upon me of my anxiety for all the churches*. It should be noted that Paul's anxiety here is not the unwarranted concern about oneself which Jesus cautioned his disciples against (Mt. 6:25–34), but rather that healthy concern for the welfare of others which Jesus himself experienced (Lk. 13:34). The Corinthian letters provide abundant examples of the anxiety-producing situations which kept the pressure upon Paul's pastoral heart. He himself cites one example: *Who is weak, and I am not weak? Who is made to fall, and I am not indignant?* This reflects Paul's concern for those who are weak in faith, and who are caused to stumble and fall because of the behaviour of those who pride themselves on being strong in faith (*cf.* Rom. 14:1–23; 1 Cor. 8:1–13). When Paul sees Christians weak in faith he feels their vulnerability, and when he sees them made to fall he burns

197

with indignation against the behaviour of those who caused it.

30–33. In this passage Paul narrates an incident from the earliest days of his experience as a Christian. This supplements the list of trials of which he has already boasted, but also seems to parody the whole business of boasting. The passage begins, *If I must boast, I will boast of the things that show my weakness.* Again the apostle shows his distaste for boasting, and foreshadows the fact that he is about to turn the whole thing on its head. Unlike the trials list of vv. 23b–29, which could be construed as triumphalist (*i.e.* 'all these difficulties I have overcome in order to fulfil my commission'), the ignominious flight from Damascus which he is about to relate contains little of which to be proud.

The God and Father of the Lord Jesus, he who is blessed for ever, knows that I do not lie. Before proceeding to his narration Paul appeals to God as witness that what he is about to relate is true. He may have wished, by this affirmation, to stress the truth of the content of the trials list also, though much of that is likely to have been common knowledge. The grammatical construction in the original demands that *he who is blessed for ever* be predicated of *the God and Father*, not *the Lord Jesus*.

At Damascus, the governor under King Aretas guarded the city of Damascus in order to seize me. King Aretas IV (9 BC – AD 39)[1] was ruler of the Nabataeans, an Arabian nation whose kingdom had once included the city of Damascus. By New Testament times the city had been incorporated into the Roman province of Syria. However, it seems that during the reign of the emperor Caligula (AD 37–41), when a policy of reinstituting eastern states of the empire as client kingdoms was followed, Aretas was given control over Damascus and thus would have been able to appoint a governor there. If so, Paul's escape from Damascus must have occurred between AD 37–39.[2]

According to the account of Paul's escape in Acts 9:23–25, hostile Jews who reacted against his forthright preaching of Jesus as Messiah plotted to kill him and were watching the gates

---

[1] It was the daughter of Aretas IV who was the first wife of Herod Antipas, and whom the latter divorced to marry Herodias, the wife of his half-brother, Philip (Mt. 14:3–4).
[2] See discussion in R. Jewett, *Dating Paul's Life* (SCM, 1979), pp. 30–33.

of the city so as to seize him when he tried to leave. Paul's testimony in the present passage identifies the governor as the one who guarded the city. We may conclude that the Jews had succeeded in getting the governor to take action against Paul, just as Jews in other cities were to convince the authorities to do the same on later occasions.

But I was let down in a basket through a window in the wall, and escaped his hands. Paul's departure from Damascus on this occasion was very different from his earlier approach as persecutor. Then he came as a zealous Jewish crusader 'breathing threats and murder against the disciples of the Lord', and carrying letters to leaders of the Jewish synagogues in Damascus authorizing him to bring bound to Jerusalem any 'belonging to the Way' (Acts 9:1–2). But now he found himself being hunted down by his fellow Jews because of his preaching of Jesus as Messiah. Thus he was forced to flee from Damascus, escaping by being lowered down over the wall in a basket like a bundle of merchandise. This may have been Paul's first taste of the ignominy of persecution, and it must have left an indelible imprint upon him. It was a humiliating experience, and his including it here seems to constitute a parody of the whole purpose of boasting. Be that as it may, it helps to prepare the way for what he wants to say about authentic boasting in 12:9b–10.

3. *Visions and revelations* (12:1–10)

Paul's boasting now moves from apostolic trials to visions and revelations. He recounts, in the third person, an experience in which he felt himself taken up into the third heaven, into paradise, where he heard things not permissible for a person to relate. The latter part of the section tells of the thorn in the flesh given to keep him from becoming too elated. It tells how he sought God in prayer for its removal, but in response was told that God's grace was sufficient for him. Through this revelation Paul learnt of the simultaneity of weakness and power which is one of the great surprises in God's way of doing things. Paul's emphasis upon the coincidence of weakness and power is almost certainly intended to undermine the triumphalist ideas about power and authority held by his opponents, and to sup-

port his own claim to apostolic authority, despite imprisonments, persecutions and rejection which may seem to be inconsistent with that claim.

1. *I must boast; there is nothing to be gained by it.* While the
apostle is convinced that there is nothing to be gained by boasting, he probably recognizes that in the present situation there
is much to be lost if he does not. His opponents have drawn
up the agenda, it has been adopted by his converts, and he
must now respond to the next item therein. *I will go on to
visions and revelations of the Lord.* We are accustomed, perhaps,
to the occurrence of visions and revelations in the stories of
God's dealings with people in Old Testament times. It is surprising just how much they are a part of the accounts of God's
dealings with Christians in New Testament times as well.
Zechariah received a vision while serving in the temple, and
was told that his prayer had been heard and that his wife
Elizabeth would bear a son whose name would be John (the
Baptist) (Lk. 1:8–23). Jesus' transfiguration is called a vision
which was given to Peter, James and John (Mt. 17:9). The
women who went to Jesus' tomb reported that they had seen a
vision of angels who said that Jesus was alive (Lk. 24:22–24).
Stephen, just before his death, saw a vision of 'the Son of man'
standing at the right hand of God (Acts 7:55–56). The Lord
spoke to Ananias in a vision when he instructed him to seek
out Saul of Tarsus after the latter had been struck blind on the
Damascus road (Acts 9:10). Peter was made ready to receive
the call to visit Cornelius' household by a threefold vision of
unclean animals descending from heaven in a sheet (Acts
10:17, 19; 11:5). On another occasion when he was released
from prison by an angel Peter thought he was seeing a vision
(Acts 12:9). The book of Revelation is the description of revelations made to the author on the Isle of Patmos (Rev. 1:1).

Paul himself received *many visions and revelations of the Lord.*
The first and most important was the revelation of Jesus Christ
to him on the Damascus road (Acts 22:6–11; 26:12–20; Gal.
1:15–16). Subsequently Paul saw the vision of the man of Macedonia calling him to come over and help (Acts 16:9–10). When
he was carrying out the pioneer evangelism in Corinth he

received encouragement from the Lord through a vision (Acts 18:9–11). Paul claimed to have received his gospel by revelation (Gal. 1:12), and that his insights into the mystery of the gospel, his access to true wisdom, and his understanding of particular eschatological truths were based upon revelations from God (*cf.* Eph. 3:3–5; 1 Cor. 2:9–10; 1 Thes. 4:15).

2–4. Of the many visions and revelations he had received Paul now singles out one which had taken place *fourteen years ago*. This places the experience several years after his conversion and thus it cannot be equated with the revelation of Christ to Paul on the Damascus road. *I know a man in Christ.* Paul describes the experience in the third person, perhaps as a way of indicating its sacred character for him, or alternatively because he wants to maintain a distinction between the Paul who was granted this superlative experience and the Paul who boasts of weakness (*cf.* 11:30). In fact the account is so consistently cast in the third person that the reader may even wonder whether the apostle is relating the experience of another person, rather than his own. However, a careful reading and appreciation of the thrust of vv. 1, 5, 7 confirms that Paul is speaking of his own experience. The reference here to *a man in Christ* can be taken to mean simply Paul as a Christian.

The apostle says he *was caught up to the third heaven* (v. 2) and a little later that he *was caught up into Paradise* (v. 3). He used the same verb, 'to catch up' (*harpazō*), in 1 Thessalonians 4:17 when speaking of Christians who are alive and remain until the coming of the Lord and who will be 'caught up' to meet the Lord in the air.

Among Paul's contemporaries differing cosmologies were in vogue, variously portraying three, five or seven heavens, which were spoken of as a series of hemispherical strata above the earth. It has been suggested that the reference in Solomon's dedication prayer to 'heaven and the highest heaven' (lit. 'heaven and the heaven of heavens') in 1 Kings 8:27 gave rise, among the Jews at least, to the notion of the heavens in three strata. However, the text itself is probably no more than an ordinary Hebrew superlative. In the pseudepigraphical writings (*e.g. Testament of Levi* 3) there is reference to several heavens, and in rabbinic writings seven heavens are mentioned (Str-B 3, p. 531).

The identification of *the third heaven* and *Paradise* which is made by Paul in the present passage has a parallel in the *Apocalypse of Moses* 37:5, where God hands Adam over to the archangel Michael and says: 'Lift him up into Paradise unto the third heaven, and leave him there until that fearful day of my reckoning, which I will make in the world.'

In the literature of both the Jewish (*e.g.* 1 Enoch 39:3f.) and Gentile (*e.g.* Plato, *Republic*, 10:614–621) worlds there are parallels to the apostle's experience of rapture. And in the Babylonian Talmud (*Hagigah* 14b) there is the story of four rabbis who were temporarily taken up into Paradise, but so awesome was the experience that only one, Rabbi Akiba, returned unharmed. The story post-dates Paul (R. Akiba died *c.* AD 135) but indicates nevertheless the sort of accounts that were circulating in the first and second centuries of the Christian era.

All these literary parallels, whether in terminology, concepts or the experience of being taken up, serve to show three things. First, that what Paul spoke of was understandable to his contemporaries. Second, that the experience of being taken up into Paradise was believed to be awe-inspiring, and this explains in part Paul's great reticence in describing it. Third, the experience of being taken up to the third heaven would place the apostle on a level with the great heroes of faith, and by claiming such an experience Paul could completely outflank his opponents. It is therefore all the more remarkable that he did not make maximum capital out of it. But instead, having disclosed the bare fact, he quickly directs attention away from it and to his weakness as the only safe ground for boasting.

Speaking of his experience of being caught up into the third heaven or Paradise, Paul says twice, *whether in the body or out of the body I do not know, God knows* (vv. 2–3). If Paul himself did not know the exact mechanism whereby his rapture occurred, there is certainly no way in which we can. However, some effort must be made to understand the two possible means which the apostle mentions, *in the body* and *out of the body*. In the Old Testament tradition two men were translated bodily to heaven, Enoch (Gn. 5:24) and Elijah (2 Ki. 2:9–12), but their translations were permanent not temporary. It is also said of Elijah that he was carried off bodily from one place to another by the Spirit of the Lord (1 Ki. 18:12).

In the New Testament the accounts of Jesus' temptation tell of him being taken by the devil to the pinnacle of the temple and to a high mountain (Mt. 4:5, 8), but the mechanism (whether bodily or in the imagination) is not specified. The writer of Revelation tells of his being carried away 'in the Spirit' to a wilderness (Rev. 17:3), and to a great high mountain (Rev. 21:10). Whether being 'in the Spirit' means *out of the body* or simply denotes a visionary experience is not clear.

Philo appears to have believed that heavenly experiences necessitate being *out of the body* for he explains that should the strains of heavenly music ever reach our ears irrepressible yearnings and frantic longings would be produced in us causing us to abstain from necessary food. And alluding to Exodus 24:18, he says that Moses was listening to heavenly music 'when, having laid aside his body, for forty days and as many nights he touched neither bread not water at all' (*On Dreams* 1, 36). Such an idea of non-bodily rapture would be in line with Gnostic beliefs that there cannot be any contact between the heavenly and material worlds, the latter being regarded as evil by definition. When Paul says that he does not know whether his temporary translation was in the body or out of the body he keeps open the possibility of *both*, and thereby makes clear that he would not accept the Gnostic view that the material world is inherently evil. At the same time he does not exclude the possibility of a spiritual experience out of the body.

And he heard things that cannot be told, which man may not utter. The expression *that cannot be told* (*arrēta*) is found only here in the New Testament but is common in ancient inscriptions. It is associated with the mystery religions and describes things too sacred to be divulged. Such secrecy concerning things that had been revealed was a commonplace among devotees of the mystery religions of Paul's day, but quite unusual in Christian circles. Paul did speak of the 'mystery' of the gospel but that was something which, though previously hidden, had now been made known to the apostles and prophets through the Spirit for the express purpose that they should proclaim it to all men (*cf.* 1

Cor. 2:1 mg.; Eph. 3:1–9; 6:19–20; Col. 1:25–27; 4:3). It is only in the present context that Paul speaks of something revealed to him which he could not utter, presumably because it was so sacred and intended for him alone.

Paul's account of his rapture differs markedly from other such accounts from the ancient world both in its brevity and the absence of any descriptions of what he saw. Paul refers only to what he heard.

5–6. *On behalf of this man I will boast.* Although the brief account is finished, Paul continues to speak of the subject of the experience in the third person. He is prepared to boast on behalf of the Paul who fourteen years ago was privileged to receive such an experience from God, but on his own behalf he says, *I will not boast, except of my weaknesses.* Having felt forced into the futile exercise of boasting about spiritual experience, Paul returns (*cf.* 11:30) to the one safe ground of boasting – his personal weakness, and this idea he develops in vv. 7–10. However, before he does that he makes a point of saying, *Though if I wish to boast, I shall not be a fool, for I shall be speaking the truth.* Paul's meaning seems to be that if he did wish to boast on his own behalf of that experience, he would not, in one sense, be acting foolishly, because all he has said about it is true.

But I refrain from it, so that no one may think more of me than he sees in me or hears from me.[1] The apostle's reason for making less of his past experience than he might is that he wishes people's evaluation of him to be based upon what they see of him and hear from him now. Both the verbs *sees* and *hears* are in the present tense, emphasizing that it is upon present performance that Paul wants to be judged. This stress upon the present lends some support to the suggestion that Paul's use of the third person in the account of his experience of fourteen years ago was a device to distinguish between the Paul of that past experience and the Paul as people see and hear him now. It is on the

---

[1] It is possible that the words, 'by the abundance of revelations' (*kai tē hyperbolē tōn apokalypseōn*) (v. 7a), which in the Greek text follow immediately at this point, should be seen as part of the explanation why Paul refrains from boasting, *i.e.* 'that no one may think more of me than he sees in me or hears from me, and particularly because of the abundance of revelations'.

latter, and in the light of all his weakness, that he wishes any evaluation of him to be made.

7. *And to keep me from being too elated by the abundance of revelations, a thorn was given me in the flesh.* Instead of making capital out of his rapture, as his opponents obviously did out of their spiritual experiences, Paul immediately explains how he was kept from becoming too elated about it. A *thorn* (*skolops*) was given him *in the flesh*. The word *skolops*, found only here in the New Testament, was used for anything pointed, *e.g.* a stake, the pointed end of a fish-hook, a splinter or a thorn. The fact that Paul speaks of a thorn *in the flesh* suggests that the imagery is of a splinter or a thorn, rather than a stake, as some have argued.

In the LXX *skolops* is used figuratively in Numbers 33:55 ('But if you do not drive out the inhabitants of the land from before you, then those of them whom you let remain shall be as pricks [*skolopes*] in your eyes'), Ezekiel 28:24 ('And for the house of Israel there shall be no more a brier [*skolops*] to prick or a thorn to hurt them among all their neighbours who have treated them with contempt') and Hosea 2:8 (ET, v. 6) ('Therefore I will hedge up her way with thorns [*skolopsin*]; and I will build a wall against her, so that she cannot find her paths'). In each case *skolops* is used to denote something which frustrates and causes trouble in the lives of those afflicted. That Paul's *thorn* was a trouble and frustration to him is clear from his thrice-repeated prayer for its removal (v. 8).

The apostle further describes the thorn in his flesh as *a messenger of Satan, to harass me, to keep me from being too elated*. In the story of Job, Satan is allowed to harass that great hero of faith and endurance, but only within the limits set by God (Jb. 1 – 2). In 1 Thessalonians 2:17–18 Paul tells his readers how he longed to revisit them after he was forced to leave Thessalonica (*cf.* Acts 17:1–10), but could not do so because Satan hindered him. And in the present context Satan is allowed to harass the apostle by means of a thorn in the flesh. It is important to recognize that, in both the Old and New Testaments, Satan has no power other than that allowed him by God. In the Gospels Jesus has complete power over all the forces of darkness. Satan has no power over him (Jn. 14:30–31), and demons must obey his will (Mk.

1:21–28; 5:1–13). This power Christ gave to his disciples (Mk. 6:7). And yet we see in the case of Paul that Satan is allowed to hinder the apostle's plans and harass him with a thorn in the flesh. However, it must be said that in both cases the actions of Satan, while in themselves bad things, are made to serve God's purposes. In the first case the hindrance kept Paul on the move and that meant the gospel came to Beroea, Athens and Corinth. In the second case, the harassment served to keep Paul spiritually well-balanced. It was a weight upon his spirit preventing him from being blown away by excessive elation.

Many suggestions have been made concerning the nature of Paul's 'thorn in the flesh'. They fall into one of three broad categories: (a) some form of spiritual harassment, *e.g.* the limitations of a nature corrupted by sin, the torments of temptation, or oppression by a demon, (b) persecution, *e.g.* that instigated by Jewish opposition or by Paul's Christian opponents, (c) some physical or mental ailment, *e.g.* eye trouble, attacks of fever, stammering speech, epilepsy, or a neurological disturbance. However, the plain fact is that there is simply insufficient data to decide the matter. Most modern interpreters prefer to see it as some sort of physical ailment, and the fact that Paul calls it a thorn *in the flesh* offers some support for this. Galatians 4:15 is appealed to by those who want to identify it as an eye problem.

8–10. *Three times I besought the Lord about this, that it should leave me.* Although there is no essential similarity between Paul's experience and that of Jesus in Gethsemane, nevertheless it is interesting to note that both prayed three times that something be removed, and in both cases the removal requested was not granted. However, just as Jesus was strengthened to face his dreadful and unique ordeal, so encouragement and strength were made available to Paul: *but he said to me, 'My grace is sufficient for you'*. Paul uses the perfect tense in the expression *but he said to me* (*eirēken*), which indicates that the Lord's response to his prayer, once made, assumed continual applicability for him. In the response itself the use of the present tense *is sufficient* (*arkei*) denotes the continual availability of grace. Essentially the word of the Lord to Paul was that while the thorn would not be removed, his grace would enable him to cope with it. To this was added the explanation, *'for my power is made perfect in weakness'*. In 1 Corinthians 1:26–31 Paul pointed out to his converts that it was by God's deliberate choice that not many of them were wise according to wordly standards, nor powerful, nor of noble birth. The reason was that God had chosen the foolish in the world to shame the wise, the weak in the world to shame the strong, and the low and despised in the world to bring to nothing those who were considered somebodies. This he did in order that no human being might boast in his presence, and so that those who do boast might boast of the Lord. So the Lord's response to Paul's request for the removal of the harassment was to remind him that his power is manifested in the weak. It also provides, in this context, justification for Paul's rejection of the type of boasting indulged in by his opponents, and for his own practice of boasting in weakness.

I will all the more gladly boast of my weaknesses, that the power of Christ may rest upon me. Having been taught that Christ's power is made perfect in weakness, Paul is glad to boast of his *weaknesses*. This does not mean he enjoys weaknesses as such; what he delights in is the power of Christ that rests upon him in these weaknesses. The verb 'to rest upon' (*episkēnoō*) is quite rare. It is found only here in the New Testament, and not at all in the LXX or the papyri. Before Paul, its only known use is by Polybius the Greek historian (*c*.201–120 BC) who used it twice of the billeting of soldiers. It may, therefore, be better to translate the verb as 'dwell in' or 'reside' rather than *rest upon*. Either way it is the experience of the power of Christ in Paul's weakness that enables him to boast gladly.

For the sake of Christ, then, I am content with weaknesses, insults, hardships, persecutions, and calamities; for when I am weak, then I am strong. Here in v. 10 Paul applies the lesson he learnt from the Lord through the experience of the thorn in the flesh to all the various difficulties he experienced in his apostolic mission.

While Paul's readers could have gained much by learning of the simultaneity of weakness and power which Paul sets out in vv. 7–10, the apostle's motive in setting it out was not limited to that. His opponents had criticized his claims to apostleship on the grounds of his weakness (*cf.* 10:10), and very likely they regarded the many persecutions and insults that Paul experienced as inconsistent with his claim to be an apostle of the exalted Christ. By setting out the divine principle of power manifested through weakness, Paul has at once defended his own claim to apostleship and cut the ground from under the claims of his opponents.

4. Signs of an apostle (12:11–13)

With these verses Paul brings his 'fool's speech' to an end. He says that the whole exercise was an act of folly, but one he was forced into by the failure of his own converts to speak up on his behalf. They ought to have commended their apostle, rather than Paul having to indulge in the folly of boasting on his own behalf. For in fact he was in no way inferior to his opponents, the so-called 'superlative apostles'. The Corinthians had been favoured by the performance of apostolic signs, the only thing they had missed out on was being burdened financially by Paul. He concludes ironically by asking their forgiveness for this wrong!

11. *I have been a fool!* Paul, at the end of his extended boasting, is conscious that it has been an exercise in foolishness. But in a sense the Corinthians themselves are to blame. He says: *You forced me to it, for I ought to have been commended by you.* Paul places particular emphasis upon the words *You* and *I.* In effect he says, 'You Corinthians forced me to indulge in self-commendation when in fact I ought to have been commended by you.' If, instead of accepting the criticisms of Paul made by his opponents, the Corinthians had spoken up on his behalf, testifying that it was through Paul's preaching that they had been converted (*cf.* 1 Cor. 9:1b–2), that God had confirmed that preaching with signs and wonders, and that the apostle's behaviour among them had been exemplary, then Paul would have had no need to boast on his own behalf. People do not need to indulge in the unpleasant act of self-commendation when their friends, or those to whom they have ministered, take positive action to defend their integrity.

For I was not at all inferior to these superlative apostles, even though I am nothing. Paul uses the aorist tense of the verb *hystereō* ('to be inferior'). This points to a particular time in the past in which evidence had been provided which the Corinthians should have recognized as proof that Paul was in no way inferior to the *superlative apostles.* What the apostle had in mind was his first visit to Corinth, the period of pioneer evangelism in that city, when the power of God had been seen at work through him. When Paul adds, *even though I am nothing,* he could be making ironic reference to what his opponents were saying about him, or revealing in a straightforward way his own sense of unworthiness to have been entrusted with an apostolic commission (*cf.* 1 Cor. 15:9-10), or quite likely doing both.

12. *The signs of a true apostle were performed among you in all patience.* The word *true* is an addition in the RSV for which there is no counterpart in the original. While its inclusion, therefore, is strictly unwarranted, it does draw attention to the fact that Paul is here concerned to show that he is a *true* apostle, even according to the criteria espoused by his opponents. He claims that he is in no way inferior to these men in the matter of the performance of apostolic signs. And these Paul itemizes as *signs and wonders and mighty works.* The account of Paul's first visit to Corinth in Acts 18 records no miracles, but obviously such had been carried out, otherwise his appeal to them here would be nonsense. In Romans (written shortly after these chapters) Paul speaks of his ministry in terms of 'what Christ has wrought through me to win obedience from the Gentiles, by word and deed, by the power of signs and wonders, by the power of the Holy Spirit' (Rom. 15:17-19). Clearly the performance of *the signs of a true apostle* was the normal accompaniment to Paul's ministry, and in this respect Corinth had been no less favoured than others.

13. So Paul then asks, *in what were you less favoured than the rest of the churches, except that I myself did not burden you?* Paul had determined not to burden the Corinthians with the cost of his support while he laboured among them. The significance of this fact had been twisted and used against the apostle as evidence that he did not love the Corinthian believers, a suggestion Paul refused to grace with a reasoned rebuttal (*cf.* 11:7-11). And here in the present context Paul once again refuses to take seriously criticisms to the effect that his unwillingness to accept support from the Corinthians was evidence that they were less favoured than other churches. In response he says with great irony, *Forgive me this wrong!* By so saying Paul implies that it is a strange thing indeed that they should object to being *not* burdened and *not* exploited by him, as they had been by his opponents (*cf.* 11:20).

G. Paul Refuses to Burden the Corinthians (12:14–18)

Here Paul informs his readers that he is ready to make his third visit to Corinth, and continuing the theme introduced in v. 13, assures them that he will not burden them with requests for support. As far as Paul is concerned, it is the (spiritual) parents' part to lay in store for their (spiritual) children and not vice versa. He declares that he is prepared to expend both his resources and himself on their behalf. And yet he is aware of the most insidious constructions that have been placed by others upon his attitude and action in all this. For them, Paul's refusal to accept support serves only to veil a devious scheme to extract a far greater amount for himself by means of the collection ploy. The section closes with Paul asking his readers quite bluntly whether he, or any of those whom he had sent, had ever taken advantage of them. The expected answer is 'Definitely not!'

14. *Here for the third time I am ready to come to you.* This statement is ambiguous both in the original and the RSV translation. It could mean either that this is the third time Paul has been ready to make a visit (without indicating whether he actually made all the visits for which he was ready), or that he is now ready to make his third visit. Fortunately 13:1 resolves the question, confirming that he is about to embark on his third visit. The two previous ones were the pioneer missionary visit and the 'painful' visit (see Introduction, pp. 21–22). Paul's intended third visit is mentioned in several other places in this letter (10:2; 12:20–21; 13:1, 10), and from these references it is clear that the apostle was ready for a showdown, though he still hoped it would not come to that.

And I will not be a burden, for I seek not what is yours but you. On the third visit Paul will adhere to his policy of not accepting support from the Corinthians. His purpose in coming is to win them back, not to tap their resources. There may well be in this statement a veiled contrast between the apostle's motives and those of his opponents, who could not claim to work on the same terms as Paul did (*cf.* 11:12).

For children ought not to lay up for their parents, but parents for their children. Paul draws upon the obvious fact that in family life it is the parents who are under obligation to provide for their children and not vice versa. The apostle uses the verb *thēsaurizō* ('to lay up'), which is found also in his response to an enquiry about the collection in which he advised the Corinthians: 'On the first day of every week, each of you is to put something aside and store it up (*thēsaurizōn*), as he may prosper, so that contributions need not be made when I come' (1 Cor. 16:2). This advice, it seems, had been falsely construed by Paul's opponents to mean that he really wanted his spiritual children to lay up money for him. Paul denies any such accusations by saying that it is the parents who should lay up for their children and not vice versa.

15. As parents willingly provide for their children, so Paul says *I will most gladly spend and be spent for your souls.* Two cognate verbs are used, *dapanaō* ('to spend') and *ekdapanaō* (passive, 'to be spent'). The word *dapanaō* is used several times in other parts of the New Testament, where it usually refers to the spending of money (Mk. 5:26, the woman with the haemorrhage spent all she had on doctors; Lk. 15:14, the prodigal spent all his inheritance on riotous living; Acts 21:24, Paul spent money to pay for the sacrifices offered by Jewish Christians; but *cf.* Jas. 4:3), and this is its common use in the papyri as well. So here, consistent with the context and in parallel with these other uses, Paul employs the word to express his glad willingness to spend his resources on behalf of the Corinthians. By spending his resources Paul probably means meeting the costs of his support while labouring among and for the Corinthians.

The word *ekdapanaō* is found only here in the New Testament, and means 'to spend' or 'to exhaust'. In the passive voice and applied to a person, as here, it means 'to be spent' in the sense of the sacrifice of one's life. Such is the apostle's commitment to his converts that he is prepared not only to spend his resources but even to sacrifice his own life for their sakes. Such a statement of extreme commitment to the well-being of others is not an isolated one in Paul's writings. He felt the same way, we know, about his Jewish fellow countrymen (Rom. 9:3) and the Philippian church (Phil. 2:17).

After such a statement of his love and commitment to the Corinthians, Paul understandably asks, *If I love you the more, am I to be loved the less?* The apostle who is prepared to exhaust his own earnings so as not to be in any way a burden on the Corinthians, who is prepared even to sacrifice his life for them if necessary, asks whether his more abundant love is going to mean that he will be loved the less by them.

16. And Paul knows why the greater love for them on his part means less love for him on theirs. It is because one expression of his love (refusing to be a burden to them) has been misconstrued by his opponents. So he confronts his readers with the charge levelled against him: *But granting that I myself did not burden you, I was crafty, you say, and got the better of you by guile.* The words *you say* are not found in the original, but are supplied by the translators of the RSV. This is unfortunate as it suggests the criticism originated with the Corinthians themselves, whereas it is more likely that it originated with Paul's opponents, and was only entertained for a time by his converts. The craftiness and guile of which Paul was accused was that of using the occasion of the collection for the poor Judean Christians as an opportunity to benefit himself substantially as well. That this was the nature of the accusation is confirmed by vv. 17-18.

17-18. Here Paul confronts his readers. *Did I take advantage of you through any of those whom I sent to you?* To increase the impact he reminds them of the ones he sent to them. *I urged Titus to go, and sent the brother with him.* Paul refers to the sending of Titus and the 'earnest' brother foreshadowed in 8:16-17, 22.[1] Having

[1] Paul omits any reference to the 'famous' brother who also accompanied Titus (8:18-19), possibly because he was less an associate of Paul and more an appointee of the churches.

reminded them, he then asks his second question. *Did Titus take advantage of you?* Both this and the previous question, by their form in the original, demand the answer, 'No.' Paul concludes his defence against this sort of allegation by asking, *Did we not act in the same spirit? Did we not take the same steps?* These questions, as both their form in the original language and the translation provided in the RSV show, require a positive answer. Both Paul and those whom he had sent to Corinth on the business of the collection had acted in the same way, with complete integrity. The apostle expects his readers to acknowledge this fact.

H. The Real Purpose of Paul's Fool's Speech (12:19–21)

In these verses Paul seeks to make clear what was the real underlying motive of his boasting. Certainly he had felt forced into it because his readers had been influenced adversely by the boasting of his opponents, and he had to show that he was in no way inferior to those men. But underlying that, his real aim was to promote the upbuilding of his converts (v. 19). And this he did because he was afraid that when he came for his third visit, neither he nor they would find in one another what they would desire. They might find Paul acting with bold authority against them, and he might find himself mourning over the fact that many of them were still caught up in the sins of the past (vv. 20–21).

19. *Have you been thinking all along that we have been defending ourselves before you?* This has been translated in the RSV (and also in the NIV) as a question. It could also be translated justifiably as a statement: 'You have been thinking all along that we have been defending ourselves before you.' But in either case Paul's point is the same. He wants to correct a view of his boasting which interprets it simply as an effort to defend himself before his readers. Essentially Paul does not feel the need to defend himself before the Corinthians or anyone else, because it is before God that he stands or falls (*cf.* 5:10), so he adds, *It is in the sight of God that we have been speaking in Christ.* The apostle does not want his readers to misunderstand his boasting, as if it meant he personally was somehow dependent upon their approval (*cf.* 1 Cor. 4:3-4). His underlying motive was not to gain approval from them, but to make possible their spiritual upbuilding. It was, he says, *all for your upbuilding, beloved*. When Paul says it is *all for your upbuilding*, he refers, most likely, to all that he has said, done and written (particularly in the present letter) which they might have mistakenly construed as mere self-defence. He also reiterates thereby the purpose of apostolic ministry: to build up the church (*cf.* 10:8; 13:10). It should be noted that after all the strong words and irony of chs. 10 – 12, Paul's true feeling for his converts emerges again in the appellation *beloved* (*cf.* 11:11; 12:15). It was Paul's love for the Corinthian church, as much as his dismay because a false gospel was being proclaimed, that accounted for the strength of his attack against his opponents and the extent of his boasting.

20-21. Paul laboured for the upbuilding of the Corinthians because he loved them, but also, he says, *For I fear that perhaps I may come and find you not what I wish*. He is ready to come to them for the third visit (v. 14), and does not want to be disappointed in his converts when he arrives. If what he fears is in evidence when he arrives, then he warns, *you may find me not what you wish*. If there is no improvement, then Paul must act with boldness and authority against the church (*cf.* 1 Cor. 4:21), as he has threatened to act against his opponents (10:2, 6; *cf.* 13:1-4).

In vv. 20b-21 Paul spells out in detail what he fears he may find among the Corinthians when he comes. *Perhaps there may be quarrelling, jealousy, anger, selfishness, slander, gossip, conceit, and disorder.* The list may owe something to traditional lists of vices that Paul makes use of elsewhere (*e.g.* Rom. 1:29; 13:13; Gal. 5:19-21; Col. 3:8-9). However, it is significant that the first two items on Paul's list here (*quarrelling* and *jealousy*) are the very things he mentioned when dealing with the problem of party spirit in 1 Corinthians (*cf.* 1 Cor. 1:11; 3:3). Also in 1 Corinthians 13 he spoke by implication against anger, selfishness, slander and conceit when extolling the way of love as the only proper context for the use of spiritual gifts. And the last item of Paul's list, *disorder*, was a problem addressed in 1 Corinthians in relations to women's behaviour and the celebration of the Lord's Supper, as well as the use of spiritual gifts, all in the context of the worship of the Corinthian church.

It seems, then, that Paul was by no means convinced that the problems he had addressed in 1 Corinthians were now things of the past, and this is confirmed by the apostle's words in v. 21. In this verse Paul expresses the fear *that when I come again my God may humble me before you.* In 9:3–4 Paul spoke of the humiliation he would feel if, when he came to Corinth with some of the Macedonians, the Corinthians proved to be unprepared in the matter of the collection. But here he faces the possibility of far greater humiliation, that of seeing the results of his labours in Corinth marred by serious moral breakdown. He envisages having *to mourn over many of those who sinned before and have not repented of the impurity, immorality, and licentiousness which they have practised.* In 1 Corinthians 5 – 6 Paul dealt at length with the arrogance of the Corinthian Christians *vis-à-vis* the immoral practices in their midst. These included a case of incest (a man living with his stepmother) and the use of prostitutes, both of which appear to have been justified by appeal to the slogan 'all things are lawful'. Paul called for disciplinary action against the incestuous person (1 Cor. 5:3–5) and argued that sexual immorality was incompatible with the Christian's status as the dwelling-place of the Spirit (1 Cor. 6:18–20).

If it is correct to identify the incestuous person with the one who questioned Paul's authority and led the personal attack against him during the 'painful' visit, then we know that he was eventually disciplined severely, so much so that Paul urged the rest to turn and forgive him (2:6–8). In that case it is unlikely that this person is included among *those who sinned before and have not repented.* It is more likely that Paul refers to those who formerly practised immorality and who may have desisted for a while (in deference to his appeal in 1 Cor. 5 – 6) without truly repenting. But in the new crisis situation where Paul's authority was called into question again, this time by Jewish Christian opponents of the apostle, he fears these people may be engaging in immoral and licentious practices once more.

I. Paul Threatens Strong Action on his Third Visit (13:1–10)

The apostle speaks here in threatening terms of his third visit to

Corinth. He informs his readers that when he comes again to Corinth he will not spare offenders. They want some proof that Christ is speaking through him, then they shall get it! He tells them that just as Christ was crucified in weakness but now lives by the power of God, so too he (Paul), though sharing the weakness and suffering of Christ, will act with the power of God when he deals with them. Alluding again to their demands for proof, Paul responds by challenging his readers to prove themselves to see whether they are holding to the faith. He assures his readers that for his part he could never act contrary to the truth.

1. *This is the third time I am coming to you.* The first visit was that of Paul's pioneer evangelism in Corinth, and the second the 'painful' visit made after the writing of 1 Corinthians (see Introduction, pp. 21–22). The third visit has already been foreshadowed several times in chs. 10 – 13 (10:2; 12:14, 20–21), and it is clear from these references and the present context that Paul is prepared for a showdown.

Any charge must be sustained by the evidence of two or three witnesses. Paul here introduces, without any introductory formula, a slightly abbreviated version of Deuteronomy 19:15 (LXX). The requirement that accusations must be supported by the evidence of at least two witnesses was stressed in first-century Judaism. The same requirement was incorporated by Jesus into his instructions to the disciples concerning church discipline (Mt. 18:16), and is also reflected in a number of places elsewhere in the New Testament (Jn. 8:17; 1 Tim. 5:19; Heb. 10:28; 1 Jn. 5:8).

Paul's introduction of this quotation here has been understood in various ways. Some draw attention to Paul's reference to his second and third visits to Corinth in vv. 1–2 and suggest that these are somehow analogous to the two or three witnesses demanded by the law. The evidence provided by these visits will justify the disciplinary action Paul intends taking in Corinth. However, Paul's first visit can hardly be seen as a witness to Corinthian misdemeanours (it was the pioneer evangelistic visit during which the church was founded). Further, the third visit could hardly be regarded as a 'witness' when it was on that visit Paul intended taking disciplinary action. Such an interpretation also makes Paul do strange things with the text of Deuteronomy 19:15, which clearly refers to the witness of persons (not events), as allusions to it elsewhere in the New Testament testify.

Another suggestion is that the warnings Paul gave (v. 2) constitute the witnesses required. The difficulty in this case is that despite the multiple warnings given, only one person is involved as a witness. A third possibility is that Paul, determined to take disciplinary action when he arrived, is here simply assuring his readers that he will do so in accordance with the instructions of Jesus and the judicial procedures accepted by the churches.[1]

Finally, the apostle could be issuing a challenge to any of his readers who may have been inclined to bring a charge against him. If so, Paul is saying they must be prepared to sustain their accusations by the evidence of two or three witnesses. This suggestion takes note of the fact that it is not only the Corinthians who are under scrutiny (by Paul) but also Paul himself (by them) (vv. 5–10).

2. *I warned those who sinned before and all the others.* Paul uses the perfect tense (*proeirēka*, lit. 'I have warned'), which locates the warning in the past while underlining its continuing applicability down to the present. In what follows, Paul both updates his warning and pinpoints for us the time when he first issued it: *and I warn them now while absent, as I did when present on my second visit.* The occasion of the original warning was the apostle's 'second visit', *i.e.* the 'painful' visit during which he had been attacked by the offender (*cf.* 2:5; 7:12). From the present context we learn that Paul did not conclude his second visit before uttering dire warnings to those who were still unrepentant for their previous sins.

Paul's reference to *those who sinned before* may be understood as a reference to the unrepentant sexual offenders of 12:21 (*cf.* 1

---

[1]Against this view it has been argued that personal witnesses are needed only to bring to light secret sins, not public scandals with which Paul is concerned here. In response it can be stated that the role of witnesses is not only to bring to light what was secret but also to bear responsibility before the judiciary for the charge brought.

Cor. 6:12–20), while *all the others* is possibly a reference to those who condoned the sexual offences (*cf.* 1 Cor. 5:2, 6).

The content of the apostle's warning is: *if I come again I will not spare them*. Paul had threatened that on his second visit he would take disciplinary action (1 Cor. 4:18–21), but in the event he withdrew without doing so, preferring rather to write a 'severe' letter. But now, ready to make his third visit, the apostle warns his readers that he will not spare them this time.

3. Paul here gives a reason for the action threatened in v. 2b: 'I will not spare them', he says, *since you desire proof that Christ is speaking in me*. The Corinthians, influenced by Paul's opponents, had adopted various criteria for testing the validity of apostolic claims. One of these criteria was that through a true apostle the word of Christ should be heard, and proofs which would indicate that this criterion was being fulfilled were sought by them. Such proofs included an impressive presence and powerful speaking (10:10), and the performance of signs and wonders (12:11–13). Paul would not have objected to the criterion, but would have taken strong exception to the proofs sought. He had learnt that the power of Christ rested upon the weak, not the impressive, and that Christ spoke through his servants when they proclaimed the gospel, not because of their high-sounding words.

In response to the demands for proofs, Paul threatens to provide evidence of Christ's speaking through him, but it will be evidence that his readers will not find to their liking. He will not spare them. He will be severe in his use of apostolic authority (*cf.* v. 10). In this regard he warns the Corinthians: *He is not weak in dealing with you, but is powerful in you.* Christ had worked powerfully by the Spirit among the Corinthians when Paul performed the signs of an apostle in Corinth (12:12; *cf.* Rom. 15:18–19), but in the present context Paul has in mind the power of Christ revealed in disciplinary action against those Corinthians who persisted in their sins. Paul's words in 1 Corinthians 11:30–31, written in response to news of abuses at the Lord's Supper, perhaps provide a clue to what he has in mind here: 'That is why many of you are weak and ill, and some have died. But if we judged ourselves truly, we should not be judged.'

4. *For he was crucified in weakness, but lives by the power of God.* Paul reminds his readers that the Christ who now lives by the power of God was once crucified in weakness. This provides a paradigm by which they should understand the paradox of Paul's own apostolic ministry: *For we are weak in him, but in dealing with you we shall live with him by the power of God.* The many evidences of the apostle's weakness (*cf.* 1:3–11; 4:7–12; 11:23–29) should not blind the Corinthians to the fact that Christ's power is being manifested in his apostolate. While acknowledging his weakness in Christ, Paul threatens to use the disciplinary power of Christ when dealing with his readers.[1]

5. *Examine yourselves, to see whether you are holding to your faith. Test yourselves.* The positioning of the reflexive pronouns (*heautous*, 'yourselves') shows that Paul is emphasizing that it is themselves that the Corinthians should be examining rather than him. He wants them to see whether they are holding to the faith, *i.e.* the gospel, and conforming their lives to it.

Do you not realize that Jesus Christ is in you? – unless indeed you fail to meet the test! In a previous letter Paul had stressed the importance of the presence of the Holy Spirit in the congregation and the individual believer, and the moral implications of this (1 Cor. 3:16; 6:19–20). In the present context, where the prospect of moral failure on the part of the Corinthians has stimulated Paul's concern (*cf.* 12:21), the ethical imperative of the presence of Christ by the Spirit is implicitly invoked by Paul's question. *Do you not realize that Jesus Christ is in you?* The Corinthians appear to have been quite confident that Christ was in them, so the purpose of Paul's question is to reawaken them to the moral implications of that great fact.

6. *I hope you will find out that we have not failed.* Just as Paul emphasized in the previous verse (by the use of reflexive pro-

---

[1]Some have argued that Paul's words, *we shall live with him by the power of God*, refer to the eschatological future when Paul and his colleagues are raised by the power of God to live with Christ. However, Paul does not have the eschatological future in mind here. The words, *in dealing with you* (*eis hymas*) show that the apostle has in mind action he threatens to take in the near future.

nouns) that the Corinthians should test themselves to ensure that they are holding to the faith, so he stresses here (by the inclusion of the emphatic pronoun *hēmeis, we*) his hope that he and his colleagues will be found not to have failed the Corinthians' test. This comes as a surprise, for the context leads us to expect that Paul's hope would be that the Corinthians would be the ones who would pass the test. The explanation of this is: by testing themselves and reaching the conclusion that they do hold to the faith and that therefore Christ is in them, the Corinthians will at the same time be acknowleding that Paul and his colleagues have not failed. For if they hold the true faith and are indwelt by Christ, that is so because of what they received through the ministry of Paul and his fellow workers, and that in turn proves that Paul is a true apostle, one who has not failed the test.

7. *But we pray God that you may not do wrong.* Paul discloses the content of his prayer and this disclosure not only reveals his concern for the Corinthians but also functions as an exhortation to them. The wrong he prays they will avoid is best understood in this context as failure to hold the faith (v. 5) and a falling back into immorality (12:21).

Lest his motives be misunderstood, Paul explains that his reason for praying is *not that we may appear to have met the test, but that you may do what is right, though we may seem to have failed.* Though he hopes they will find out that their apostle has met the test (v. 6), this is not his main concern. He wants them to avoid wrongdoing, not because his own reputation would suffer, but simply because he wants them to be found doing what is right.

Those who may deem Paul to have failed the test would probably do so on the grounds that he failed to provide proofs that Christ spoke through him, *i.e.* he lacked an impressive presence, his speech was of no account (10:10), and there was little evidence, as they thought, of spiritual power in his ministry (*e.g.* visionary experiences and the performance of signs and wonders, *cf.* 12:1, 11–13). In his 'fool's speech' Paul provided such evidence as they demanded, even though he gave it his own special twist (see commentary on 11:21b – 12:13). However, as far as Paul is concerned, the true legitimization of his apostle-ship belongs not with such displays of power but is seen in the changed lives of his converts. When they pass the test of holding the faith, and that finds expression in moral renewal in their lives, then the genuineness of Paul's apostolate will be confirmed (*cf.* 3:1–3).

8. Lest his statement 'though we may seem to have failed' (v. 7b) should be misconstrued as an admission that he has acted wrongly, Paul adds, *For we cannot do anything against the truth, but only for the truth. The truth* is best understood here as the gospel, and what Paul asserts is that he could never act in a way that is contrary to the gospel or its implications.

9. *For we are glad when we are weak and you are strong.* This statement reinforces that of v. 7, and recasts it in general terms. Paul is prepared, as he said in v. 7, to appear to have failed as long as the Corinthians do what is right. Now in more general terms he says that he is prepared, even glad, to be weak if that means strength for his converts. During his ministry, Paul had discovered that very often weakness in himself was the concomitant of power at work in others (*cf.* 4:11–12; 12:7–10), a fact which rested upon God's decision to use the weak things of this world to achieve his purposes (*cf.* 1 Cor. 1:26–29). The sort of strength Paul looked for in his converts was the strength of commitment to the gospel and the outworking of that commitment in moral renewal in their lives.

What we pray for is your improvement. It is a mark of the apostle's Christian maturity and commitment to the purposes of God that in the face of the defection of his converts, and their calling into question of his own apostolate, his overriding concern is not self-justification, but rather their improvement.

10. Paul sums up the purpose of his letter: *I write this while I am away from you, in order that when I come I may not have to be severe in my use of the authority which the Lord has given me.* This statement of purpose fits well with the content of chs. 10 – 13, in which Paul has repeatedly threatened a severe use of authority (10:5–6, 11; 12:20; 13:1–4). Despite these repeated threats Paul hoped all along that it would not prove necessary to carry them out (10:2; 12:19–21). We may say, then, that the purpose of chs. 10 – 13 was to recall the Corinthians to their senses so that they would reject the false gospel and false claims of Paul's opponents and also live out in their lives the moral implications of the gospel and so forestall a severe use of authority by Paul.

Paul describes his authority as that *which the Lord has given me for building up and not for tearing down.* It is true that elsewhere in his writings Paul speaks of an exercise of authority which constitutes a *tearing down* (*e.g.* handing people over to Satan for the destruction of the flesh, 1 Cor. 5:3–5; *cf.* 1 Tim. 1:20), nevertheless the primary function of that authority is for building up Christ's church. This is stressed again and again in this letter (*cf.* 10:8; 12:19).

II. CONCLUSION (13:11–14)

A. Final Exhortations and Greeting (13:11–13)

11. *Finally, brethren, farewell.* The word *brethren* is used generically to denote all Christians (so also in 1:8; 8:1). *Farewell* renders the Greek *chairete*, which could also be translated 'rejoice'. The word is used with the latter meaning in 1 Thessalonians 5:16 as part of a similar list of brief exhortations. However, the simple *farewell* fits better at the end of a letter punctuated with expressions of anxiety, self-defence, castigation of opponents and sarcasm, than does an exhortation to rejoice.

Mend your ways, heed my appeal. What Paul required by way of amendment is clear enough. He wanted the Corinthians to reject the different gospel brought by his opponents (11:1–6), to recognize his rightful claims to be their apostle (10:13–18; 11:21–23; 12:11–13), and to make sure no immoral practices were allowed in their midst (12:20–21). Paul's appeal to the Corinthians is that they should examine themselves and amend their ways so that when he comes he will not have to be severe in the use of his authority (vv. 5–10).

Agree with one another, live in peace. This too must be included as part of Paul's appeal to the Corinthians, and it reminds us that the disharmony which marred the church when 1 Corinthians was written (*cf.* 1 Cor. 1:10–12; 3:1–4), was still a source of trouble in the church (*cf.* 12:20). To this exhortation Paul adds the assurance, *and the God of love and peace will be with you.* This promise should not be understood as a reward that will be given if the Corinthians obey Paul's exhortation. It is best taken as an encouragement to those who set themselves to obey, as well as an indication of the source of power by which they will be enabled to do so.

12. *Greet one another with a holy kiss.* In the New Testament the kiss was a sign of greeting and respect. So, for example, Jesus reproached Simon the Pharisee because he gave him no kiss when he entered his house (Lk. 7:45). It was also used as a symbol of affection, as in the case of the woman who, being forgiven much, kissed Jesus' feet repeatedly (Lk. 7:38, 45), and in the case of the father of the prodigal who embraced and kissed his wayward son when he returned home (Lk. 15:20). Paul repeatedly exhorted members of the churches to *greet one another with a holy kiss* (apart from the present context such exhortations are found in Rom. 16:16; 1 Cor. 16:20; 1 Thes. 5:26; *cf.* 1 Pet. 5:14).

The fact that the kiss was described as *holy* indicates that erotic overtones were excluded, the kiss was a greeting, a sign of peace and Christian *agapē*. In post-New Testament times the use of the holy or cultic kiss in early Christian liturgies, especially the eucharist, is found. However, quite early there were objections voiced against the practice because of the suspicions of non-Christians and because of the danger of erotic perversion.[1]

13. *All the saints greet you. All the saints,* whose greetings Paul conveys, are to be understood either as all the Christians of Macedonia or those Christians in the particular Macedonian city from which Paul wrote this letter.

[1] G. Stahlin, '*Phileō*', *TDNT* 9, pp. 142–143.

B. The Benediction (13:14)

14. The closing invocation of God's blessing is especially significant because of its triadic formulation. It is the only place in the New Testament where God the Father, Son and Holy Spirit are explicitly mentioned together in such a blessing.

The grace of the Lord Jesus Christ. In 8:9 Paul wrote: 'You know the grace of our Lord Jesus Christ, that though he was rich, yet for your sake he became poor, so that by his poverty you might become rich' (see commentary on 8:9). This is the nature of the grace of the Lord Jesus Christ which Paul invokes upon his readers, a grace completely undeserved, yet overwhelmingly generous and astonishingly committed to the well-being of sinful human beings.

The love of God is a major theme in Paul's whole theology. Supremely it was demonstrated in that God provided and was involved in the great reconciliation effected by Christ so that human beings might live at peace with God (Rom. 5:6–8; 2 Cor. 5:18–21). This is the nature of the love of God which Paul invokes upon his readers. One again, what is involved is completely undeserved and astonishingly generous.

The fellowship of the Holy Spirit. The word *fellowship* is a translation of *koinōnia*, which means essentially 'participation'. The expression *fellowship of the Holy Spirit* can be construed so as to mean participation in the Holy Spirit where the Holy Spirit is understood as the object in which Christian people share (objective genitive construction). Alternatively it can be construed so as to mean a fellowship created by the Holy Spirit (subjective genitive construction). Both ideas are true and are found elsewhere in Paul's letters (*e.g.* 1 Cor. 12:13 where Christians are said both to have been baptized *by* one Spirit into one body, and to have been made to drink *of* one Spirit). In any case Christians can share 'objectively' in the Spirit only if the Spirit himself as subject makes that participation possible.